A BREED APART

A BREED APART

**A Tribute to the Hunting Dogs
That Own Our Souls**

An Original Anthology
Edited by Doug Truax

COUNTRYSPORT PRESS
New Albany, Ohio

This edition of *A Breed Apart* was printed by Jostens Book Manufacturing, State College, Pennsylvania. The book was designed by Angela Saxon of Saxon Design, Traverse City, Michigan. The text is set in Berling.

© 1993 and 1994 by Countrysport, Inc.
First published in hardcover as *A Breed Apart* volumes I and II

Paperback Edition 1996

Published by Countrysport Press
15 South High Street, New Albany, Ohio 43053-0166

Printed in the United States of America

Library of Congress Catalog Card Number 96-084191

ISBN 0-924357-61-4

CONTENTS

INTRODUCTION

I trained my first bird dog armed, as I often am, with too many books, too many theories, and only the vaguest idea of what I was doing. I was soon convinced by a high-octane English setter puppy and all the vagaries of the grouse woods that this dog training business was less of an exact science than the books had made it out to be. Much less.

But despite frustration, confusion, and occasional moments of sheer chaos, I quickly came to see that hunting birds without a canine companion was not hunting at all. Humans, if they minded their manners and were close friends, were sometimes fun to have along. The dog, however ill-mannered or unruly it might be that day, was *always* welcome.

The high white tail of a setter bounding through the thickets and occasionally, God willing, bounding back in my direction, could illuminate the depressing gray of a November afternoon. I came to live each autumn to see the white form etched, high-headed and motionless, in a weave of saplings, to enter the mysterious scent world that stretched ahead of her nose guided only by her eyes and impossibly taut body, to feel the air explode.

I enjoy the company of other hunters, but I enjoy it most after the hunt, or during the winter and summer months when we recall tales of hunting, which are as often as not tales of dogs and their deeds and misdeeds. The process, I am sure, is like that of support groups for recovering alcoholics or compulsive gamblers, except that hunting dog owners, while they may enjoy consolation and can even tolerate a little mild advice, seldom if ever are willing to take the cure. In fact, the solution to many folks' problems with gun dogs is more of the same. You can't quite keep that raw-boned pointer in the same congressional district you are in, so rather than taking up golf or sending him off to boarding school, you come to the conclusion that another pup might be just the answer. Maybe if you bred ol' Jess into a more sedate line, the new dogs would hunt like oiled machines. The problem, of course, is that most of us will never live long enough to see a happy end to this logic. With gun dogs, most of us are dealt only a few hands in a lifetime; we settle for something less than a royal flush.

Which is why this is such an endlessly fascinating game. In few fields is the Platonic ideal so raggedly approximated by reality. Sporting dogs are sublime when everything falls beautifully into place—abundant game behaving in predictable ways, a skilled hunter, a dog that performs flawlessly. Seldom is it so. So we struggle with imperfection, with dreams that never quite materialize, with promises we can never quite fulfill.

That, of course, makes sporting dogs the perfect material for good story making, and telling. Good writers thrive on ambiguity; great stories get told when there is a need to explain the inexplicable.

So when the opportunity to put together an anthology of original stories on hunting dogs presented itself, I jumped at it with enthusiasm. Here was a chance to gather old writer friends, whether they were ones I've shared the field with or writers whose stories I'd read often enough to think I had, and listen to them spin a yarn or two. The problem was, I confess, that my enthusiasm for gun dogs got the better of me.

We made no attempt to structure this book around particular themes or to systematically cover every type of hunting dog. My own prejudice in dogs matches that of Glen Sheppard, whose opinions are never meek—you hunt birds (grouse and woodcock) with a setter, mainly white, and a gun with two barrels. But, hell, a gun dog is a gun dog: a creature to be admired. Some of my most enjoyable days in the field have been behind springers (a fact I am loath to admit to my springer-owning friends) and if I were more of a duck hunter I'd own another golden retriever in a minute. Some of the best dog stories I ever heard were about a bird hunting beagle.

So we went to some of the finest writers we knew working today and simply asked them for the best dog story they had to tell. The writers come from the chukar country of the West to the Green Mountains of Vermont, from the northern grouse woods to the southern quail fields and duck marshes. Here you'll meet some familiar writers whose stories we've all been enjoying for over forty years, and some young writers whose work you may not have yet had a chance to read. Among them are novelists, professional outdoor writers, newspapermen, dog trainers, and writers you may have thought wrote only about big game or fly fishing. But they are all writers, through and through, and they all share a love of the hunting dog. One writer, who breeds and trains pointing dogs, even ended up writing about his horse...and in the process tells us much about dogs.

Each story here, by the way, was written especially for this book. What you'll read is intended for pure enjoyment, although do not be surprised if you find, as I did, that you come away learning more about handling and training a hunting dog than you have through the conventional manuals. I think back to those armfuls of technical books with which I started training my first setter and realize that none of them contained the training medicine I found in these stories. That medicine has nothing to do with electronic collars, whoa commands, or whistle blasts. It has much to do with commitment and defeat, with obsession, acceptance, and even joy.

So pull a chair up close to the fire, sit back, and listen to a talented group of writers discuss one of the most enjoyable, perplexing, and endlessly fascinating subjects I can think of—the hunter and his dog.

Doug Truax
Traverse City, Michigan

Philip Bourjaily was born in Iowa City and has lived in the area all his life, with time out for high school in Barcelona, Spain, and college in Charlottesville, Virginia. After vigorously resisting his father's early attempts to turn him into a hunter, he took up the sport on his own after college and began writing about it shortly therafter.

His work has appeared in Field & Stream, Sports Afield, The American Hunter, *and other national and regional publications. He is also co-author (with Vance Bourjaily) of the book* Fishing by Mail.

He lives in Iowa City with his wife, Pamela, sons Charles and John, and his German shorthaired pointer (ret.), Sam.

SAM

by Philip Bourjaily

Somewhere up ahead I heard the very conspicuous sound of a bell not ringing. Bending over double, I ran down a deer trail through a thicket of young willows, holding the gun in one hand and fending off branches with the other—you don't want to dawdle when your dog is pointing a pheasant. Breaking into the open I found Sam standing rigid in the knee-deep grass, the tip of his tail beginning to flag. I released him with a tap on the back of the head, and he resumed the chase with me chugging along right behind him. A hundred yards down the trail he pointed again. I tapped him, he took a few mincing steps, then locked into a third point, his quivering intensity leaving no doubt the bird was right under his nose this time. The pheasant waited only a split second before flushing, but it was warning enough. I'd skidded to a halt, flicked off the safety, and was raising the gun in anticipation as the cackling rooster flew straight into the low afternoon sun. Pulling the trigger as he disappeared into the blinding glare, I was rewarded first by a heavy thump, then the sound of Sam rustling forward through the grass to make the retrieve.

You'll hear sometimes that pheasants will turn pointing dogs into nervous wrecks, running out from under the dog's noses instead of sitting obediently like proper game birds. I have to differ: Sam was born a nervous wreck, but he handles wild roosters just fine. If anything, pheasant hunting seems to calm him down.

At eight years old, Sam still has the look of a young German shorthair waiting to fill out. Until he turned five or six, people invariably guessed his age at under a year. Even today, no matter how much I feed him, I can still encircle his waist with my hands. In the past two years, however, his muzzle has turned white. What he looks like now is a year-old shorthair with a white muzzle, the white hair as much at odds with his appearance as sideburns and a mustache on a ten-year-old boy.

Nor has the passage of time conferred much in the way of wisdom or serenity upon Sam. He still barks frantically at every slow moving farm vehicle that passes by. Ditto for dinner guests. Outside, he patrols the yard at top speed and points feral cats with frightening intensity. In the house, he keeps to himself, coiled like a spring on his dog bed. Occasionally he'll check in for a quick, reassuring pat on the head, then turn around and leave the room. Only when summer thunderstorms rattle the windows does he cling near to us, trembling.

Years ago I watched Sam's grandfather, Peter Gunn, run in a shoot-to-retrieve trial with Vern Zach, the trainer who later gave Sam to me. Vern and Peter were up against another man and his setter, who were, incidentally, the only dog and owner I've ever seen who actually did resemble one another. At the starting line, the rail-thin reddish setter whined and strained against a lead in imitation of his tall, gaunt, red-haired owner, who paced nervously while stuffing shells into a pump gun. Vern joked with the gallery, a Remington 3200 broken open over his shoulder. Peter lay at Vern's feet, regarding the other dog with drowsy contempt, on the verge, it seemed, of falling sound asleep. At the blast of the judge's whistle, Peter was transformed instantly into a ground-eating blur of energy that outran, outhunted, and outclassed every other dog at the trial. In the field, Sam has every last ounce of Peter Gunn's drive and style. What he lacks is an "off" switch.

I have other interests besides birds and gun dogs, and while I'm sometimes a little pressed to remember what they are, I can enjoy life between pheasant hunts. Sam, on the other hand, simply marks time between outings, unaware that there will ever be an end to the cycle of running and waiting to run. I am burdened by the knowledge that these cycles are indeed finite, and I'm reminded more and more these days by that whitening muzzle that sometime soon I'll have to start thinking about the next dog.

I may not have the nerve to try my luck with another high-octane burner like Sam. He has been more of a project than any first-time trainer deserved, and our successes together were many years in coming. The rewards of hunting pheasants with a stylish, wide-ranging pointing dog are great, but so are the frustrations. I find myself torn between wanting the next dog to be an exact copy of Sam or wanting it to be his opposite in every way. I'm writing this in full knowledge of the fact that I won't choose the next dog at all: someone will offer me a pup and I'll take it reflexively, whether it be another shorthair, a hunting cocker, or Chesapeake Bay retriever. There are people, to paraphrase, who are born to choose their dogs. Others have their dogs thrust upon them. I belong to the latter group.

Sam was thrust upon me by Vern, who called out of the blue one day to say he had a dog to give me, repayment for some favor my father had done for him long ago. The dog, Pee Wee, was just a year old, he said. Pee Wee had been returned by an indignant buyer who complained that the dog wouldn't gain weight, had an underbite, and, the final insult, his testicles were too small. Too small for what the man didn't say.

"He was kinda the runt of his litter," Vern admitted, but he'll make you a good little bird dog."

My previous "free hunting dog" was Betsy, a beautiful black and white springer spaniel from bench stock who, it quickly became apparent, had had all the nose and sense bred out of her in favor of flawless conformation and a lovely gait. Once she did actually blunder into a sitting rooster, which subsequently flushed and, to Betsy's horror, crashed dead to the ground in front of her when I shot. I found her a good home in the suburbs and vowed not to take any more free dogs. But when Vern called I had no money to spend on a pup and I wanted a hunting dog in the worst way. This dog, I told myself, would be different because Vern's shorthairs were proven hunters. I'd seen Peter Gunn tear up the field at NSTRA events and killed my first rooster over him, too. Besides, my wife, who believed her German shepherd was enough dog for the two of us, was conveniently out of town. What else could I say but yes?

I drove over to Vern's house the next day and he led me past pen after pen of lean, athletic shorthairs, tails cut long, their predominantly white coats suggesting more than a trace of English pointer somewhere in their bloodlines. Vern had sixty dogs at the time. Fifty-nine of them ran to the wire when he passed their pens, wagging their tails, sticking their noses through the mesh. One sat off in the background, barking suspiciously.

"That's the dog I had in mind for you," said Vern, pointing past the crowd around the fence to the bony little dog sitting against the back wall. Vern went into the pen, caught Pee Wee, and clipped a leash to his collar. The dog immediately pulled and strained as hard as he could, so Vern showed me how to loop the lead once around the dog's middle to keep him under control.

Out in the yard, Vern produced a fly rod with a pigeon wing on the line and flipped it in front of the dog. I'd seen him do this before with tiny young puppies, and had watched them lock into stylish points. Pee Wee dove on the wing and ripped it to shreds.

"Well," said Vern, yanking the tattered wing out of the dog's mouth and putting the rod away quickly, "that doesn't mean anything. Let's take him for a run."

I nodded, at a loss for words. We let Pee Wee loose in the field behind the house.

"Look at that tail," Vern murmured in admiration, as Pee Wee streaked for the horizon, "Straight up in the air. Now that's style."

How could he tell? The dog was already out of sight. He came tearing back into view moments later from an entirely different point of the compass, no doubt having just completed a quick circumnavigation of the globe. I'd never seen a dog this fast in my whole life.

"Will he retrieve ducks?" I asked.

"Nope," said Vern, "He's a bird dog."

"I'll take him," I heard myself saying. Here we go again, I thought.

Despite my reservations, I accepted Pee Wee with genuine gratitude; Vern's pups aren't cheap and the dog's papers were full of field trial champions. I loaded Pee Wee and a bag of dog food into the back of my Super Beetle, said goodbye, and there I was. I changed Pee Wee's name, which I hoped would raise his self-esteem, and bought a book on how to train pointing dogs.

What followed was disaster, frustration, and despair. One incident sums up our early hunts together. I was walking the bean field behind the house. Sam was tearing along as usual, happily bumping and chasing birds a couple of hundred yards ahead of me. Finally, I managed to catch his attention with the whistle and he swerved slightly in response. (I would whistle at Sam that year with the same vague hopefulness I feel when blowing a call at ducks. "Look, I've turned him!" I would sometimes exclaim to my long-suffering hunting companions in delighted surprise.) Just then a small plane flew over us, low, maybe five hundred feet off the ground.

Sam flashed me a look, almost a shrug that said, "Hey, I've got a plane to catch" and took off. He chased the plane across the huge expanse of plowed black earth until he was just a tiny white speck in the distance. I whistled and screamed myself hoarse. I was hoarse most of the time that fall.

The next year, I worked Sam on a checkcord all summer with marginal results. Off the cord, he would respond to the whistle at close range, but inevitably something in the distance would catch his eye and he'd bolt. As a countermeasure, I ordered a pair of rubber balls on nylon rope to hang from Sam's collar. These "Dog Compensators," the catalog copy explained, would slow the dog down by interrupting his gait and thwart his efforts to run big. Eagerly ripping open the package, I had the Dog Compensators snapped on Sam's collar while the UPS truck was still backing out the driveway. I watched with ill-concealed glee as he hobbled slowly around the house, confused by the nylon ropes tangling around his legs and the rubber balls bouncing off his shins. Incredible, I thought, almost lightheaded with euphoria and relief, my dog problems are solved for just $4.95, plus shipping and handling.

I should have known better. The first time I hunted Sam with the compensators on, he nearly caught a rabbit in a pure, straightaway footrace in an open field, the rubber balls streaming behind him like an aviator's silk scarf in an open cockpit.

A shock collar, purchased the next summer for considerably more than $4.95 plus shipping and handling, finally brought Sam under control. There was, he soon came to realize, something out there that could hurt him and he started checking back, looking to me for protection. Our bond strengthened. My blood pressure lowered and my temper improved. Sam still ranged wide, but from then on I knew his wanderings would be roundtrips instead of one-way.

The electric collar served its purpose, but Sam became collar-wise, behaving in the field only if he wore the real collar or the dummy. I always felt as if I were cheating with the collar and that Sam was restrained rather than trained, so after the collar broke down one time too many, I sold it and bought a pair of track shoes. When Sam stopped responding to the whistle, I'd put on my running shoes and took him to a twenty-acre grassy field that was clipped so short there was no cover anywhere but along the fencelines. Sam liked to race down the fence and around the square, looking for birds.

I'd start him in one corner, whistling until I was satisfied he wasn't responding, then sprint diagonally across the field to cut him off at the far corner. If Sam paused to sniff around the locust tree, I could beat him to the brush pile near the old gate. Then I'd hide in the corn across the fence and leap out yelling when Sam arrived. He now believes I am faster than he is, which has done wonders for his obedience.

Other than the sprints, the collar work, yard work, and force-learning to retrieve, the rest of Sam's training consisted simply of turning him loose on wild birds before, after, and during the season. I may not have had any experience as a dog trainer myself, nor money to hire a pro, but I did have time to walk the dog every afternoon and there were wild pheasants on tap right across the road.

While my son was young enough to fit in a baby carrier, I'd strap him on my back almost every day from mid-July until mid-October and again from the end of the season in January until the hens began nesting in the spring. We'd follow Sam around the fields, letting the dog learn everything there was to know about pointing pheasants—when to creep, when to chase, how to push roosters hard without making them flush.

My dog remains far from perfect. He chases birds he flushes. The aggressiveness he's learned from pheasants carries over very poorly to woodcock; he crowds them and bumps as many as he points. He has a hard time picking up dead roosters because he invariably stands on one wing with both feet while trying to lift the body. He refuses to swim. Even today, at the dog middle age of eight, the sight of a pheasant flushing still sends a jolt of adrenaline to his brain that often renders him totally uncontrollable for several minutes afterwards. But the experience he gained in those seasons of working wild pheasants eight months a year, combined with a nose handed down from field trial champions, adds up to an uncanny talent for finding and pinning roosters.

During those afternoon runs, as I huffed along behind Sam with my son bouncing up and down and chortling in the backpack, I learned how to read my dog. Ever stylish, even joyous in the field, Sam's expressive body made it easy for me to understand what his nose was telling him about the hidden world of birds and scent beneath my feet. Soon I could read his every twitch the way an expert fisherman reads the slightest movement of his bobber.

Watching him track birds, I came to understand pheasants, too. When I hunted without a dog, I imagined pheasant hunting as a sort of walk through a minefield. Pheasants were hunkered down everywhere in the coverts, I assumed, heads pulled in like turtles, hoping you would walk past without noticing them. If you stepped close enough to a sitting bird, it would explode in your face with a disconcerting rattle of wings. When, after miles of tramping, a bird finally flushed at my feet, invariably I would repeat the dogless hunter's bromide to my companions: "We must have been walking by birds all day." I'd say it sagely, and my partners would nod in assent. Years later, with Sam's educated nose as my guide, I realized that pheasants slink, sprint, and double back, usually only sitting when trapped. If hunting with a dog increased the weight of my game bag, it also increased my respect for the wiles of pheasants.

As Sam has changed from liability to asset, and the Conservation Reserve Program has fueled a boom in pheasant populations, we've begun to enjoy the kind of success I'd always dreamed about. Where in previous years a three-bird limit was at best a biannual event, some days we're back home in little more than an hour after shooting our three birds over hard points. Other days there are long, satisfying chases through the CRP fields as Sam points and breaks over and over again on the trail of long-spurred, wise old roosters. I keep up as best as I can, breathless with exertion and anticipation both as Sam tiptoes after the birds and, more often than not, holds them until I arrive.

These latter outings invariably leave me drenched in sweat, and by late November I've usually shed a good ten pounds. Sam, always scrawny to begin with, looks positively cadaverous after a month of hard hunting. Effective predators, I'm well aware, must not only capture dinner, they must expend fewer calories in the chase than they gain from the kill in order to survive. By that measure, Sam and I would be doomed to quick starvation in the wild no matter how many birds we killed in a year, a thought which lends a certain wry perspective to our success in the field.

Two seasons ago, on the day after a blizzard had buried my place and the birds were sitting tight below the new-fallen snow, I caught myself taking a pheasant from Sam and stuffing it into my game bag with my right hand while signaling the dog to hunt up the next bird with the left. Any rooster pheasant, I have always maintained, is a trophy, and here I was cramming the bird into my vest without pausing to pay respects. We'd been hunting so much and killing birds so fast in the previous weeks that I realized I'd come to view a rooster as little more than one-third of a limit. Chastened, I took a break for a few days of deer hunting—which unfortunately counts as a nonconsumptive activity for me these days—before returning to the fields with Sam and my shotgun. The pheasants had grouped up into big, skittish late-season flocks while I was off sitting in trees, and they remained unapproachable until the last days of the season.

"That's what we get for feeling sorry for them," I told Sam on a mid-December day when the only pheasants we saw were tiny specks scaling off into the distance.

Our luck finally changed after Christmas, beginning on the drizzly afternoon I took Sam to hunt an eighty-acre CRP field a couple of miles from my house. I parked on the shoulder of the gravel road by the field's edge and at the sound of the truck door closing, pheasants poured out of the field, flying almost directly over the hood of the green Dodge pickup. One, two, three, four...at least four roosters in the gaggle of ten pheasants who'd survived this long by learning precisely what that metallic "clunk" meant.

I lifted Sam over the fence, then followed, loading the gun after I'd crossed. The sound of the breech closing over a pair of low-brass 6s was the last straw for one more tense rooster, who flushed out of range and followed the rest to the safety of the heavily posted cornfield across the road. The minute I put him down, Sam began snuffling through the grass where the pheasants had flushed.

"Sam," I said, "You're wasting your time. They're gone."

In answer, he locked on point, then broke and began trailing. In front of the dog I caught a glimpse of a black shape slinking in the direction of the fence we'd just climbed. I turned and ran back towards the fence myself, anticipating a wild flush. Now we had the bird trapped— the shorthair creeping in behind him, the open road to his front, me in easy gun range of his escape route if he didn't stop and crouch when he ran out of cover. The rooster flushed ahead of the dog, and I let him fly across the road and dropped him among the cornrows, then put one foot on the bottom strand of wire and pushed down so Sam could scoot back through the fence to make the retrieve.

This time the bird was duly admired, his feathers smoothed, the long tail carefully arranged to protrude from one side of the game bag, not merely for the benefit of passing road-hunters, but so he'd look as good hanging up in the kitchen as he'd taste on the dinner table. I gave Sam a hand signal. "Hunt 'em up." I said, pointing left. Sam went right. I put the whistle in my mouth to turn him, then let it drop back to my chest. Why make him come back? The rooster in the game bag was compelling evidence that Sam, as usual, had a better idea than did I as to where the birds were going to be.

"All right, all right, we'll do it your way," I said in affectionate, feigned resignation. Taking a few steps after him, I realized the sound of the bell had faded away; Sam had either crossed the county line or was pointing a bird nearby. I climbed to the top of a small rise, conditioned by years of frustration to scan the horizon for a small white dot coursing distant fencelines. What I saw instead was Sam locked on point, just below the crest of the rise. Breaking open the gun to make sure I'd reloaded, I walked down to join him, wondering if the bird he held in the brome grass for me was a rooster or a hen. I've known for a long time now that my job in the field is not to run the hunt but to carry the gun and see what happens. Most of all, Sam has taught me that wherever your dog leads, it pays to follow.

John Barsness was born and raised in Montana, where his grandparents homesteaded, and he shot his first game bird as soon as legally possible. With his wife, the writer Eileen Clarke, he lives on a trout stream in an obscure part of the southwestern quarter of the state. He's never held a real job for a whole year, instead devoting his life to hunting, fishing, and gazing at long vistas. In addition to writing for a number of national magazines, including Gray's Sporting Journal, Outdoor Life, Sports Illustrated, *and* Sports Afield, *he's presently a contributing editor of* Field & Stream *and* Petersen's Hunting. *His books include* Hunting the Great Plains, Montana Time: The Seasons of Trout Fisherman, *and* Western Skies: Bird Hunting on the High Plains and in the Rockies. *Though he has shot wild birds over a dozen breeds of pedigreed hunting dogs, a half-dozen accomplished mongrels, and dropped a francolin flushed by a baboon in Africa, his own dogs have been Labrador retrievers. He sees no reason to change and is working heartily toward an opinionated old age.*

A ROUGH- SHOOTING DOG

by John Barsness

The British have a term for what Americans do when we bird hunt. They call it "rough-shooting," meaning we stomp around in the woods and fields— as opposed to standing in a blind or butt with a gun handler reloading our matched Woodwards as red-legged partridge fly by like skittish kamikaze. I gather this term is not exactly an honorific, and is often used to describe the sporting habits of not only Americans (who on frequent occasions use, gasp, repeating shotguns) but the Irish. What the Irish have to say about the sporting habits of the Brits is not appropriate for this treatise.

Over here the dichotomy between classes of bird hunting is not so vast, though as land disappears into the maw of the mall, some of our rough-shooting seems to have become more stylized. I was born, raised, and still live in Montana and have watched the process occur even here. Why, just down the road in the Gallatin Valley there are several shooting preserves, offering stocked pheasants and chukar, and dog clubs where the members stand around on Saturday injecting the little thrill of electricity into their pointing dogs' necks. All of these gentlemen use double guns, and while none as yet wear ties while chasing Hungarian partridge, at least one adds the subtitle "Esq." to his name.

Luckily, when I was growing up out here three decades ago, there were no such role models around. The primary method of bird hunting was to drive around on logging roads and shoot ruffed grouse with a .22 rifle, or take their heads off with a .30-06 while out after elk. My father was antibird hunting, not because he didn't like to kill or eat them, but because unlike shooting mule deer, it wasn't cost efficient. He was an English professor but had grown up during the Depression on a Montana homestead and still saw any sort of game in utilitarian terms. If pheasants had come wrapped frozen in threes down at Heeb's Grocery then he might have been interested, particularly during weekend sales.

My first real live sporting idol was a friend of my father's, one of his fellow professors who lived in the house across the alley from us. He killed his deer every year, had a genuine six-point elk head sitting out in his garage, and caught trout on flies he tied himself. When pheasants first grew numerous enough to hunt in the valley, around 1960, he bought a bolt-action 20-gauge, then walked through a local cattail slough until a bunch of roosters flew. He was as good with the 20-gauge as his "sporterized" Springfield, and as the birds got up he killed a limit of three with three shots, afterwards declaring "there wasn't much to pheasant hunting." My father used this as further evidence in his antibird campaign.

So my main education came from outdoor magazines, books like *The Old Man And The Boy*, and even worse.

I was under the impression that there were two kinds of bird dogs in the world. The first were not only able to do mathematics with day-old scent (E+nose=quail/12 ga.) but could run all day, hold a point as long as the Statue of Liberty, and save drowning babies. The second type ate chickens and pecan pies, busted coveys, and belonged to young boys who didn't wear ties and probably never would.

So it was something of a surprise to meet my first real live bird dog. This was a Brittany spaniel that belonged to a student of my father's, who lived in a tiny cabin in one of the local canyons so he could hunt deer and grouse and catch trout. (Somewhat typically, he was from New York City. Montana kids usually wanted to move to the city, meaning Spokane.) I really didn't have much interest in bird hunting, but the student invited me out one day during my first legal hunting season, at age twelve. We each carried a double gun, quite by accident, and followed Duchess the Brittany up a side draw in the canyon. This was before Brittanies had been bred into schizophrenic imitations of Southern pointers and learned to run like hell; Duchess meandered quite placidly from side to side across the bottom of the draw, almost always in sight, once in a while flash-pointing at the bottom of an aspen.

Twenty minutes up the draw she pointed hard, nose uphill. The student pointed too, at the dog, and pantomimed for me to move up behind her. While I did, brain full of adrenalin and sixty-three *Old Man And The Boys*, Duchess held as steady as the mounted black bear in the window of the Stockman's Bar. Then I was right behind her, and nothing happened. No thunder-flush, no gray ghost ripping through the trees, none of the stuff I'd read about. Then Duchess tilted her head up a little, looking at an aspen a few feet away, and barked.

I had never read of this. It was as if my phys. ed teacher had lined us up for calisthenics and then recited Robert Frost. The student walked up beside me, shotgun ready, looking up in the tree. "Get 'em, Dutch," he said, and Duchess leaped up and bounced her front paws against the aspen. A ruffed grouse fell out of the top, gliding almost silently across the coulee, until the student's shotgun went boom and the grouse fell in the leaves.

Almost thirty years later, Duchess is still the most useful single hunting dog I've ever known. In today's terms, when Hungarian-loony western hunters like their Brits to cover counties as large as Delaware in a morning, she would be considered almost as slow as Dan Quayle. When she decided the wisest move was to break point and bark, she did so, though never without a gunner in range. She also was quite passable in a duck blind, though Canada geese were a little large for a forty-pound dog. She hunted every legal bird out here, which includes five different grouse, Huns, pheasants, snipe, and ducks, and always seemed a little smarter in that capacity than any human she ever accompanied. If doves had been legal then I suspect she'd have figured a way to toll them.

The next rough-shooting dog I met belonged to my grandfather-in-law, an old Sioux Indian from the Fort Peck Reservation in northeastern Montana. Ben was not only a hunter and angler of nearly seventy years experience, but a highly practical scavenger as well. When he visited the local landfill, odds ran about fifty-fifty that he'd come back with more than he took. One day he returned with a black puppy that someone had abandoned. He claimed it was a Labrador retriever, and indeed there may have been some in there because Suzy Dump (as he named her) retrieved anything that fell down, including the walleye and channel cats Ben pulled out of the Missouri River.

But she specialized in putting sharptailed grouse and pheasants out of the thick buffalo berry and wild rose thickets of the reservation. From the first of September on through December, these are the favorite houses of those birds. Ben showed me how to tell when they'd set up shopkeeping in a particular thicket, pointing out the "chicken trails" the birds pushed underneath the branches and grass, creating archways not unlike those found in old Mexican cathedrals. By then Ben was too old to walk the longer coulees, so he'd drop me and Suzy Dump off at one end, then drive his pickup to the other, anywhere from a half mile to two miles away, and wait for us to drive birds toward him, picking off what we could along the way.

Suzy's technique was to push her way along a chicken track until she'd chased all the birds into the thickest part of the brush. Early in the season many of the birds would flush quite readily, and I'd often have a full game bag by the time I met Ben, but later—particularly during pheasant season—they grew more wary and adept at worming their way like feathered ferrets under the matted grass and wild roses. Then Suzy used her patented Heinz 57 technique, named not only for her heritage but her motion: she jumped up and down on top of the matted roses like a newly opened bottle of steak sauce some giant was trying to unplug. Often this was in brush shoulder high to me, and all I could see were her pointy ears at the apex of each jump, flipping skyward like two lapping black tongues before she disappeared again. The cover was so thick that sometimes I could hear a bird starting to claw its way out for what seemed like a full minute (and may have been six or seven seconds) before it appeared, looking as nonplussed and disheveled as a banker suddenly thrust into a mud wrestling contest.

But unlike Duchess, Suzy Dump was a specialist, not much use at anything else. As a waterfowl dog she lacked attention, quite often abandoning the bird in the last thirty feet of the retrieve, which in the Missouri River rendered her quite useless. She was very attentive to whomever she hunted with, so much so that on one cold November day, when Ben and I were jump-shooting a series of stock ponds for mallards and whatever else we might find, she almost drowned me. We sneaked to the edge of one cattail-rimmed pond and when six mallards jumped, killed one in the pond and one on the land.

The one on the land was no problem, but the cattail margin was frozen, the ice just thick enough that Suzy couldn't break it. I wore hip boots and decided to break trail to the edge of cattails and open water, so she could swim out, get the duck, and, I hoped, bring it all the way back. (By that point in our career, I always carried a stout spinning rod and several huge treble hooks to snag any ducks Suzy abandoned in midretrieve, so field-trial behavior wasn't necessary.) When I entered the water Suzy came with me. The bottom was typical black muck, and by the edge of the cattails I was up to my ankles in ooze and almost to the top of my hip boots in icewater. I tried to step aside to get out of Suzy's way but was stuck. She was swimming in a narrow track through the ice and couldn't back up, so she swam right up my jeans pockets. We both went down and experienced a new low in physical sensation. On my life list I'd put falling into thirty-two-degree mudwater somewhere between being kicked in the crotch and a Scotch hangover. The recovery period was somewhere between, too; when we slogged back to the truck Ben just said, "The next pond's a couple miles. You'll have time to dry out." Oddly enough, both Suzy and I did, partly because we had to wait a half-hour for the mallard to drift to the dam end of the pond where she did retrieve it. That is rough-shooting at its finest.

There have been other rough-shooting dogs over the years, ranging in skills and heritage between Duchess and Suzy Dump. One was Norm Strung's Boykin spaniel, Pistol, who went along on beach expeditions and learned to dig clams. Another was a German shepherd who not only flushed and retrieved pheasants but on one occasion ran down a wounded deer, throttled it, and came back to lead his master to the deer. ("Search, Lassie, and destroy!") Bill DeShaw has a Brittany that is the closest genetic throwback to Duchess I've seen in this age of jet-powered pointing spaniels. She's come up with yet another approach to rose-and-grass thickets; she gets down on her belly at pheasant height and points under the brush. Bill waits until the brush quits rustling, then walks in and kicks out the bird. Eli Spannagel, a rancher I used to work for in southeastern Montana, had a bassett hound that did much the same thing, except he didn't have to scrunch down much and when he got close to a rooster he bayed at it, which was quite effective.

My own two rough-shooting dogs have both been Labs, which is the safest way to go when bird work gets varied and unpredictable. The first was a very lean black dog with a white chest-blaze named Gillis. He didn't care for water (though he'd jump in and dive after wounded mallards) but really liked to insinuate his skinny body between rosebushes to scare the hell out of sharptails and pheasants. I toted it up once and in his almost fourteen-year existence he retrieved around twenty species of game birds, from doves to Canada geese, and a number of rabbits and hares. My present is a chocolate at the opposite end of the spectrum, a one-hundred-pounder named Keith who likes water as well as any pilot whale and prefers to go over pheasant cover rather than between it. In his first year I saw him slam head-on into several trees and fenceposts. He'd back up, look at them as if memorizing the exact diameter that had stopped him, then step aside and zoom onward. He has flushed everything from Huns (which he does rather well, quartering naturally in a grainfield) to a Shiras moose, which came out of our local pheasant cover late last season. Since I didn't shoot the moose, he didn't retrieve it, though if asked he would sure as hell try.

It may seem as if my experiences with rough-shooting dogs have tended toward flushers and off-breeds rather than pointing dogs. This is true, perhaps because pointing breeds have grown more specialized in the past couple of decades. This is, of course, because bird hunters have grown more specialized and stylized in the past couple of decades. A couple of seasons ago I took a friend up on his invitation to hunt his personal bird ranch. Upon arrival I found two huge pens full of pheasants, and soon learned that his private pheasant ranch is privately stocked. He ran German shorthairs, and looked a little askance at Keith. We worked several overgrown fields and some cattail creeks and, predictably, the pointers did better in the open cover and Keith did better in the cattails. At the end of the day my friend remarked that he could always put his pointers in a field worked by Labs or springers and find a few more birds.

I nodded and didn't say what I thought, which is that damn few of the pheasant places I hunt have roosters living in fields. Maybe on opening day, but after all the one-day wonders have worked the easy places, killing the easy birds, my pheasants seem to live in places a trifle more difficult than even overgrown fields. Cattails are one of the easier places, willow swamps being the hardest. My grouse tend to live in buffalo berry thickets or along alder-choked creeks. Doves and geese fly around fields, but the work is a little different than stylish pointing. I have known pointing dogs that did all these things, but not since Duchess have I seen one do all the rough stuff really well.

This is not to say that I don't enjoy walking a few 120-acre strips of wheat stubble behind a good English setter, talking to my friends and waiting for that classic point on a covey of Huns. This gets done, quite frequently. But the kind of bird hunting I do more often is a less stylized, more random. Despite early brainwashing by *The Old Man And The Boy*, my bird hunting has evolved into something much more akin to the Pleistocene than wearing a tie and standing around in groups watching several dogs work pen-raised birds. It has gotten so a great many bird hunters I know seem to expect similar experiences each time they go out. I listened to one such complain that he'd paid for four dozen quail for him and his three buddies, and they'd only gotten thirty-seven. This seems similar to what my father expected from the wild: a cost-effective hunt.

What Keith and I like to do is have adventures. My wife, Eileen, Keith's other alpha, says we get up in the morning like two goddamned chipmunks, tails wagging and looking forward to another day full of new scenery and unexpected thrills. We like to pick out a certain piece of western landscape—willow bottom, durum wheat field, sagebrush, or ponderosa ridgetop—and go across it at a pace designed for nothing in particular. Like Duchess and all the other really good rough-shooting dogs I've ever known, Keith seems to be adapting to the terrain and bird rather than a gun club's notion of what an AKC Labrador retriever should be. When in willows, he circles the pheasants. When in sage, he snuffles the sage. When in wheat, he trots back and forth in front of me, nose higher and eyes alert. Wherever we go, we expect the unexpected, which is what dogs and men did a few millenia ago when

they made their first looping travels along the unpredictable path of evolution. Perhaps that's the reason
there aren't many rough-shooting dogs left these
days; there aren't many rough-shooting hunters. Keith
and I are regarded as recidivist mutations, which is
just fine with us. There's more room out there for aim-
less drifters, and once in a while, past the fourth or
fifth ridge, the sun falling at that four o'clock angle that
makes every piece of buffalo berry or peachleaf willow
or big sage seem ripe with expectancy, we even find
a wild bird.

George Bird Evans was born with English setters eighty-six years ago and has never been without them. He had to be away from them while studying art, and then in New York working toward being an illustrator, and arriving, but even then there were the grouse seasons with his father and the setters in southwest Pennsylvania. Kay was introduced to Speck as seriously as to George's parents, and until 1935 Speck was with George and Kay whenever they could be at the mountain cabin. In 1939 they realized their own place in the Alleghenies, named it Old Hemlock, and bought Blue, the beginning of their Old Hemlock line. His son Ruff pointed and retrieved grouse from 1947 to 1962, sired three litters, and saw George put away paint brushes and start writing. Twenty-two books and many anthology and magazine pieces later, Quest and his son, eleventh-generation Manton, now live and hunt with George and Kay, who could not exist without a setter.

BITTERSWEET

by George Bird Evans

Without the alchemy of Indian summer the shooting man would have only gray days from August to December, deprived of hazy afternoons and the war paint of the mountains; no glow of sugar maples progressing into flame, no newly minted aspen copse atremble in soft winds, no wincing yearning for days and moments like lemon-yellow leaves coming down counting Time that won't come back; no fermentation stirring primordial memory, no pungency of October's rot, no expectation. None of those smells and agonies and visions would be here to make it good, to make us go on living it after it has passed, remembering, wanting, hungering for it to come again.

It had come again and we were driving out our long lane with black lace of hemlocks a fairyland against sugar-maple gold, and I felt somehow that everything was going to be like the old days. Belton and Quest peering out the tailgate window seemed to know it was the week of the season when generations of Old Hemlock setters from Ruff through Dixie and Bliss and Briar had come under the spell of the big woodcock coverts of the Blackwater/Canaan, and we were off.

Partway to the Valley, Kay turned the station wagon into a side road and up a hill leading to high coverts that had to hold flight woodcock this last week of October. Winding up the dirt road doubling back on itself, we could look down through gnarled apple trees to the empty unpainted house where the old man, gray as the clapboards, used to wave to us where now his makeshift ladder still leaned against the roof.

We topped the last bend through vines blue with wild grapes, and leveled along the straight stretch with all things beautiful until we came to the yellow No Hunting notices plastering our first covert. We drove on with them glaring at us for half a mile, even at the Poplar House where the entrance had been plowed into a hostile barrier with one more yellow rectangle nailed on the wooden gate.

Farther down the hill we parked with the station wagon canted on the side of the rough road. I at least had a permit marked "lifetime" in my shooting vest that said I could hunt here.

While I was changing into rubber pacs a car labored up the stony grade and stopped and a white-haired man in a Stewart tartan shirt—why do some old men look like some old women—inquired if I wasn't Mr. Evans. There was a patient-looking woman on the seat beside him instead of a dog and she listened quietly while he told me he was from the southern part of the state. It seemed a West Virginia game biologist had said he could find woodcock in here, and had marked his map *George Bird Evans's cover*. I thought of Col. Peter Hawker's

Diary and "that green-livered son of a bitch, the lawyer." He finally left, after telling me there weren't any birds in there.

We cast Belton and Quest and they leaped the sagging wire fence and began quartering through leaves too dry and noisy. The old man had been right: we didn't move a feather all the way to the hemlock swamp in the bottom. Crossing back over the road, I was certain we'd find 'cock among the hillside hawthorns but both dogs covered them well and there was nothing, not even in Belton's rail fence corner.

Waiting for Kay, who had gone for the station wagon, I sat on the top rail with memories of the birds in Belton's younger days and tried to make some sense out of it. Today was cool, forty-five degrees, and partly sunny, and it was the last day of October, when my setters and I had so many times been mesmerized by flighting woodcock in this sleepy Rip Van Winkle hollow. This season there were no cattle grazing around the Poplar House, but could woodcock anticipate that and bypass a covert such as this? The charm of the old road was beginning to work its hypnosis when Kay pulled the station wagon to a stop and brought me out of my reverie.

At the bottom of the hill we crossed the stream and let the dogs out. There was a barbed wire fence and we took turns spreading the strands for the other to squeeze through. There were cow pads—big, juicy, lovely—and a hen woodcock came back over us fast and sassy and was gone.

Here in the open lowland it was windy and colder and we worked cattle paths through the red-berried hawthorns. Out ahead I saw Quest on point in a dense spinney below a small shed. This was what I had waited for all summer, with daily therapeutic drymounting the new little 28-bore AyA. Ten days ago there had been a reinjury of the right shoulder, bringing back the old pain, but now it was going to be all right. I couldn't see Belton, but Quest was holding—a high-headed angel, his bloody tail tip vivid in the sunshine. A woodcock, another hen, gave me everything in a rising straightaway over the spiky thicket and my shoulder atrophied with the gunstock partway out from under my arm. Some things are more bitter than pain.

We hunted higher into good cover, stepping around more cow pads, but had no reflush. On top we came to what from a distance had appeared to be out-of-scale sheep—off-white Charolais, lots of them. Quest had a point that proved empty and Belton, the rascal, wouldn't honor—*there was no bird, was there?*

Just before we left home I had discovered a suspicious swelling on Belton. He was approaching thirteen and in apparent good health, but our vet had sent off a specimen for biopsy. With a week to wait for the report, we had come on this trip as the best way to get through the uncertainty until diagnosis, and I was grateful for any pleasure Belton had.

Quest gave us another point, a hot one, but the flush wouldn't have been a shot, even with a good shoulder. It was nearing end of day when we reached the station wagon, and Kay put Belton into the rear and stayed with him while I took one more turn with Quest in search of the first 'cock that had flushed to the north side of the road.

The thicket was too dense to penetrate, but I heard Quest's bell go silent. I made a short circle into swamp grass on the outside, and then the bell spoke again, and the woodcock came out against the sunset and bloomed into vision, whizzing past me. I wheeled and tried to mount and again the shoulder just wouldn't do it. The stock felt a foot too long, and I was still subconsciously trying to start the mount by the Churchill method, high up under the arm against the ribs. You can't unlearn years of habit in a day.

It was well after dark when we reached our rented Canaan Valley cabin, but we were soon set up with Belton and Quest fed and spread out on their blanket on the sofa. This was the end of October, the flights would logically be in; if Belton's report proved negative, it would seem we just about had everything.

Next day was cloudy and sunny by turns with a wind that made the forty-seven degree temperature seem cold. We parked inside a rickety iron gate leading to a huge pasture grown to copses of hawthorns and red maples, with a draw of spruce and fir and alders tapering into tundra.

There was a rutted trace of road and Belton and Quest went on point at the very cluster of thicket where they'd had a point last season. As I circled in front, a woodcock flushed head high and to my delight I got the gun up and fired. I felt I might have hit but Quest bored out, and although we got both dogs back to search carefully they found neither bird nor feathers. To a man for whom a shot like that would normally have almost certainly been a hit, such misses are devastating.

With Belton and Quest wild with excitement, we hunted south into alders bordering the balsam swamp. I remember Bliss pointing there on a day when she and Dixie were in their prime, with Bliss's tail straight up; I also remember that I missed the 'cock, and there was nothing wrong with my shoulder then.

On Quest's next point with Belton backing, a woodcock went up before I reached the dogs, and soon after, Quest had another productive in the edge cover. Woodcock may not like to get their feet wet, as I am told, but there was whitewash floating in a small puddle. I splashed to Quest, who was rigid, then took two more steps and heard a bell-like twitter-up behind me and wheeled and fired at a silhouette topping the alders. The muscle spasm threw the pattern to the right and I watched the 'cock disappear, dropping a departing token. Old Alaric Alexander Watts advised: "try to draw the trigger just as you at the gun's end the object view. Nine times in ten the gun is right." I was having too many tens, and becoming a little vocal about it, then recalled Nash Buckingham at ninety, gamely trying to shoot with vision in only one eye.

We had come to an area new to us, with tundra sweeping into the south and alders delineating a tiny run, which was widening into a series of beaver dams, with blue Cabin Mountain scalloping the sky to the east. We reached a low rise with a view of hawthorns ahead of us and stopped to eat lunch sitting on an outcrop of rock under two of the larger trees. Unlike the hawthorns we hunted yesterday, these spiky branches held no haws where there would normally have been red or yellow globes, but woodcock would be there for the leaf-pack on the ground, not the fruit.

It was sunny on this big plain, with huge cumulus repeated in shadow on Cabin Mountain. Kay got some pictures of Belton seriously watching her for the biscuit he knew she would have brought him, and here in this glorious land it seemed he just had to be all right.

Starting after lunch both dogs reached out—Belton as far as Quest—but on our way north we felt he needed resting, and Kay led him on leash while Quest and I skirted tall woods with excellent thorns. When we came to the far end Kay released Belton, who hadn't taken his eyes off me, and he worked the damp leaf-pack under the big hawthorns with Quest. There were almost always 'cock in here and Belton soon gave us a nice point that Quest honored loyally. Woodcock were nervous this season, going up like killdeer. There were two birds, one a climbing flush I would normally have tried for, but my clumsy misses on this trip had robbed me of my confidence and I didn't take the shot. That was the end of the action. Regrettably I gave Belton and Quest nothing to retrieve but Quest made do with a couple of deer legs he delivered to me religiously, souvenirs of the bow hunting that goes on throughout the bird season in the Canaan.

In the night it began to snow and we awoke to a white Canaan Valley with Cabin and Canaan mountains fogged out in the upper elevations. By late morning it was up to fifty-five degrees with a flawless sky but still breezy. We had saved one big covert in the upper Valley for such a day as this, a place we discovered only the previous season.

Taking time to pack for the drive home after the hunt, it was past 1 P.M. when we cast Belton and Quest. The area was an expanse of flatland dotted with hawthorns— big as hawthorns are big in this strange highland. Quest was moving wide, fitting himself to the scale of the covert but Belton found the first woodcock in a corner nearby, a bird that bored out like a bullet.

It has been my experience that 'cock act differently in open situations, refusing to hold for the gun, and I wondered if it was the lack of overhead cover or pressure from recent gunners making them spooky. When I first came to the Canaan, one of the regulars, a shooting M.D. who reserved a room throughout the season at the old Worden's Hotel in Davis, used to say: "There is no such thing as a private covert in this Blackwater country," and it is true. Curiously, you don't always see the other hunters, but I can tell by the action of my dogs and sometimes by the behavior of the birds when other gunners and their dogs have been there.

Wind was at our backs, seeming to gain velocity out in the bottom, and although Quest was trying to work with it in his face, he ran onto a woodcock in a small copse of hawthorns and stopped conscientiously at the flush, the strong breeze ruffling the hair the wrong way on his back.

He stood watching the bird disappear, followed by another and another, until five 'cock had lifted from the one thicket, flushing in as many directions. One crossed up the slope in front of me, a nice chance that I passed—I don't shoot at woodcock unless they're pointed—and Quest moved on, trying to avoid my look.

There were so many points and wild flushes that counting separate woodcock was difficult. Belton hunted hard, even ranging too wide but keeping in touch, while Quest, stimulated by so much action, had to be checked at times.

We made a big circle, and at the south-end woods ate sandwiches as we sat on twin stumps. Quest had pointed a 'cock at the head of the little draw and Kay had got some pictures; now she took more of our blue/orange brace resting.

Starting out after lunch we almost immediately had a double point among small hawthorns—a male bird that came out low-crossing right, a shot I tried too close and missed and missed again as it banked, but it is odd that two empty shots can be an event to a man with atrophied shoulders, and I rejoiced that I shot at all. I recalled how I used to handle my $7^3/_4$-pound Fox in dense grouse cover, and I can still see 'cock folding in puffs of tan feathers when I was using the little Purdey—split-second shots in dense alders and spiraea jungles.

Quest had another point breathing fire—a hen looking larger than hens look and right-quartering through the orchard-size hawthorns. My mount was so cramped I shot from my right biceps and the bird looked as if it had no intention of ever stopping.

In our three days of gunning we had been in more hawthorns than I can remember anywhere, with almost no aspens, which normally spell woodcock to me, but the 'cock were there.

By this time Quest was pointing again in dead golden-rod beyond the station wagon. I got to him and stepped past and the woodcock darted for the edge of beech woods. I like to think I might have dropped it *if*, but Quest made a dash in my line of fire, high on adrenaline from seeing too many birds fly on unhit. Lady Luck is a fickle hussy, irresistible and charming, and there was a time when she and I were on more intimate terms.

I had an urge to continue, but Belton was showing signs of tiring, and I knew, without facing it too squarely, that I was not going to make any shots with my humerus and acromion grinding bone-on-bone each time I mounted my gun. The little 28-bore was a delight to carry and the 2 dram ³/₄-ounce No. 9 loads were pleasant to shoot, but merely hearing them go off was not what I came for.

Changing out of my boots, we headed the station wagon up Canaan Mountain, pausing at the top to look back down on the wild spread of aspen and spruce bogs with the Blackwater winding from one beaver dam to the next, each a piece of misplaced evening sky. It was a land Robert W. Service wrote about without ever having seen it: *I am the land that listens, I am the land that broods…* . Behind me I could hear Quest licking his wet coat and Belton trying to find a comfortable position for his tired bones. We drove homeward toward Old Hemlock with the old gibbous Woodcock Moon changing from right to left and back again as we unwound the narrow curving road.

On Monday we got the report on Belton's biopsy. But we had given him three more wonderful days.

Michael McIntosh is one of the world's best-known writers on shotguns and shooting. He is shotgunning columnist for Sporting Classics, Shooting Sportsman, *and* Gun Dog *and a regular contributor to* The Double Gun Journal *and* Wildlife Art, *as well. In addition to best-selling gun books—* Best Guns, The Big-Bore Rifle, A.H. Fox, *and* Shotguns and Shooting*—he also has written books on sporting artists Robert Abbett, David Maass, and Herb Booth.*

His love for dogs began with a pointer named Cookie, who was born just a few weeks before he was. "My mother bottle-fed us both," he says. "Probably from the same bottle, which would explain some things." For the past twelve years, his constant companion has been the sweet-faced Brittany he calls October—or Doofus, depending on what she's rolled in recently. They're growing old together on their farm in the Missouri hills, though neither one shows any real signs of growing up.

TALES FROM THE DARK SIDE

by Michael McIntosh

If memory serves me right, I have lived with dogs I could call my own for just about forty-three years now. With few exceptions, they have been gun dogs of one stripe or another; without exception, I have loved them all, loved them as fiercely and completely as they have loved me, shamelessly and without reserve. The roster of my dogs is fairly short—minuscule, by some standards—for I have always preferred to know them one at a time, two at the most, and nearly all have mercifully been long-lived and unprone to fatal accident.

By contrast, the list of dogs that have laid some claim on a place in my heart, however momentary the affair, is enormous and would include almost every one I ever met. I have gone out of my way to make their acquaintances all over the world, gone out of pocket to see them fed and cared for when no one else was willing, gone half out of my head with grief at each loss of a dear old friend.

Simply put, I love dogs, large or little, yeoman or sissy, working stiff or pampered pet. I have to confess, though, that I love gun dogs most of all. They like what I like, which is to poke around any shaggy piece of countryside where certain birds are likely to be found and to test our collective skills of nose and gun against their capabilities for survival and flight—exercises performed in the sheer animal exuberance of taking part, of being immersed in a world whose rhythms and mysteries are so vast that the deeper we penetrate, the more its margins fade away.

As my progress toward fifty years of being a hunter is about to come down to counting on a single hand, I can no longer tally all the dogs I've known. Some stand out sharp and clear. Others come to mind only in brief images. Many more shift and blend until I haven't a clue where one might end and another begins. I've known a few geniuses, a lot of competent craftsmen, and a handful of duds whose witlessness was mitigated only by their being lovable fools. I've known some men who deserved better dogs and some dogs who deserved better men. I've learned how easy it is to blame a dog for our own shortcomings, expecting too much and offering too little, how shamelessly we take credit that rightly belongs to them, how heart-crackingly and purely damn *good* it feels to see a piece of work pulled off with a flash of brilliance.

Fond as I am of dogs, I fancy it's not an unrealistic affection—though it certainly could be. We have a penchant for glorifying dogs beyond all the limits of reality and good sense, burdening them with fantastic presumptions of nobility and then growing disappointed and blameful when they can't possibly live up to it. We do the same to women, I'm afraid, although I'd just as soon not get into that right now. Suffice it to say, we might be better off all around if we kept our romantic notions more closely in line with the way things really are most of the time.

I can't think of a better way to illustrate just how far off the deep end we can go than simply to cite the lunkhead, whoever he was, who once observed that dog spelled backwards is god, as if it proved something. In response, I can only point out that buzzard spelled backwards is drazzub, polecat is tacelop, and the whole thesis strikes me as being so much tihsesroh. Dogs are not gods—unless, of course, we're willing to accept gods whose shortcomings sometimes are more than a match for their virtues. Dogs are simply dogs, which is enough to ensure that their concomitant disasters are more than sufficient. If I've learned anything in all these years, it's this: no creature that breathes is capable of delivering a wider range of realities more pointedly or more inescapably than a gun dog.

Now, I don't know if I've witnessed everything a gun dog can do that's either distressing, disgusting, disgraceful, disagreeable, distasteful, or some combination of two or more. Sometimes I hope so, because I'd hate to think it could get any worse.

I'm not talking about everyday lapses like tracking up the house with muddy feet, nor even such garden-variety misbehavior as selective deafness, breaking up other dogs' points, eating birds, or barreling out of a duck blind before called upon to do so. If those were the worst things dogs were capable of, then they truly would be candidates for the pantheon. The fact is, though, they are capable of much worse—acts of a magnitude to make saints fall a-cursing, behavior so vile and proclivities so foul as to gag a vulture at the very thought. Like the thorn beneath the rose, the dark side of the dog looms ever near the surface and manifests itself not so much when you least expect it but rather when it's least convenient, most embarrassing, or in some way certain to have maximum effect.

The fundamental themes that govern this shady realm are remarkably few. Perhaps this is because dogs are essentially simple creatures—and possibly because those who insist upon living with them are too. At any rate, these themes offer means as good as any for organizing a survey. In the interest of keeping this both accurate and in manageable proportion, the incidents I shall use by way of illustrating the points are strictly from my own experience or from reports by people I know to be reliable. Hard as it may be to believe, some men have been known to take liberties with the facts when relating dog stories, whether about their own dogs or others'. What you're about to read, though, is absolutely true, much as I wish most of it wasn't.

Gastrointestinals, Upper

Strictly speaking, dogs are carnivores, just like their original ancestor, the wolf. Somewhere in the long evolutionary descent from *Canis lupus*, however, *Canis domesticus* acquired a gene, possibly several, that expanded its gustatory horizon considerably. The present-day dog is omnivorous in the broadest sense of the word, which is made up of two Latin words—*omnis* or "all" and *vorare* or "devouring." Together, they denote an organism willing to consume anything, and if you looked it up in an illustrated dictionary, you'd find a picture of a sporting dog.

Exactly which breed wouldn't really matter, although among the ones I've known, the most truly catholic tastes have belonged to setters, Brittanies, and Labrador retrievers. Sorting the big-leaguers from the amateurs isn't easy, but I'd have to give Burly a slight edge on all the rest. Burly was a big black Lab who belonged to an old friend of mine. He was a grand hunter and fearless retriever. He also was a first-rate companion—usually.

The thing about burly was his appetite, both in quantity and variety. He was the only dog I ever knew who truly would eat *anything*. Which was fine so far as dog food and table scraps were concerned; we never had to go out of our way to keep him happy with what he was fed. The problem was all the stuff he'd find for himself, and even that would have been okay if his digestive system had been a match for his taste, or lack of same.

If I really put my mind to it, I probably could remember one or two trips that ended without Burly throwing up in the back of Jim's station wagon, but none occur to me right off the top of my head. And it never was just some little wad of green grass, like every other dog hurls up now and then. No, when Burly unloaded, you just had to marvel that a mere eighty-five-pound dog could hold sixty pounds of dead fish, road-kill possum, deer guts, or whatever else he'd polished off while nobody was looking.

You could tell it wasn't going to be any dainty little burp just by listening. He'd suddenly stand up, pace back and forth a couple of times to find the exact geographical center of the cargo compartment, and then give forth a chorus of rumbling and churning that sounded like a volcano giving birth to New Zealand. This would culminate in the delivery of some wet, steaming, stinking mess that invariably arrived before Jim could get the car stopped alongside the road. Pulling over always gave old Burl the idea that we weren't through hunting yet, so he'd charge up to the front seat and give me one or two good slurps up the side of my face before I could fend him off. Nobody who ever went hunting with Burly had to ask twice why Jim carried an old shovel in the car.

On one occasion I wish I could forget, he even managed a double-header. Jim had moved to western Iowa by then, and I was up for a long weekend with pheasants. We let Burly out of his kennel the first morning, and he dashed around the house to air out. While Jim got the last of his gear loaded, I walked around to see if Burly was ready and met him coming the other way, just finishing breakfast, which in this case was a full-grown squirrel that he'd either caught fresh or found in the street out front.

Either way, it was impressive. I guess he didn't want to waste any hunting time, because he was in the process of swallowing the damn thing whole, and when I came along it was all down except one hind leg and the tail. Burl sort of humped up, took a couple of mighty heaves, and even those disappeared, tail and all. Not for long, though. It all came back about twenty minutes later.

I don't know what it was he got hold of that afternoon; I'm not even sure a histologist could have made any sense of it, although he certainly would've had plenty to work with.

The last time I hunted with the old boy before he died, we parked the car next to a creek, which Burly naturally had to investigate while we uncased our guns. We could hear him still splashing around as we started off, so Jim whistled to get him moving. And he came lumbering up the bank happily chewing on what I took to be a muskrat, judging from the tail.

"Burl's eating a muskrat," I called over to Jim.

Jim kept on walking. "That son of a bitch. There's probably a Number Four Victor trap on the other end of it." He sighed. "We'll find out on the way home."

I never thought I'd meet Burly's equal—and I still haven't, really—but my Brittany, October, is no slouch when it comes to omnivorousness. Living on a farm as we do, she's developed a fine taste for cowflop, relishes the odd placental repast at calving time, and come fall, has an infallible knack for finding the gut pile where my neighbor field-dressed his deer.

This wouldn't be so bad if she could just keep it down, but as with Burly, her stomach has better sense than her head. Except for once when she was a pup, she's never tossed her cookies in the car, but I haven't found that to be any particular comfort when I wake up in the middle of the night to the sounds of imminent eruption—or step barefoot into the results next morning on the rare occasions when she's quiet about it.

Whenever she barfs up some godawful mess, I send her straightaway outdoors. I realize it's too late by then, but it makes me feel better to do something just in case there's more. I did that one night, and in the few minutes it took me to clean things up, she wandered out by the barn and got crossways with a skunk. At least she didn't eat it.

Possibly the most unusual thing I've ever seen a dog eat was a little package consumed and subsequently returned by a setter who belonged to my old pal Spence. We were hunting grouse in Minnesota one fall, sharing a motel room. Spence got up in the middle of the night, stepped in something, and awakened most of the local population in the process of explaining acceptable behavior to his dog. Sam the setter was not known for this sort of thing—and I didn't have anything else to do at the moment, anyway—so I asked what she'd eaten. Spence took a look and said he wasn't sure, so I had a look, too.

Nearly as we could tell, it was his underwear.

Intraspecific Infelicity

One of the things in this life that I never asked for but got anyway is a strange knack for being nearby when two dogs decide to try tearing one another limb from limb. Rarely is one of the combatants mine, since I haven't had a male gun dog in more than twenty years, so I really don't understand why I'm always the one closest to the action. Just lucky, I guess.

I do know that I have little patience with dog fights and even less with the hammerheaded types that seem to make careers out of starting them. I am therefore apt to take draconian measures.

Water, I find, is a splendid tool for sorting out a donnybrook. I discovered this one day when two Labradors began disputing ownership of a dead duck in the bottom of a boat. (These fools had just spent four hours together in the same blind without raising an eyebrow or a hackle. Besides, the damn duck was *mine*, but try to tell that to a dog.) They were in opposite ends of the boat, and I had one foot in and one in the water when they met more or less between my legs and started snarling at one another. I grabbed the nearest collar, lost my balance, dragged the dog over the gunwale, and somehow managed to get him underneath me before I hit the water. I know it sounds amazing, but holding a Labrador's head underwater for about five minutes makes him lose all interest in fighting.

I witnessed a really clever variation on this once in South Dakota, when somebody else happened to be closest to the fray for a change.

There were three of us, hunting sharptails, and two dogs—a handsome setter and an equally handsome Brittany who also happened to be one of the dumbest dogs I ever met. This specimen was competent enough, but he could make the proverbial bucket of rocks look like a Rhodes scholar. The two dogs hadn't met one another before, and by the end of the second day, it was obvious that the setter, also not overly burdened with brains, was just biding his time before starting a fight.

The sun was about half a gun-barrel's length above the western horizon. We had our birds dressed and packed away and were toasting sundown from the tailgate of the Suburban, parked atop a rise in that great, gorgeous sweep of sky and grass. Both dogs had been repeatedly admonished for their interest in the gut pile and, being dogs, were doing everything they could to circumvent their orders. They weren't even paying much attention to each other, until they met nose to nose with fresh grouse guts between them.

It was just the straw the setter was waiting for, and in about two seconds he had hold of the Brittany's ear and was settling in to punch some tickets. Without a moment's hesitation, the Brit's owner leaned over, tilted the setter's head up as delicately as a midwife handling a newborn, and poured half a can of beer right down his nose. End of fight. The setter was still snorting up the odd gobbet of foam next morning and couldn't smell birds worth a damn, but it turned out to be the pleasantest day of the trip.

On the whole, there's nothing funny about a dog fight until it's over, but I did see one that almost put me on my knees. It happened at a duck club in the Missouri River bottoms and involved two splendid young Labs and a newspaper sportswriter I used to hang out with in my teaching days.

Bill Bennett, whose name will come up again before we're through with this, is a man who should never even have owned a picture of a dog. He loved them, but they were his Nemesis. He was, for instance, the only man I've ever seen knocked flat on his face in a puddle of his own urine by a dog—but that's another story for another time. The fight I'm thinking of came after he bought the Labrador he named Ebony of Nghaerfyrddin, or some equally inscrutable Welsh word that translated as "black dog with tail." Don't ask me why.

Even as a yearling pup, Ebby, as we called him, was magnificent, big and sleek and strong, and he showed all the promise of becoming a first-rate hunter. The day we shot at Greenhead Farm, we showed up about ten minutes late and found a local physician in our blind. While he very graciously apologized for having misread the blind assignments on the clubhouse wall, his dog, who was somewhat older than Ebby and grouchy as a Cape buffalo with a case of jock itch, growled and snarled. I was not unhappy to see him led away across a field of cut corn.

We gave neither of them a thought until the end of the day, when the good doctor winged a mallard that sailed way out into the corn before going down. Since we had a better view of where it fell than he did, I suggested we go help him retrieve it. Bill put Ebby on a leash, and we waded across our pool and into corn stubble almost knee-deep with the slick, gluey northwest-Missouri mud that is a major factor in what holds the world together. Miserable stuff to walk in.

Doc and his dog were out of their blind, too, headed down the field, and when the Lab saw us coming, he wheeled around and charged straight for us. He wasn't making very speedy headway, but we couldn't, either, so I told Bill to get a good grip on the leash and I'd try to stop this maniac before he reached Ebby.

It almost worked. I got my fingertips on his collar but he ducked his head and I lost him. In the next instant, he bowled into Bill and Ebby, and all three went down in one massive tangle of arms, legs, dogs, flying mud, snarling, snapping, and half-coherent shouting.

Even if he hadn't had the leash wrapped around his wrist, Bill was as helpless against the mud as a turtle on its back. The whole pile kept rolling over and over, although somehow Bill managed to stay mostly on the bottom. For all the uproar, the dogs were scarcely touching one another, but between them they were literally stomping poor Bill into the mud. Everything he tried to say ended up choked off in midphrase—which was just as well, because none of it was fit for tender ears anyway.

It was a great show, and I enjoyed as much as I dared, but finally it was clear that I either had to do something right then or drag Bennett's carcass out of the field later. Big as the dogs were, they were flyweights compared with him, so I waded over and grabbed the first collar that came to the top of the heap. Mercifully, the other dog was wearing it. By the time I got the collar twisted into a passable form of tourniquet and managed to turn Old Crusher's attention from trying to fight to trying to breathe, Doc came slogging up, red-faced with exertion, eyes the size of teacups. I handed over his dog, and the last we saw of them, they were headed back for the clubhouse, Doc delivering a very loud lecture on aspects of Labrador parentage that I'm sure aren't listed anywhere in the Field Dog Stud Book.

On the way home, Bill rehearsed a similar dissertation that may have included some observations on my own ancestry, but I'm really not sure. It's hard to understand a man who's trying to talk and spit at the same time. Besides, all I did was suggest that if he ever got tired of journalism, he could have a great career in mud wrestling.

Commedia Sexualis

I'm sure everybody's heard the old story about the young man, invited for the first time to Sunday dinner with his girlfriend's parents, who drops a piece of food in his lap and to divert attention while he retrieves it, looks out the window and says, "Well, my heavens, look at that," pops the morsel back onto his plate, realizes that everyone is glaring at him, and looks for himself—to see two dogs mating on the lawn.

This is not a true tale, but rather a piece of modern myth, like the Cadillac convertible filled with fresh concrete or the lady who attempts to dry her French poodle in a microwave. But like all myth, it bespeaks a fundamental truth, because whatever else dogs may be guilty of, sexual inhibition is not among them. For the most part, this is an admirable, if somewhat clownish trait. Where it tends to go wrong is when some backyard breeder gets involved because he wants a pup out of Old Bolter. (In ninety-nine cases out of ten, the bird-hunting world would be vastly better off if Old Bolter's gene pool were drained, paved over, and used as a toxic-waste site, but that's another matter.)

Generally speaking, these liaisons quickly turn to comedies of error. Sometimes the dogs are the principal players, and sometimes it's the people. I knew one chap who made his garage into a love nest for a male Brittany (his) that hadn't the foggiest idea what he was supposed to be doing. When Charlie looked in a while later, he found the female sound asleep and the male busily servicing his water bucket.

Another guy I know, fearing that the female in question was going to pass out of estrus before his male could get the job done, turned the matter over to his vet and then promptly departed on a hunting trip, leaving his wife to see that things went as planned. What he didn't know was that in vitro fertilization is not widely practiced on dogs. The vet later described to me a scene you might find in some Mexican porno movie—the wife holding the female, some teenage girl who was the veterinary equivalent of a candystriper holding the male, while the vet took matters literally in hand. And none of it worked because the two women were so busy trying to look everywhere but in front of them. I've always figured the happy ending, such as it was, came about solely because the wife didn't know any divorce lawyers.

Another gentleman of my acquaintance had a male pointer he wanted to breed and arranged the services of a well-pedigreed female from a friend. When the friend called one Saturday morning in late September to announce that the female was ready, he drove across town to pick her up, taking the male along. As it turned out, she was a bit more ready than anyone realized, and by the time Tom got stuck in the traffic surrounding the local high-school homecoming parade, the dogs were well engaged in the back of his pickup. Some of his friends later presented him with a special award for having the most unusual float.

Finally, there was the time I went grouse hunting in northeastern Iowa with a couple of guys, one of whom had a male Brittany and the other a female setter that had just gone out of heat. We drove up in one chap's old Mercedes, which naturally had no place for crates, so the dogs rode in the back seat. All during the drive and the first afternoon's hunting, they paid little attention to one another.

We got showered that evening, asked about a good local restaurant, and were directed to a dinner-theatre supper club on the edge of town. The parking lot was empty when we got there, so we parked right in front. Our table was butted up against a front window, and when the waitress came back to serve our drinks, she looked out, did a double-take, and said, "Are those dogs?"

We looked and, sure enough, they were—ours, going at it in the back seat like two kids at a drive-in movie. Not knowing quite what else to do, we ordered another round of drinks.

By this time, the dinner-theatre crowd began to arrive. I don't know what the production was to be, but it definitely was something of interest to the geriatric set, because about twenty carloads of blue-haired ladies showed up and every last one had to totter over to our car to see the nice doggies. And every last one got a good look, spun around on her heels, and marched away stiff-backed as a colonel on parade. Once inside, I'm sure they thought they'd been invaded by perverts in the form of three men sitting by the window and choking to death laughing. We didn't stay to see the play.

Interspecific Infelicity

Dogs that fight with one another are annoying enough; those that tangle with other animals are usually disasters. I'm not thinking here of such mundane irritations as porcupines or housecats nor even skunks (although one skunk episode from my experience certainly qualifies; more about that in another section); what I have in mind is the kind of completely gratuitous nonsense that makes you want to grasp your gun like a baseball bat and line-drive some blockheaded mutt right over the left-field fence.

Actually, I know a man who tried just that one time. He and his big male pointer were hunting pheasants on a farm in western Iowa. He'd worked his way around a field and was nearing the farm buildings when pandemonium broke loose somewhere up ahead. Hurrying to the scene, he found his dog attacking a goat that was tethered to a tree outside a little shed. Having gone to some effort to find good hunting grounds and seeing his welcome wearing thinner by the second, he took his Winchester 21 by the barrels, charged up, and aimed a mighty swing. Unhappily, he missed the dog—also, fortunately, the goat—and smashed his gunstock to matchwood against the tree.

In the days before he bought Ebby, Bill Bennett had a nice young female Brittany who was a dandy quail dog. Prospecting one Saturday morning, he knocked on the back door of a farmhouse and was making good headway toward getting permission to hunt when his dog trotted up bearing a surprised-looking Leghorn hen. She had a wonderfully soft mouth, so the bird wasn't harmed in the least. Bill turned an intense shade of scarlet, grabbed the bird, and whacked his dog over the head with it.

Which killed the chicken dead as a hammer.

He looked at it and then at the farmer, who hadn't said a word since the whole scene began, and handed it over.

"I expect you'll want to dress this for dinner," he said. "And would you mind if maybe I came hunting some other day?"

Few breeds of men are as taciturn as north-Missouri farmers. "Son," he said, holding the now-limp fowl by the legs, "why don't you come back Friday. I was *plannin'* to kill chickens then."

Aromatica

Sometimes I look at my dog, a stunningly beautiful creature who is the product of bloodlines as classic as Brittany blood can be, and wonder what exactly we think we've accomplished: umpteen generations of careful breeding to arrive at an animal whose greatest joy is break dancing in cow manure?

I know all the genetic blueprints that prompt dogs to roll in foul-smelling matter. What I don't know is why, or more to the point, why still. It isn't as if Tober has to cover her own scent in order to go off in the woods and successfully scrag a deer to get something to eat. She couldn't catch one if her life depended on it, or kill one even if she could catch it, and she's never gone a day in her life without a healthy ration of good, nutritionally balanced food served up right on time—so why the hell does she insist on smelling like a buzzard's crotch?

To me this is one of the world's greatest mysteries and it probably is so because my aging puppy is one of the world's great practitioners of draping herself in an aura of stench. I've seen her turn from orange and white to a uniform brown in just one trip through a pasture. Just the other day, she went on a binge of such enthusiasm that one ear was packed completely full of cowflop. It has occurred to me more than once that I should have named her Meadow Muffin instead of October First.

At other times she has come to the door wearing essences of everything from rotting flesh to coyote urine to skunk musk to stuff I couldn't possibly identify except that it just smells awful. Perhaps what bothers me most is her utter lack of contrition; she loves it and clearly expects me to love it, too.

I suppose any dog is apt to roll in something vile once in a while, although I've known a few that seemed to have no interest in such activity. On the other hand, some, like mine, can't seem to live without it. Maybe it has something to do with the keen desire for hunting that we have taken such pains to preserve and enhance in the gunning breeds, or maybe it's just downright perverseness.

In any event, gun dogs probably have more opportunities for this sort of thing than most others do, and while some level of stink is pretty much routine, it sometimes gets entirely out of hand.

Wendy, for instance, once got involved in the second-worst case of rolling I ever knew. Wendy was a young, exuberant black Lab who, on a grouse hunting trip in northern Minnesota, rolled on a dead skunk.

I don't know if you've ever smelled a dead skunk, but if you haven't, you don't want to. The difference between a dead skunk and a live one is roughly the same as the difference between a live skunk and Chanel No. 5. It's enough to make a maggot retch.

Anyway, Wendy found *Mephitis mephitis* remains somewhere in the woods and coated herself with it from chin to rump. There was no place to clean her up except the bathtub in our motel room, so we were faced with the additional challenge of getting the job done in a way that left the place livable. We opted for tomato juice as the first mode of attack and literally cleared the shelves at the local Red Owl. I've since learned a much better approach, which is to mix tomato juice with liberal doses of vodka and use it for moral support while treating skunk stink with white vinegar, but I didn't know this at the time—or at least not the vinegar part.

Anyway, with the tub about half full, the bathroom looked like the set of a third-rate chainsaw movie, and we took turns laving Wendy, working in shifts just slightly shorter than the maximum span in which each of us could hold our breath. Finishing off with two big bottles of shampoo ameliorated the situation to the point where Wendy was tolerable company so long as she stayed in the back of the truck while we stayed in our room and didn't breathe too deeply.

The worst case of rolling I know occurred on a quail hunting expedition in north Missouri. Mercifully, I was not present, but I got the story from an eyewitness. It seems that two members of the party overindulged in the consumption of beer one night and upon arriving at the hunting ground next morning were both taken with a sudden, urgent need to find a men's room with minimum delay. Being where they were, the grader-ditch offered the only option, using their car—a nearly new Suburban—as a screen against the chance of any passersby. Thus presently relieved, they all went off a-hunting.

Back at the car in late afternoon, they set about field-dressing their birds. Left for a while to their own devices, the dogs, two Brits and a setter, found the morning's latrine, practiced some zealous gymnastics on the site and then hopped into the back of the 'Burban. By the time anyone realized what was happening, they'd done what every dog does when loose inside a vehicle—which is to say, explored every inch and tested the comfort level of every seat. It was not, I'm told, a scene fit for small children or the faint of heart.

The same day I heard this story, October came in from some cow-diving and was thoroughly taken aback when I gave her a biscuit for being a good girl. I never did tell her why, and I'd appreciate it if you wouldn't, either.

Gastrointestinals, Lower

Regardless of what a dog eats, anything that makes its way past the stomach is going to reappear sooner or later. This simply is a fact of life and isn't any particular problem unless you keep a large number of dogs or restrict one to a small space. Even at that, the worst thing likely to happen is for a dog to step in its own waste and then jump up on you, but teaching a dog not to jump on people is so easy and so fundamental to good manners that anyone who gets foot-wiped by his own dog deserves it.

Coprophagia can be a problem, mainly because it promotes horrible breath, but I believe it is most often a sign of some dietary deficiency, which isn't the dog's fault.

To my thinking, the most disagreeable product of lower gastrointestinal activity is gaseous rather than solid.

Down here in the Ozarks, asking whether a fat dog farts is the equivalent of enquiring if the Pope is Catholic or if a pig's butt is made of pork. The answer, of course, is yes; fat dogs fart. So do skinny dogs, old dogs, young dogs, and especially, gun dogs. This often is directly related to an appetite for carrion and cow pies, but I've known some dogs who could manufacture an endless supply of noxious gas on a diet of cornflakes. My father had one of those once, a big pointer who always got to ride home on the front-seat floorboard. This was in the days when automobile heaters were boxlike units installed under the dash on the passenger side, and when old Boy cut loose a measure of toxic emission, the heat and fan combined to create an atmosphere that could make your eyes water.

As with other things dogs do that result in noisome odors, the culprits themselves don't even seem to notice, which I find perennially amazing for animals whose stock in trade is their sense of smell. But I don't think obliviousness is truly the case. Waldo, my old farm dog, was a great farter in his later years, and when he'd cut one, I had only to look at him. His face would take on a sheepish expression and he'd wag his tail in an apologetic way. It isn't that dogs don't notice; they just don't care.

Moreover, I can scarcely remember ever smelling a dog-fart outdoors, which suggests some element of free will at work. October, now entering her own later years, is becoming a world-class gas-passer herself, and she clearly has some favorite times to practice. She likes evenings, when she can catch Susan and me sitting together somewhere, and late nights, especially nights when she's sleeping in her own bed, which is on the floor next to my side of ours.

Intensities naturally vary according to what miserable thing she might have eaten earlier, but in top form she can lay down a barrage that brings even me, who could snooze peacefully through the apocalypse, wide awake and gasping for fresh air.

At first, I thought she was doing this in her sleep, but after a few episodes that took place while I was still awake, I noticed that every attack is invariably followed by the sound of my dear old girl heaving a deep, heartfelt sigh of utter bliss and contentment.

I'm not entirely sure, but I think I've even heard her snicker once or twice.

As I said at the outset, I truly do love dogs, although it hasn't always been an easy affection to maintain. If, like mine, your canine mileage amounts to something over half our allotted threescore and ten, then all this probably has rung some familiar bells—as it would for any hunter of any time since man and dog first set out together in search of game. In his diaries covering the first fifty years of the nineteenth century, the great English sportsman Peter Hawker includes this note, cryptic and yet perfectly clear: "Finished my day with shooting the dog, at the express desire of Mrs. Hawker, and to the great satisfaction of all who were with us."

If by chance you're a more recent convert, perhaps working with or even anticipating your first gun dog, then you probably still harbor some romantic notions tinged with firelight and pipesmoke, the amber glow of good malt whisky and a pair of loving eyes gazing up by your side. Cling to these, and cherish them, because you're going to need them, sooner or later.

Charles Fergus is a freelance writer whose articles have appeared in many publications, including Shooting Sportsman, Game & Gun, Sporting Classics, Pennsylvania Game News, Science, Harrowsmith Country Life, *and* Audubon. *He is the author of four books. His first,* The Wingless Crow, *is a collection of essays on nature and country living. His historical novel,* Shadow Catcher, *deals with the 1913 Rodman Wanamaker Expedition of Citizenship to the North American Indian; a selection of the Book-of-the-Month Club, it is now out in paperback. Fergus has written two hunting books.* A Rough-Shooting Dog *chronicles the training and first hunting season of his English springer spaniel, Jenny;* Gun Dog Breeds *describes the more than thirty canine breeds used to hunt game birds in North America. Fergus lives with his wife, son, and spaniel in a stone house he built himself, on a mountain in central Pennsylvania, where grouse strut next to the woodpile and deer browse in the front yard.*

THE HEART
OF MY HUNTING

by Charles Fergus

It never seemed convenient. Hunting season was always just around the corner, and I didn't want her nursing puppies, or out of shape after having raised a litter, when the first day of grouse rolled around. I did not want a puppy for myself; I felt she should be my sole companion until she grew too old to put in a full day afield. So I kept putting it off, even though my hunting partners—after she'd made a particularly stirring flush or fetched a runner that surely would have fed the foxes—would scratch Jenny behind the ears, look at me, and ask, "When are you going to breed her?"

Jenny is an English springer spaniel. She is six years old, almost seven. Her coat is white, with patches of dark brown (technically, "liver") arrayed along her back and flanks, in what had looked to me, when she was a puppy, like the silhouette of a flushing grouse. Her tail is docked to about a foot in length, brown with an eye-catching white tip. Her eyes are golden-yellow. She has brown ears, a brown head, a white muzzle with a small brown mustache, and a symmetrical blaze on her forehead. Her shoulders reach to my knees. She is solid and muscular and, on the veterinarian's digital scale, weighs thirty-seven point six pounds.

Jenny is a rough-shooting dog. "Rough-shooting" is a British term that describes striking out across the land and taking whatever game the dog rousts out—precisely the sort of hunting Jenny and I practice here in central Pennsylvania.

To be sure, she is more than a hunting dog. She sounds the alarm when anyone drives down our lane. She can be counted on to join any sort of outing, be it a canoe trip, the one-hundred-yard walk to the mailbox, cross-country skiing (her first time out, she plunked down in the track to bite ice from between her pads, and suddenly we were both head-over-heels in the snow), my daily jog, picking blueberries (she strips them daintily from the stems with her front teeth and declines to drop them in the pail), hiking, bird watching, or simply puttering around in the yard. Jenny is a full-fledged member of our family, and confident in that status, but there is no question that she is my dog. Whenever the spirit moves her, which is often, she worms into my arms. She interposes herself between me and my four-year-old son when he and I are playing. Since she is not allowed on the furniture, she lays her head on my foot while I am sitting on the couch, reading. When I'm in my office writing, she curls up next to my chair.

Though she is not there now.

The house seems strangely empty. It has been like that all week. No friendly tail thumps when I lower a hand to pet her. No wagging and spinning at the door, as she lobbies to go outside. No gobs of white fur collecting in the corners, as my wife noted last weekend. However, I would bet that my wife, though she might not admit it, also misses Jenny.

On the bulletin board in my office is a list of five hunters who want a Jenny of their own. I would not have bred her just to satisfy these friends. But as Jenny matured—as she demonstrated the depth of her hunting instincts, her biddability and goodness of nature—I edged toward it. I did not make the decision lightly. I weighed and pondered and analyzed (and probably anthropomorphized) before I acted.

I remember how long it took me to pick a breed of dog in the first place. Before I got Jenny, I hunted with acquaintances who ran pointing dogs: Brittanys, English setters, and pointers. I enjoyed watching those dogs work. They were terrific at pointing woodcock, less adept at handling pheasants and grouse.

When a dog went on point, all too often I would spy the pheasant or grouse, its head down and its body hunched, legging it off through the brush. Or the dog would "bump" the bird, flush it prematurely. My friends warned me not to shoot at birds so bungled: It would encourage the dogs to run riot. On the days when everything clicked and we managed to shoot a bird over a point, rare was the dog who would then go and fetch it. A dog might point a dead bird, helping us locate it, but that technique failed when a wounded bird took off running. All of this puzzled me greatly. I had always thought that one of the reasons for hunting with a dog—perhaps the main reason—was that it would fetch the game.

I considered what was being asked of a pointing dog: upon encountering scent, to freeze, fight down the instinct to rush in and grab the prey; and then, after the shot, to abandon this static stance, perhaps chase down a runner, pick the bird up gently but firmly, and bring it back. From what I had read, some paragons consistently managed those contradictory tasks. But I felt I lacked the skill and patience to train a pointing dog to that level.

I wanted a more basic sort of canine, one that simply flushed the game, hustled it into the air with a sudden, dramatic rush. More important, I wanted a dog I could depend on to retrieve the game I downed. My dog would hunt the gamut of upland birds: grouse, woodcock, pheasants, doves. Since I planned to expand my hunting to include ducks, I needed a dog that also would dive into the swamp and recover what I shot. According to the books I read, the English springer spaniel could do all of those tasks, with aplomb and good cheer. And I was charmed by the breed's looks: trim, efficient, rough-and-ready, a touch feral-looking with those raggedy high-set ears.

It was a cool day in August, a day that spoke of autumn, when I went to pick up Jenny. The breeder let the mother and the puppies—three of the litter were left—out onto the lawn. I knelt and clapped my hands, and this double-handful of enthusiasm came tail wagging, ears flapping, as fast as her legs could carry her. I found it remarkable that a dog would so trust a strange human; but such is the nature of a puppy, open to love and to being loved. I have read about how early experiences imprint a creature and affect its behavior for the rest of its life. I became imprinted on Jenny at that moment, on that day in August of 1986.

I was thinking of that auspicious meeting—of the trust that Jenny had invested in me, and how it had grown and deepened—when I took her to the vet two weeks ago. I still had not decided whether to breed her, but I knew her time was limited. A six- or a seven-year-old bitch is far more likely to have problems whelping a litter than a three- or a four-year-old. If I was to breed Jenny at all, it would have to be during her next estrous.

What the veterinarian said added to my ambivalence. After examining her, he told me that Jenny had a constriction in her vagina. Some dogs, he said with a shrug, are just built that way. She might be able to accept a male, and she might not—in which case she could be bred through artificial insemination. That raised new questions in my mind. Once impregnated, would she be able to whelp? Probably, the vet said; and if need be, they could do a Caesarean section, a safe and routine procedure, some risk from the anesthesia, but usually without complications.

When Jenny and I got home that day, I grabbed my whistle and a pair of retrieving bucks. Down to the meadow we went, Jenny wagging her whole body and leaping for the dummies. This is old hat, but she loves it, loves to work, to do her job. I hupped her with a single blast on the whistle, threw a buck to one side, and heaved the second in the opposite direction. With a hand signal I sent her for the first buck; she raced to it and brought it back. I hupped her. *"Jenny!"* I said, releasing her for the second. She fetched it. I took the bucks, laid them down, and sat in the warm sun. Jenny sniffed the dummies, picked up one, and came and sat next to me.

When she was a puppy, she would carry all sorts of things in her mouth: sticks, pine cones, crumpled envelopes, corncobs filched from the compost heap, desiccated toads, songbirds that had broken their necks against the windows. Just holding something between her jaws seemed to make her feel secure. And how she loved to chase after the puppy buck—a small, kapok-filled boat bumper. She would pick it up with a flourish; her eyes knowing and her tail proud, she would dance it back to my hand.

One day—during her first October, when she was still too young to hunt—I shot a woodcock, carried it home, and hid it in the meadow. *"Jenny!"* I called, and waved her toward the bird. All gangly limbs and big paws, she romped along until she hit a tendril of scent—an essence she had never before encountered. She slammed to a halt, her body tense, her tail whipping from side to side. Guided by her nose, she sprang straight at the scent. Finding the source of that irresistible essence, she picked up the woodcock. I blew a few pips on the whistle. Fetching back, all the way she tried to stare at the strange feathery bundle between her jaws; it proved so enticing that she ran smack into my knee.

We spent hours in the meadow with whistle, buck, and gun. The guiding concept I drilled into her was *hup*. "Hup" is the traditional spaniel command for "sit." "Hup!" rockets out with authority to a dog on the edge of shotgun range, where "Sit!" may not be heard—or at least can be conveniently ignored. With that cornerstone firmly established, I could stop my spaniel on the trail of a running bird, so that I might get into position for a shot. Set her down when she got too near a road. Hide her at my side when ducks were flying. Halt her on a retrieve, then signal her to the bird.

I accustomed her to gunshots, to swimming, to riding in the canoe. Using planted birds (pigeons made dizzy and then hurled surreptitiously into the weeds), I tried to persuade her that the game always lay within twenty yards of the master's boots. Many were the Saturdays spent at a nearby shooting preserve run by a professional spaniel trainer; many were the pigeons, and finally the pheasants, that Jenny flushed and fetched. As we approached her second autumn, she had emerged as a spirited, hard-driving, raw, and promising young hunter.

One brisk October morning, we drove upstate in the dark, Jenny and I, and a friend and his young, equally inexperienced Labrador retriever. Dawn found us on the meandering headwaters of a stream, sneaking along, my friend and his dog on one bank, Jenny and I on the other.

We crept past yellow-orange maples and deep green pines, through broad openings carpeted with tan grass and wine-red huckleberry. Frost lay heavily on the ground, and wisps of fog floated above the water.

Out ahead, we spotted a flock of wood ducks on a beaver pond. My friend and I crouched and began edging forward. Whispering fiercely, we held the dogs at heel. Soon our sneaking developed into a hunched-over race with the ducks' and the dogs' increasing awareness—until the flock finally took to the air with a chorus of keening cries. Our shotguns rang out. Two ducks fell.

My friend's duck was killed outright, but mine was only wounded. The dogs splashed around in a state of gleeful confusion. My duck, a wood duck hen, swam off into the brush. Coming in from the side, I spotted it only five yards ahead. Not wanting to obliterate it, I aimed a few inches in front of its bill. I pulled the trigger, the water spouted—and when it subsided, nothing was afloat. We searched for an hour. We combed the alders lining the banks. The dogs stuck their noses in every clump of brush, every patch of sedge. We looked upstream and down. Finally we gave up; we continued on with our hunt, but after a few hundred yards, we retraced our steps for one last look.

Jenny sniffed through a strip of grass we had searched maybe half a dozen times. The fur across her shoulders stood up. She pounced. The duck, peeping, went skidding down the bank in front of the spaniel and splashed into the run. Jenny crashed in after it but came up empty. I got her out and hupped her on the bank. After several minutes, my friend noticed two small bumps emerging from the water beneath the overhanging bank: the wood duck's eye and bill-tip. He shot. Jenny made the five-yard fetch.

I drove down the valley. The windshield wipers snickered. The creek, its surface dimpled with rain, ran brown and full on the south side of the road. Jenny sat on the floor, on the passenger's side, her front paws canted up onto the gearshift housing. She looked at me, then out the rear window. The trees along the road whisked by, the gray hills behind shifting more slowly. A crow flew across the road, and Jenny spotted it, her eyes widening, her ears raising, her tail sweeping the floorboards.

I had decided. This was her chance, her first and last chance, to pass on that marvelous hunting sense, that loving merriness, that instinct coming down through countless generations. That much she deserved.

The highway led past farms, houses, a lumberyard, a car dealership, a gravel pit. Beyond the creek, the land sloped upward toward Brush Mountain. Although it was late April, the mountain still looked like November, the trees gray-brown and bare. In the valley the lawns were greening, and weeping willows showed their tender yellow leaves. We left the main road and drove along a winding street. My friend's house, an old stone farmstead on three acres, is surrounded by newer homes. The settlement lies on the fringe of a small city that has been slowly crumbling for the last half-century, ever since its shops and yards—for repairing rail cars and building locomotives—shut down.

My friend let out his springer, and we went down by the creek. The male came after Jenny right away, sniffing at her tail, bumping her with his shoulders. She kept spinning around to face him. When he got too familiar, she growled him off.

The rain had slackened; my friend got a pigeon out of the bird pen, dizzied it, and threw it into the pond. Jenny swims like an otter (she has swum like that ever since she was a puppy—never that nervous forepaw-plunking that you see with some youngsters). With the male hupped on the bank, she paddled out, grabbed the pigeon, pirouetted in the water, and started back. Her white legs churned.

Her eyes switched this way and that. She snorted water drops out of her nostrils. Her ears streamed back. Only the top of her head stayed dry.

We gave the male a retrieve. Then we let the dogs run. The male raced along close to Jenny, his side nudging hers. He licked Jenny's muzzle. He dropped to his belly, his rear end high and his tail wagging. She disdained to play with him. She came up to me, panting and wagging, a puzzled look on her face.

My friend's male, named Sky, is a young dog really coming into his own. Earlier this month, he placed third in a national pheasant competition held in Minnesota. Four years ago, my friend had gone to the Isle of Anglesey, off the coast of Wales, and bought the dog at the kennels of Talbot Radcliffe, the foremost springer spaniel breeder in the world. Sky's impeccable bloodline and his hunting prowess were not the only reasons I chose him: He is an experienced stud whom I hoped could effect the mating.

No luck that evening, though. Jenny would not stand for him; apparently she was not yet fully into estrous. It was dark when I said good-bye to her, there in the kennel by the creek. She barked plaintively as I crossed the lawn. I got in the truck and started for home. The traffic was light, and the rain had stopped.

The lights from a convenience store reflected off the black waters of the creek. Beyond loomed the mountain, dark and massive, probably with some good game cover tucked into its wooded folds. The combination of waters and woods got me thinking of another first from Jenny's first hunting season.

In the morning, I had shot two drake woodies on a beaver pond, with Jenny retrieving both; back home, I exchanged hip boots for Bean boots, and we went to the bottoms along the creek, where the land starts its gradual slope to the mountain. We tried a big patch of hawthorn and crab apples that always holds grouse. Halfway into the cover, she showed scent. The grouse powered up and cartwheeled at my shot. I went to my knees and spotted it crumpled on the ground beneath the crabs' arching stems. The grouse shot up its head. Its glittering eye took in the onrushing dog, and the bird picked itself up and raced off through the leaves. Jenny matched it swerve for swerve. It scuttled down over the bank toward the creek. So great was my confidence that I sat, unloaded the gun, and waited for Jenny to return. She did, with the grouse in her mouth, its eye angry and its crest upraised. My heart was pounding as I took it from her. This passing of game between dog and man is the heart of my hunting. I looked at my rough-shooting dog, and she at me.

◆

I swung the truck south at the light, gearing down for the hill. How far she had come since that first year! She had fetched many grouse—and would have fetched plenty more had I shot better. I would rather hunt grouse than any other game. One day last season, I wounded a big male and Jenny chased him down and brought him in. The grouse had his head up. He looked positively ferocious, outraged at having been apprehended. He did something decidedly ungrouselike: Turned his face toward Jenny's and pecked at her eye. I took the bird and dispatched him, then checked Jenny. She must have blinked before he got her, for her eye was unhurt. Then, on the last day of the season—just three months back, up a little hollow not two miles from where I was now driving—I flushed twenty-seven grouse in a bit under four hours, did not kill a one, and did not begrudge the birds a thing. They were wild as hawks (Did they know it was the last day?), and Jenny couldn't handle them. The last bird was an exception: She caught him hiding in a blowdown, and drove him up, straight at me. A big bird with a broad chestnut tail. I turned to take him going away. He juked behind a bushy hemlock, and I never saw him again.

I stopped at another traffic light. The light changed, and I went east. Down the valley I drove. A good brushy valley where lights are few. I passed a shuttered-up country store, an auto body shop, an old barn with a hole battered in its brick side. Across the railroad tracks from the barn, on the other side of the stream, lies the covert I call Pufferbelly.

I named the covert that day, back in Jenny's first year, when an antique steam engine came chugging incongruously down the line. A gray day, with a chill wind to hurry the clouds. Quick showers of rain pattered against the fallen yellow leaves. The smoke from the locomotive hung like a banner above the tracks, then began shredding. We started from the east, into the wind. Immediately Jenny set to work with an almost frantic busyness to her quartering. Her lithe white form coursed through the brush like a predatory fish hunting in the shallows. The clouds parted for a moment, light slanting in through the break, lending a coppery tone to the aspens' water-beaded bark. Chalk on the ground, and holes made by bills probing for worms. Things can develop quickly—and often unpredictably—when you follow a flushing dog. The scent practically yanked her around. The woodcock came up like a gusted leaf. Wings twittering, following its mud-flecked bill, it swerved a course through the close-set trunks. My shot downed it on the far side of the creek. Jenny swam across, ferreted the bird out of the dense willows, and paddled back, her first woodcock dangling loose-headed and long-beaked from her jaws.

◆

When I got back home, I looked at Jenny's empty kennel box. I sat down to read for a while, and no spaniel came to lay her head on my foot. I put the book down.

Was I tempting fate? I still did not think I wanted a pup for myself. I certainly wasn't breeding her for the money any puppies would bring. A friend once remarked that he was breeding his purebred dogs to put his kids through college. Put the vet's kids through college, is more like it.

So why press the issue? The next bitch I get, I'll have her spayed right off so I won't have to make these decisions. Had I done right by Jenny? Puppies were a tremendous drain on a dog, especially an older one. There was probably still time to call it off, the dogs were kenneled together but it didn't look like Sky would make any progress tonight.

But I didn't call. Pass it on, girl, I thought. If you can. That prebreeding exam—finding the constriction in her vagina—still bothered me. Artificial insemination? No. If she couldn't breed on her own, we'd forget it.

I sat in the quiet house, considering how much it meant to me, having Jenny. I remembered what was probably the brightest day of our first year's hunting. It was so cold that morning that my hands were alternately numb and then wracked with pain. Jenny had dipped her belly in the creek, and icicles tinkled when she wagged.

The decoys bobbed in the olive-drab water. A mallard quacked from somewhere downstream. Suddenly, there they were! Black ducks! Four pairs of wings came pumping, cupping, fluttering down—but the ducks flared up and began to flee. I managed to shove the safety off. I swung on the first duck in line, yanked the trigger, missed, shot again, apparently missed—and heard a splash. A duck, from farther back in line, floated upside down in the creek. "Jenny!"—and out she went into the frigid flow. Swimming hard, she gathered him in and was swept downstream by the current. She fought her way over to the bank. I stumbled through the brush and mud to meet her.

That afternoon, on a snowy hillside strewn with logging slash, she flushed and fetched a brace of grouse. Our hunt finished, we trudged home along the logging path as slivers of pink and yellow glowed in the gray western sky. I walked loose-limbed and weary, basking in the sense that I understood, really understood, what it meant to collaborate with a dog. To expand my instincts in partnership with a creature whose talents far surpassed mine. To let her joyousness, her simplicity, rub off on me. To shed mind and intellect for a time, to soak up the hunt, to simply be myself. I called her to me. As she danced around, her eyes on the cover, still wanting to get in there and hunt, I aimed caresses at her head. I ran my hand down her back and crooked it where her muscular hind leg joined her belly. I pulled her against my own leg, held her there for a moment, and told her what a good dog she was. With a perfunctory tail wag she broke free, and, glancing over her shoulder, tried to lure me back into the slash. I smiled and patted my palm against my thigh; reluctantly, she came back to heel. She had no need to stop and ponder, no need to hoard memories. For her, there was only the sweet now.

◆

Another evening, in the truck again; the moon was setting in the west behind coal-sack clouds as I headed for home. Tonight it was done—though she will stay with the male for a while yet.

She was ready. She was flagging her tail, wanting it to happen despite the discomfort causing her to yelp and pull away. I ended up holding Jenny, talking quietly to her, and there was blood and pain, and then calm, and, for the humans at least, elation. Who knows what the dogs thought and felt?

There will be more blood and pain nine weeks hence. I hope someday to write a postscript about healthy young

spaniels on their way to good homes, to lives that are rich
with love of master and land and game and the consum-
ing, fulfilling passion of the hunt. I hope to write a
postscript about an old rough-shooting dog back home in
the fields and marshes, the beaver dams, the thornapple
patches, the alder tangles, having passed on her brief,
glowing spark.

Datus Proper says he was born in Iowa, raised in Montana, domesticated at schools in New Hampshire, New York, and New Mexico. He survived employment in Angola, Brazil, Ireland, Portugal, and Foggy Bottom, D.C. Datus invariably preferred hunting and fishing to the alternative, such as working, and claims to have been run out of every town within four years. He lives today on the banks of a spring creek in the Gallatin Valley of Montana, surrounded by schools of trout, wisps of snipe, sords of mallards, and nides of pheasants.

LANGUAGE LESSONS

by Datus Proper

Jim McCue is partly to blame for what happened, mind you. When I was looking for a pup with the right ancestors, Jim's dog was winning the biggest field trials for German shorthaired pointers, so naturally I inquired about the champion's social life. Jim told me of a promising litter and I bought Huckleberry over the telephone—one of the quickest of life's big decisions. Jim and I met a few days later at an abandoned airport, turned the pup loose, and watched him try to catch a flock of starlings before they gained altitude. Jim said that I should let the pup tear around like that for his first year, building up enthusiasm. By the time Jim finished his sentence, Huck was out of sight and I was wondering how much more enthusiasm to expect.

Back home, I introduced the pup to a brand new kennel and concrete run—built for my wife, in a sense, because she had run out of enthusiasm for dogs that dribbled on her floors. It turned out that I should have used a thicker door for the kennel. Huck clawed a hole in the plywood and Anna thought he looked cute, peeking out for company, so she allowed him in the kitchen while I was armor-plating his quarters. By the time I was done, Anna remarked that the pup did not drool. A couple of hours later she reported that he had housebroken himself. After some few months, I sneaked out of my office and heard Huck telling Anna a tale that was making her giggle. His pronunciation was weak, you understand, especially on the consonants. What caught my attention was that he was imitating the cadence of my wife's speech and the pitch of her voice. Must have been a funny story, too, because she's Irish, with more feeling for tragedy than comedy. I'd never realized that she had such a pretty laugh.

Languages are easy to learn, at the right time of life, and that time—for humans—is before puberty. Little children can learn even Irish Gaelic, which is more than I have managed. The right timing turns out to be crucial, however. Neuropsychologists now believe that early childhood is a "critical period"—the time during which a human *must* be exposed to his or her mother tongue. A child that fails to acquire language skills does not develop the necessary brain circuits and is impaired for life. Work is being done on critical periods in dogs, too, and it is going to change the ways we raise puppies. Meanwhile, most of us have probably known dogs with circuits missing.

I do not mean to push the analogy. Huckleberry is a communicator, but neither his logic system nor his sound system has evolved in the same way as mine. What he thinks is language is, in fact, just a game. On the other hand, puppy games made him a faster learner than the kennel-raised dogs I've worked with. In particular, the way he picked up trailing seemed unusual, for a pointing dog.

During that first fall, Jim McCue's advice gave me the excuse to do what Huck and I both wanted anyhow, which was to run wild. There were bigger things than puppy training for me to worry about just then. I needed an optimistic little bundle of energy to exorcise my emotions, focus them at infinity. Optimism was part of Huck's personalities—both of them. "House angel, field demon," Anna called him. When Huck glimpsed our pond for the first time, he took a flying leap into it and swam toward my wife, who thought he was drowning. "My puppy!" she screamed. I had not heard that tone in her voice since our baby rolled down the stairs (with similar results). Anna waded in to save Huck. He climbed out on his own, shook water all over her, then jumped back in and swam across the pond to me.

A pup this bold would not have been daunted by more early training in obedience. On the other hand, I do not regret my failure to train Huck on the usual tame bob-whites and pigeons. In lieu of them he pointed the meadowlarks, flustered the ducks, and chased the mag-pies. It might not have been everyone's idea of fun but the most important thing in matching man and dog, I suppose, is temperament. Part of me was right out there running with the pup,eyes shining, tongue hanging out.

The first pheasant that Huck pointed was a hen, which I of course flushed with fanfare. There were not many cocks around but he started pointing those he ran into. I took the finds as serendipitous—gifts from the angels. Any pup can run into a bird, and a pup of the right breeding is always going to point strong scent. It's in his genes. You don't know that you've got a real pheasant dog till he learns trailing.

When Huck was six months and eleven days old, however, my enthusiasm and his reached the same level. He started trailing in grass that was, I thought, too low for a pheasant. I watched for a while, concluded that he was doing a good job of hunting the wrong thing, and decided to ignore him. Hiked fifty yards. Realized that I was alone, looked around, and saw the pup on point. Ran back, caught the bird between us, waited out a great noisy glittering flush, and dropped a rooster in plain sight. Huck pounced and retrieved. He had done it all, seen it all, made the connection.

Two days later, almost at dark, he went on point in cattails. I tried extra-hard to shoot well, which is of course the best way to miss, and the rooster came down winged. I saw it land in a patch of brush and heeled Huck to the place. He tore off across an open field. I kept whistling him back, making him hunt the brush. The stars came out. We did not find the bird till the next day, by which time it was bones and pretty feathers, the rest eaten by a skunk. The bird had in fact headed across the open field and Huck had been on its track, if only I had let him follow his nose. That was the last time I tried to teach him anything about trailing.

In his second season, when the pup was a year old, he lost none of the hundred-odd birds that my friends and I shot over him. Hardest to smell were the singles of gray (Hungarian) partridges. Members of the grouse family ran as well as the partridges but left more scent. Pheasants, of course, were the long-distance champions, covering up to a measured mile. It seemed, too, that they shared some of the partridges' ability to suppress scent in an emergency.

Huck was experienced, considering his tender age, but he was not trained by the usual field-trial rules. He remained free to creep or break point in order to stay with a moving bird. Perhaps some pups can trail as well as Huck without being allowed equal discretion. I just haven't seen them.

A year-old pup on his own discretion was, of course, often indiscreet. He would stand on point as long as his bird held, but when it moved there were various possibilities. Hardest of them to handle was a maneuver we'll call the Montana Sprinting Squat. Pickup drivers have a similar ploy called the Texas Rolling Stop, during which the truck coasts through an octagonal sign at forty-five miles per hour. You are supposed to take good intentions into account. Pheasants intend to flush but not within eleven inches of a dog's nose, so they sprint till achieving the velocity of a Texas Rolling Stop and then go airborne, total elapsed time 0.7 seconds.

Fortunately, the Montana Sprinting Squat always worked and the birds always escaped. They were wild and strong, remember. You could not let a pup chase pen-raised birds or he'd catch some of them and perhaps decide that he could hunt successfully on his own. Huck learned that he only got pheasants when we worked together. I ladled on praise when he did things right, of course, but a bird in the mouth was all the encouragement he really needed. At the end of a day we'd both tell my wife that we'd had fun but it was not fun, exactly. It was the happiness that comes with pheasant feathers.

My system (or nonsystem) might be wrong for you. You might lack wild birds or the time to work a pup on them. Your wife might not provide language lessons for the youngster. You might have a kennel-raised dog, or one with less point in his genes. Your specialty might be eastern ruffed grouse, in which case you would be wise to insist that your dog point at first suspicion of scent and hold till released. For covey birds like the partridges and quails, I'd have preferred Huck steady to wing and shot, too, because a dog that breaks can spoil a covey rise. But for the rest I wanted him to trail. I wanted him to get me shots at the old cocks that considered themselves immortal. I wanted him to find winged birds no matter how far they ran. The rewards seemed worth the risk.

A "dog that's going to be any good puts his nose where the scent is," high or low. That's what William Harnden Foster wrote about grouse dogs back in 1942, and Huckleberry reached the same conclusion. When air scent failed, he would work a patch of snowberries on ground scent till I called him off, and a cock would flush the moment my back was turned. It turns out that roosters can run around for a long time in the same half acre of brush. You might not want to waste time on such birds— if you have easier hunting available. We did not.

Working air scent, on the other hand, was anything but tedious. The pup would trail from one end to another of a two-hundred-acre field of grasses planted under the Conservation Reserve Program. Or he'd follow birds out of a brushy bottom, up weedy draws, and into wheat stubble. Some of the pheasants would hold tight at the end of the trails. Others would flush wild. It's what most owners of pointing dogs would have predicted, and what some would call disaster. The pheasants certainly considered it disaster, because we got our share at the end of the trails. I earned the shots, mind you. My wife was teaching aerobic dance classes, working out on a ski machine, and watching her calories while I was eating like a sumo wrestler and getting skinnier by the week. Huck was going through ten cups a day of the expensive high-fat dog food. If you don't want exercise, stay away from pointer pups bred for all-age field trials.

When you run a young dog almost every day, something happens to its body as well as its mind. Huck put on ten or fifteen pounds of muscles that he would not have developed if he had spent his youth in a kennel. The weight was in the right places, because running is complete exercise for a dog. Being light-boned, he did not look heavy. His brown hair was shiny as a seal's. His pads gave no trouble. His pace would have exhausted any other dog I've had in two days, but Huck kept it up all season. There was, however, a disadvantage that I learned when partridge season opened the next year on September 1: muscles hold heat. I had to whistle him in frequently, sit him down in shade, and give him water. When duck season came, swimming was harder for him too, because his body was so dense that he had to work just to stay afloat. A serious water dog needs some fat.

Perhaps trailing, the way Huck does it, really is a skill that must be acquired before puberty. I don't know. At various times, however, I have watched him hunt with seven other pointing dogs, and that's counting only the good ones. Some of the seven are competitive with him in shoot-to-retrieve trials; one is his half brother. All can follow hot body scent. When Huck takes off after a really sneaky rooster, however, the other dogs have learned that the only way to get involved is to run loops in front of him. That maneuver takes brains, too, of course.

I watch the other dogs when the realize that Huck is on a tough trail. They deduce what is going on but cannot get the hang of it themselves. They look at him as if he were speaking Gaelic, sort of.

Steve Grooms grew up in central Iowa at a time when even inept hunters without dogs could find plenty of pheasants. He moved to Minnesota when pheasants were so scarce that hunters without dogs rarely saw one. That led him to buy his first hunting dog, beginning the fourteen-year adventure told in his story, "Pirates." Grooms lives in St. Paul, Minnesota, with his wife, daughter, and two hunting dogs. The family spends as much time as possible at their cabin on the shores of Lake Superior, near Cornucopia, Wisconsin. Grooms is a freelance writer. His books include Modern Pheasant Hunting, Pheasant Hunter's Harvest, Bluebirds!, The Cry of the Sandhill Crane, The Ones That Got Away, *and* The Return of the Wolf.

PIRATES

by Steve Grooms

Last night I brought out our film projector, blew the dust off it and spooled up the film Kathe shot the day we met Brandy. Because our old Super 8 camera had no microphone, the film is eerily silent. The only noise one hears as the film rolls is the rattle of the projector itself. Dogs bark, people laugh, shotguns fire...all in pantomime. In the darkness of my basement room, jittery frames of film pour out their flow of softly focused images like a dream.

In the film, a man throws a stick across the snowy parking lot of a northwoods resort. A mob of rotund springer pups surges hither and yon, fighting over that trophy stick. It looks like they are playing rugby. The man keeps throwing the stick. Finally there is just one puppy in the film. The camera whirls giddily to show the rest of the little spaniels monkeyballed together in exhaustion in their straw bed. While they sleep off their exertions, their aggressive sister continues to chase the stick, again and again.

I have trouble now recognizing myself in the slim, dark-haired youth in that silent film. But I have no trouble recognizing Brandy. Indeed, it was all there to be seen, had I then only possessed eyes that could see: what she was, what she would become, what she and I would be together, the agony and glory of it all.

What is missing in that film is the mentor I should have brought along to advise me, the veteran hunter who would have told me, "Son, let me speak as clearly as possible: you don't know jack shit about dogs. That little springer is way too much dog for you. Hell, she's too hot for most professional trainers." But as I said, that wise man was not there the day of the filming, just a young fool who had already fallen in love with the high-spirited puppy he soon would name Brandy.

Back then there was an empty lot behind a post office not far from our St. Paul home. It is part of a shopping mall now, of course, but in the early 1970s about a dozen pheasants scratched out a living in that vacant urban lot. On winter afternoons when my college classes were over, I took little Brandy out among the snow, weeds, and broken wine bottles of the vacant lot. She and I would hack about until we managed to spook up the pheasants. As they clattered into the sky, I would leap about like a kangaroo with a hotfoot and howl, "Birds! *Birds! Brandy, get the birds!*" And this, I blush to report, was all I did to "train" my young dog to hunt.

Had I known anything about dogs—anything at all—I would have realized Brandy's blood already boiled with bird lust. Even I should have recognized that my challenge as a trainer was to gain some degree of control over my hotheaded puppy. But in my towering ignorance, I thought I had to teach her to care about birds. My training amounted to pouring gas on the white-hot embers of Brandy's innate birdiness.

Brandy was five months old when Kathe and I took her to observe a springer field trial. We had some vague notion this might be educational for her. Apart from our bizarre romps behind the post office, Brandy had no experience with birds. She had never had her mouth on one. The only field command she knew was *Get the birds!* She had never heard a gun. In spite of all that, and in defiance of common sense, I allowed myself to be talked into entering Brandy in the puppy stakes.

At a signal from the judges, I told Brandy—what else?—to *Get the birds!* Amazingly, she quartered naturally. Brandy found and flushed the first pigeon within seconds. When the gunner touched off a short magnum 12-gauge load right over her head, Brandy was too preoccupied marking the fall of the bird to mind the muzzle blast. On her own, she decided to pick up the dead pigeon and bring it back to me, just as if we had rehearsed this act a thousand times. Her work on the second pigeon was similarly perfect. Alas, Brandy's third pigeon had been dizzied too vigorously when the bird boy stuck it in the grass. That bird flew away woozily just a few feet above the grass. When the gunner missed it, Brandy continued racing along under the pigeon until she was finally stopped by a tight fence a quarter of a mile away. That mad dash cost Brandy a blue ribbon, but she did take second place in what was to be our first and last field trial.

Brandy's subsequent career was to span geography from the Missouri to Ontario and from Wisconsin to Nebraska. In addition to various species of ducks and geese, Brandy and I hunted prairie chickens, sharp-tailed grouse, Hungarian partridge, quail, ruffed grouse, and woodcock. But above all, Brandy was a hunter of pheasants. Fittingly, her first rooster was memorable.

We had been hunting some scrubby brushland north of the Twin Cities. I had managed to bag a grouse and two or three woodcock. When we came upon a little marsh near a cornfield, Brandy rushed some cattails. Up came a turkey-sized old rooster, cursing like a truck driver stuck in traffic. He was so big and raucous I lost my composure and made a tentative shot that only broke a wing. When the rooster sailed into some bulrushes in about two feet of water, I rushed to the spot in knee-deep water and began shrieking for Brandy to help me find our bird. By ignoring me, she soon found the cock where he'd run, forty yards away. But then Brandy refused to retrieve him to me even after I'd walked over to her and stood three feet away, repeatedly demanding that she fetch the bird. I gave up after fifteen minutes of comic frustration and retrieved my soggy trophy myself.

That night I confessed my disappointment to Kathe. I explained that my little springer apparently lacked the strength to handle birds as big as pheasants. Just as I spoke, the doorbell rang. Among Brandy's idiosyncrasies was a compulsion to greet visitors with some precious object in her mouth. Out of the corner of my eye, I saw Brandy streak to the pile of birds in the kitchen. She kicked away the woodcock, pawed her way past the grouse, and seized that gorgeous rooster. When our friends walked in, Brandy paraded before them like a major domo, brandishing her rooster like a baton.

She obviously had enough muscle to carry the biggest pheasant ever born. So why had Brandy stonily refused to retrieve that same bird to me when I had been so close?

I finally understood, and with that comprehension I made progress toward understanding my quirky partner. In thirteen years of hunting with me, Brandy retrieved several hundred pheasants. She fetched many across rivers and through tangles of brush. She made several retrieves at distances I estimated at about half a mile. But she consistently refused to retrieve a bird whenever I stood close to her. In Brandy's view, if I was that near

I could damn well walk two steps and pick the bird up myself. Brandy would do anything I asked of her, *if* she saw the point of it.

I made another key discovery about her character when we hunted Iowa for the first time. Kathe and I made that trip in December, right after Christmas. Seven weeks of heavy hunting pressure had made most of the surviving pheasants too jumpy to be approached. Kathe and I were able to get limits by hunting hard from sunup to sunset three days in a row, but it was exhausting work, especially for Brandy. I kept expecting her to give in to exhaustion, but every morning she was as full of ginger as she had been on the first day.

We were slowly working our way back toward Minnesota on the fourth day when I spotted a creek that had the thickest cover we had seen since entering Iowa. The creek was twisty and deeply eroded. Its banks were completely overgrown with horse weeds and willows, and its bottom was a tangled mat of marsh grasses. When I asked permission to hunt the place, the farmer broke into guffaws. "If you really want to go in *there* fella, you're more than welcome," he said, "but I'm tellin' you it's a waste of time. That cover's just too thick. Last week, six guys from Illinois went through there with three dogs, and they couldn't dig a single rooster out of all those weeds." He didn't see the furtive smile on my face as I headed back to the car.

Brandy flushed the first rooster from the willows on the south shore. Ten minutes later, she dug the second out of a thicket of horse weeds. Her third bird was a running cripple that couldn't run quite as fast as she. The fourth rooster ran for nearly a hundred yards on the high bank before Brandy caught up with him and boosted him into the sky. At my shot, he plunked down right on the frozen surface of the creek. Brandy dove off the bank to grab him. But when she tried to return she found herself confronting a sheer wall of black dirt that was about fourteen feet high and undercut near the top.

I knew she could never scramble up that wall even without the extra weight of the rooster, but I wanted to see what she would do. Brandy charged the wall three times, getting halfway up each time before gravity dragged her back. The loose soil of the bank simply could not give her madly spinning feet enough purchase to lift her. Without putting the rooster down, Brandy attacked the wall a fourth time. Her feet were a blur. Dirt clods and stones shot behind her in a torrent and went pinging off the ice of the river like birdshot. With agonizing slowness, her body inched higher and higher until she finally clawed her way over the edge.

As stupid as I was about hunting dogs back then, even I knew I had witnessed something astonishing. I had just seen a dog levitate herself by a ferocious act of will. I vowed to never underestimate her again.

That same will, over the next several years, was the glory and the agony of our hunts. Brandy hunted every moment of every day at a mad gallop, attacking the cover as if the fate of the world depended upon her shagging every bird out of it. She seemed to believe her sacred mission was to flush every bird before I could get close enough to do that myself.

It was generally a pure accident when I happened to be close enough to one of Brandy's flushes to take a desperate poke at the disappearing bird. In the grouse woods she ranged so far from me that the panicked birds sometimes flew toward me. I bagged a lot of grouse by pass-shooting birds that had no idea I was there. As much as she loved me, Brandy was mad for birds. She pursued them with maniacal energy and no regard to where I might be.

All my anguished efforts to bring Brandy under control failed. I screamed at her. I chased her. When I caught her, I beat her. That stopped when I realized the beatings were boring her. Brandy was utterly indifferent to pain. She regarded her beatings a waste of precious hunting time. When I finished thrashing her, Brandy would grin and go right back to hunting with her unique volcanic energy. After one particularly frustrating trip to Iowa, I told Kathe, "I have the worst hunting dog in the world. Her every effort is focused on flushing birds eighty yards ahead of me. She has the range of a pointing dog, only she doesn't point."

Something had to change, and I really didn't have much of a choice about what it would be. I loved bird hunting and Brandy too much to give up either one. By the time we'd put in two seasons together, I knew she was too aggressive to limit her range to the cover right around me. It was equally clear that all the bird action was happening where Brandy was. If I meant to shoot anything, I had to be somewhere near her. Since Brandy would not restrict her hunt to my proximity, I extended mine to join hers. That is a fancy way of saying I spent thirteen years running desperately in bird cover, looking less like a hunter than a man trying to catch a train that has just left the station ahead of him.

It wasn't pretty and it wasn't easy. Brandy was more fit and more fleet than I, and she didn't have to carry a shotgun. In all the years I hunted with her, my slowest pace was the fastest walk a young man can manage in heavy cover. Much of the time I had to trot, and often I gripped my shotgun like a track relay baton and simply lit out as fast as I could go.

On one typical full-tilt hunt, a friend who was chugging along beside me turned to say something. He found himself staring at the chainlink soles of my hunting boots. I had hit a wire fence at shin height, out of sight in the weeds. Because of my hurtling momentum, hitting the fence didn't knock me down but launched me into the air like a man shot out of a cannon.

Another time I was attempting to sprint through a swampy stand of willows because I could hear Brandy somewhere ahead of me putting up roosters. When I tripped on a hummock, my shotgun left my hands and flew thirty feet before impaling itself muzzle-first in the mud. The shotgun was sticking out of the ground like a spear when I retrieved it. I saw that about four inches of mud were packed in each barrel, and just then two of Brandy's roosters flew through an overhead opening in the willows. As the roosters flapped safely out of sight, I cursed my predicament in language that blistered bark off the nearest willows.

In spite of such moments, I became a specialist at hunting roosters in marshes because in such swampy cover I could stay slightly nearer Brandy than on firm ground. Grouse cover was the worst for us because it didn't slow Brandy down at all but tore me up considerably. I routinely ran into trees, frequently ricocheting off one or two before gathering control and plunging forward again. We hunted grouse with the desperate pace of two escapees from a chain gang.

Because of our strenuous hunting style, I wore a thin cotton shirt and light vest at times when everyone else was wearing wool shirts and insulated coats. Even then I sweated copiously as I stumbled along in Brandy's wake, my face a hunter orange. Once when a partner in Iowa made me stop so he could smoke a cigarette, I went into hypothermia. I used to wear out two pairs of boots each hunting season, and the nylon hunting pants I bought in September looked in December like they had been put through a food processor.

It was much the same for Brandy. She didn't know what discomfort was when hunting. Brandy was a dog who would hunt hard in sandburs. After several hunting trips, I found she had sustained cuts so deep I almost fainted when I found them, but she had given no sign of the pain. When she took a full hit in the face (and tongue, and lips, and gums) from a porcupine, Brandy merrily hunted all the way back to the car. For Brandy and me, upland hunting was a contact sport.

According to an old cliche, dogs and the people who own them come to resemble each other in appearance. It just isn't so. But Brandy and I came to resemble each other in a more fundamental way, namely our passionate and intemperate approach to hunting. In that, we were identical twins. We went out of our way to attack cover that normal hunters refused to enter. Our ferocious attack on bird cover was macho, enormously wasteful of energy and about as subtle as a chain saw.

We were twins in another sense. Not until Brandy had been dead two years did I finally understand a central fact about her. Brandy—*forgive me for saying this, old girl!*—had a mediocre nose. She hunted with cyclonic energy because that was her nature and because she simply needed to cover a great deal of ground to make contact with hot scent. Dogs with sensitive noses can trail cold scent until it becomes a hot flush. Not Brandy. Cold scent just confused her, so Brandy had no choice but to rip around in bird cover until she made a smoking hot contact. For my part, I lacked any sense of where a bird might be found. We were quite a duo: a dog with a cold nose and a man who didn't know what he was doing. Yet we each compensated for our deficiency by hunting so long and hard we found birds in spite of ourselves.

So it went for five desperate years while I waited for Brandy to get old, mellow, and slow. That didn't happen. But while Brandy could do nothing to improve her nose, she could improve her head. In her sixth and seventh years, Brandy become extraordinarily effective by applying all the lessons she had learned in her first years. It was fascinating to watch her at work; you could see the gears turning. If Brandy and another dog were looking for a running pheasant, the other dog would rely upon its nose while Brandy would draw upon the prodigious data bank of bird behavior between her ears. Time after time, the dog with the bum nose and the bird smarts was first to come up with the prize.

Just when Brandy should have been aging toward the decline that inevitably drags down all bird dogs, she hit her peak. The years she was eight, nine, ten, and eleven were the stuff of legends. While our hunting style was still queer and grossly inefficient, Brandy and I had become an exceptionally effective team. We always sought out the most difficult walking, down in the slop of marshes and the mazes of young willows. Since Brandy and I hunted twice as fast as anyone who might be with us, we always took one end of the line and worked a huge zig-zag pattern so we covered twice as much ground as our partners. People often told me we hunted too fast. Yet in all those years, I don't remember anybody finding a rooster in ground we had just covered.

A hunt from Brandy's ninth year typifies our partnership at its peak. We left home about noon to join friends for a five-day South Dakota trip. When I crossed the state line there was a little legal shooting time left. I stopped at a gas station to ask the owner if he knew of a marsh in the area with so much heavy cover that it couldn't be hunted. He did. In that marsh, Brandy flushed two roosters and caught a running cripple just before sunset. We then hunted three days in the Platte area, getting three-bird limits each day, thanks mostly to Brandy.

On our fifth morning, she and I hunted alone in the largest wildlife management area in the state. The first cock Brandy found there took us on a wild gallop across the prairie and through two separate cattail marshes before it ran out of options and had to fly. We chased the second rooster right through the heart of the marsh before Brandy caught up with him. While she was retrieving him, she ran smack into the third pheasant. We returned to the car with three handsome roosters, having hunted half an hour.

We were back in Minnesota, heading home, when I realized we were near a swampy Minnesota wildlife management area that was an old favorite of ours. I reached it with less than an hour left of legal shooting time. Brandy only needed half that time to find and flush a Minnesota limit of two roosters for me.

Please don't misunderstand. I am not boasting about how many birds we could kill in those days. What I am trying to convey is the confidence—call it cockiness— I came to feel each day we entered the field. I had spent five years fearing I had the worst dog in the world. I then savored six years of a remarkably effective and joyous partnership. As Brandy got better each year, I began to believe she had found a way to transcend the laws of aging.

The first intimations of mortality came on a South Dakota Sioux reservation near the mighty Missouri River. In that year of pheasant superabundance it should have been easy to come home with our party limit of forty-five pheasants. But my partners were not shooting well. Not to put too fine a point on it, Kathe and Jerry were each burning up a box of shells for each rooster they bagged, which meant the dogs had to flush that many more birds. Brandy hunted with her usual ferocity for five days in temperatures better suited for sunbathing than chasing footloose roosters. In that time she probably flushed between four hundred and five hundred pheasants, counting hens, and she retrieved about forty roosters.

Finally, we needed one bird to fill our limit. Brandy put up two roosters, and Jerry broke a wing on one of them. Brandy ran to the fall but did not come back. We found her staring quizzically down a badger hole, and I guessed Jerry's cock had scooted down there. Brandy was always so fond of digging we used to joke there must have been a backhoe somewhere in her family tree. I pointed down the hole and said the magic words: "Get the bird!" Dirt began to fly. After fifteen minutes, Brandy's whole body was below ground, with just the backs of her legs still in sight. (We have a photo of this.) It was obviously hopeless, so I called her back. Brandy wriggled out of her hole and turned to present me with a face comically loaded with black dirt. But she had a single rooster tail feather in her teeth. I sent her back down to finish the job.

When we had Jerry's bird, we set off walking back to the car. But I had a panicky, amorphous feeling of something being wrong. Then I understood: Brandy was *following* me. She hadn't been behind me since she was six months old. After five days of ferocious hunting in that heat, and almost half an hour of vigorous tunneling, Brandy had hit her limit. She looked embarrassed, and she soon got out ahead of me again. But in that moment I realized that even Brandy could not defy the processes of aging forever. She was eleven at the time.

One year later, Brandy still slashed through the cover with vigor and efficiency, outperforming all the dogs who shared the field with her. But that was the year Brandy and I plunged recklessly into an icy swamp that nearly claimed our lives. As I struggled against exhaustion and hypothermia that night, dragging behind me the old dog whose body had locked up tight like a statue in that cold water, I had a lot of time to contemplate the fact our partnership was nearing its end. I realized that night that if I lived to hunt again, I had to find and begin training the younger dog who would eventually replace Brandy.

Brandy's thirteenth year was amazingly strong. I could tell she had slowed down a little, but anyone else would have complained that she was roaring around out of control like any damnfool puppy. In a hellish phragmites marsh in Minnesota, Brandy found a running rooster that evaded three other dogs. She hunted heroically in an Iowa blizzard in December that left the cover full of dead birds, their beaks or feathers impacted with frozen snow.

Brandy declined tragically in her fourteenth year. By then she was deaf, nearly blind, arthritic and weak from lack of exercise. She was also riddled with cancer, although I did not know that for some time. I mostly hunted with her young replacement, leaving the old warrior to bark in frustration as she saw me leaving home dressed in the hunting garb she knew so well. I was afraid she'd get lost if I took her into the field with little vision, no hearing, and a poor sense of smell to bring her back to me.

At last I realized her career was winding to an end. In a "Masterpiece Theater" series running at that time, a father decides to buy his dying son a date with a prostitute. In much the same sense, I decided to buy my dying partner a trip to a game farm. By luck, the birds that the owner put out for us were the prettiest and wildest pen-raised pheasants I have ever encountered. Just a year earlier, Brandy and I hunted the same field. On that day, the preserve had released six birds, and Brandy had found seven of them.

The miracle I had irrationally expected did not occur. Time after time for thirteen years, I had seen the sight of weeds magically restore Brandy when it seemed she was surely too footsore, cut-up, and exhausted to hunt again. Time after time I had seen her rise, phoenix-like, to assault the cover again. Foolishly, I had expected it to happen one more time.

But although Brandy tried her hardest, she was overmatched. Three times I saw her bump into weeds that knocked her off her feet with their springy resistance.

She did manage to frighten several pheasants into flight. And one, a hen, she retrieved to me, pausing three times along the way to drop it and pant in exhaustion.

Then she got on the trail of a cock I could see sprinting down a cornrow ahead of us. Brandy's last rooster was a magnificent bird with a tail in the twenty-inch range. Brandy bustled eagerly along on his trail, snuffling frantically to suck in enough scent to tell her which way to go. The pheasant was just too quick for her. He reached the end of the row and turned the corner. I saw he would get away unless I ran at him to force a flush. But he wasn't my bird; he was Brandy's. And he had beaten her. Though I had already paid for this rooster, I knew I didn't have the right to kill him.

Brandy neither heard nor saw the bird when he flushed. Cackling with indignation, he sailed to the protection of some trees beyond a dark little river. Brandy snuffled around in confusion when she reached the spot he'd flushed from. With stinging eyes, I picked her up and carried her to the car.

Three months later, Brandy made her own passage across a dark river.

I think I now understand that bird dogs can be great in four specific ways. Three are based in natural ability: nose, heart, and intelligence. Some dogs also excel in what I've called "manners," which is how well they have been trained. With reason, veteran dog men reserve their highest regard for those rare dogs that excel in all four areas.

Yet I treasure the memory of a dog who was highly imperfect. Brandy had no manners—which was my fault—and not much more nose. In spite of that, she managed to elevate herself to a kind of greatness through courage and sheer will, much the way she once elevated herself up an impossible wall of undercut soft dirt. I can't believe any dog ever accomplished more with the gifts he or she was given than Brandy.

Although I know it is foolish, I sometimes wish the wisdom of my graying head could be installed in the resilient young body I once possessed. More realistically, I wish I could have known even a little about birds and dogs back when Brandy and I first met. But time is a river that runs only one way. One becomes wise by being foolish first, and Brandy and I were good at that. I guess most dog men have regrets about their first hunting dog.

Yet any regrets I have are trivial when set next to all the fond memories that linger of our unique partnership. I have written two books and scores of articles about my adventures with Brandy, and many stories remain to be told. After all, we had almost a decade and a half together, and those were prodigious years. I don't know how a man ever stops missing a dog like that.

Brandy represents a whole lusty era of my life, a time that is now gone just as permanently as is Brandy. We were a pair of pirates, Brandy and I, two bird-mad swash-bucklers who flailed at the sport with dull broadswords and stormed into places where prudent folk never go. I can never again be the person I was with Brandy. And this is part of what we say goodbye to when we bury a dog: a part of ourselves.

Chris Dorsey worked in Los Angeles as the senior editor of Petersen's Hunting *before becoming executive editor of* Ducks Unlimited. *He's the author of four books and his freelance works have appeared in numerous national magazines including* Writer's Digest, Sports Afield, Field & Stream, Outdoor Life, Sporting Classics, *and a host of others. He's currently working on a book about waterfowling to be published by Lyons and Burford in 1995. He's a Wisconsin native who now lives in Memphis, Tennessee. He began training his first setter at the age of nine and has had at least one setter ever since—having a collection of chewed shoes to show for it.*

EXCLAMATION POINTS

by Chris Dorsey

Do we own bird dogs to hunt birds, or do we hunt birds to own bird dogs? A hunter's answer to that question tells much about him. Bird dogs can be both a curse and a blessing and any dog can transform from one to the other in a tail wag.

There is a kind of poetry, nevertheless, in watching a masterful pointer work the air currents, guided by the muses of the uplands. Indeed, in the recesses of every bird dog owner's mind dwells the perfect dog, a creature distantly related to the unicorn and the yeti. Perhaps it's our quest for that mythical dog that keeps us in rawhide chews and leather collars.

A great bird-dog is more often defined by what it doesn't do than by what it does. I favor a consistent plodder over an occasional whizbang that's prone to fits of distant prospecting. No matter the dog work, though, a bird hunt without a dog is like a painting without a primary color, a drama without a protagonist, or a martini without an olive. For that reason, bird dogs are more than mere pets. To look at a bird dog as one would a guinea pig, hamster, or goldfish is to see no difference between a rabbit and a rabbit pellet.

There are many milestones in the life of a bird hunter but none that rival the purchase of a first pup. You don't care for a puppy as much as you give it a piece of your very being. When you invest wisely, the returns can be greater than any of Wall Street's blue chips. A new pup is either a ray of sunlight that beams all the way to your heart or a shadow of mischief that can run off with your sense of humor. It is up to you to shape the course of your dog's life, for a pointer is an unbridled desire, a form of raw energy requiring harnessing to be useful.

The next memorable milestone in a bird hunter's life occurs when the pupil first locates a wild bird and comes to a staunch point. At that moment you don't know whether to flush and shoot the bird or fall to your knees, lift your hands to the firmament, and praise the Almighty.

Such a feeling came over me once when I acquired a dog after breaking a promise to myself to never accept another person's failed pup. "If you don't want her," said old Jack, the trainer who, after having put down more dogs than a Korean chef, had developed plenty of calluses on his conscience, "I'm going to have to get rid of her." That meant the next gunfire the year-old Irish setter would hear would be her last.

"I'll pick her up next week," I said, glancing at the lever-action .22 Jack kept in his pickup for the dogs that didn't measure up. I worked daily for most of the summer with Maggie and, though she showed some promise, she was as willful as any Irish lady. I had never worked with one of the red setters but had developed a sentimental kinship with the dog whose descendants probably confounded my ancestors every since my clan answered to the name O'Darcy on the Emerald Isle. I was once told of an Irish tale that explained the unruly behavior of a dog. As the yarn goes, dogs that misbehave do so because there's a tiny leprechaun hiding under their collars, whispering commands into the dogs' ears. By the end of the summer, I no longer wondered why the Irish had developed such an infatuation for whiskey. It wasn't the dreary climate nor a lack of spuds, it was their dogs. Then, one dew-soaked August morning, Maggie must have sensed my frustration. In what amounted to a canine epiphany, she snaked a course through the goldenrod, locating six wild pheasants in a series of points spaced no more than five minutes apart. Her performance remains the most memorable single outing I've ever shared with a bird dog.

Despite such successes, rest assured that there will be setbacks on the trainer's journey. You'll likely discover, for instance, that bird dogs seem to have a particular fascination for skunks and porcupines—the same way young children can't resist writing with markers on a newly painted wall. Thor, the best dog I'd ever owned, winner of seven successive hunting dog trials, a dog that could reduce well-seasoned roosters to fricasseed pheasant with his mastery, could also locate a denned polecat anywhere on a section of head-high bluestem. If I saw a skunk dead on the road or so much as caught a faint waft of *essence de skunk* near an area I wanted to hunt, I'd load up and head elsewhere for fear the nearest town wouldn't have enough tomato juice to bathe the scent away.

Idiosyncracies aside, selecting a pup should be a matter of thoughtful consideration. Measure a dog's traits against its pedigree, the experts tell us, and carefully examine a pup's parents before making a decision in haste. Such advice, in most cases, is soon forgotten when a plump little pup wanders over and licks a prospective buyer on the chin. It's at that moment that people are especially prone to surrendering their wallet along with their common sense.

When it comes time to begin the process of molding your lump of canine clay, many people subscribe to the theory that old dogs will teach young dogs important skills critical to the success of a gun dog. I agree. My youngest setter, Frost, never knew how to dig tulip bulbs, chew door bottoms, and rearrange furniture until old Thor shared those invaluable lessons. I've often wondered if it wouldn't simply be easier to teach a pup to read a training book than to actually walk the student through the process myself. When you raise and train your own bird dog, you either share in the joy of having developed the prospect or suffer the pain of a plan gone awry. The outcome is never guaranteed, but nothing worthwhile comes without risk.

Too many modern dog handlers take the view that dog training is a testing of a dog's will against an electric collar, forgetting that the road to a finished bird dog is a scenic path traveled but once. The difference between a thoughtful approach to teaching and the work of an impatient trainer is the difference between taking time to smell the roses and simply mowing them. I've studied most of the so-called "new" methods of training bird dogs and, at the elemental level, they differ little from the advice given by old-timers decades ago. I suspect the methods haven't changed much because bird dogs and bird men haven't changed markedly over the years either.

We often romanticize that when our pointers are resting, their paws twitching in the depths of sleep, that they are dreaming of splendid days afield. In actuality, though, they're probably thinking of putting a choke collar on their owners and are wondering what it would be like if their trainers—albeit only for a moment—swallowed their whistles. Some of my most entertaining days in the uplands were spent watching otherwise sane men reduced to frothing idiots as they sprinted through cover in a desperate attempt to collar their runaway pointers—dogs seemingly deafened by an incessant chorus of whistle blasts.

One particularly lively hunt took place on a Wisconsin public hunting area—one of those places where 179 hunters and their dogs compete for the twenty roosters the state releases the day before the season opens. One of the birds—pheasants often referred to as "liberated," but about as free as an East German used to be to scale the Berlin Wall—flushed to face what amounted to a military maneuver. The bird fell instantly to one or more of the ten or twelve shots that rang out and, at the same moment, a half-dozen dogs descended on it. A pointer reached the bird first and took two steps toward its master before being tackled by a yellow Lab. The Lab and the remnants of the pheasant were soon ambushed by a larger Lab and a setter, and two German shorthairs joined the fray like a pack of famished wolves fighting over a lemming dinner. It was the last time I opened the Wisconsin pheasant season on a public hunting area.

I once thought I had owned some pretty rangy pointers until I attended my first field trial. I reasoned any dog that could outrun a horse was too much canine for me. My surmising was confirmed when I asked one of the trial men how many dogs he'd run at one time. He replied, "As many as I can afford to lose at one time."

No matter how well devised one's training techniques might be, frustration has a way of clouding even the most patient regimens. There isn't a dog trainer alive who, at least for a fleeting instant, hasn't wanted to strangle his dog with its ears. But I've seen as many dog owners as dogs who've needed an electric collar. We so commonly create a dog's fault and, in our haste to correct it, we too often make matters worse.

Given the precipitous peaks and expansive valleys of emotional terrain that accompany training a bird dog, prospective dog owners often ask me how long it takes to develop an effective pointing dog. The answer lies not in age but in experience—both the dog's and the trainer's. It's a matter of tabulating a dog's encounters with birds, for a young pointer with scores of introductions to birds will be more apt to cope with fowl than an older dog shy on exposure to game.

No amount of yard training can replace a dog's experience with birds. And a thousand pen-raised birds can't teach a dog the behavior of wild game. The difference between a pen-raised dupe and a wild bird is the difference between a birdbrain and a brain surgeon. That's a fact readily apparent with a pup's first hike into those magical places we call coverts. That's one reason I'm particularly fond of hunting with older dogs. Such veterans tend to use their wits more and their legs less. What the years take from them in speed they give back in savvy, and when you hunt with a sagacious pointer you never want for entertainment, for bird and dog are seldom long separated.

There have been reams of drivel devoted to the topic of which dog to use when hunting your favorite game bird. For instance, I've never owned a truly great ruffed grouse dog—at least not one that could consistently and stalwartly find and point grouse. But then, when it comes to hunting grouse, perhaps the most important trait a dog can possess is a sense of humor. The dog that can point grouse with regularity is, indeed, the four-leafed clover of the canine world. New England and the Great Lakes states are the hunting grounds of would-be grouse specialists that ended up woodcock general practitioners. Many mediocre pointers, in fact, owe their dog chow to timberdoodle.

When it comes to quail dogs, the best ones are the pointers that have never had their confidence shattered by the shenanigans of a sprinting pheasant. Who can blame a pheasant pointer for being a little neurotic and slightly hard-mouthed? After desperately chasing a ring-neck through marsh and meadow, a dog lucky enough to retrieve a rooster deserves a little revenge for its efforts. There's a fine line, however, between a little revenge and disemboweling a bird, a subtlety a friend's springer never quite mastered. If you didn't get to a fallen bird before the dog did, the best you could hope for was to have enough leftover for soup stock.

Perhaps you hunt your pheasants with one of the breeds termed "versatile" hunting dogs? I've been fascinated by this designation that's found a seemingly permanent place in the contemporary gun dog owner's lexicon. A versatile hunting dog, most often, is a moniker worn by any of the various pointing breeds originating from continental Europe. As a lifelong setter disciple, I've taken the term as a bit of an affront—sort of feeling the way I did when a Lutheran acquaintance used to refer to me as a mackerel snapper because of my Catholic heritage. I once owned a setter that could dizzy a pheasant with his wizardry, retrieved geese in ice water, and was rock staunch on raccoons. What's more versatile, I ask, than that?

Regardless of what breed of pointer graces your life, a good bird dog is the spice of any hunt in the uplands, adding a special flavor to the main course that is autumn. A bird dog is an interpreter of the air currents, relaying the story in the breeze through the cock of its ears or the wag of its tail. One is especially proud of his dog when those interpretations translate to more birds in the hand. Though I'm always appreciative of good dog work, I'm not prone to spoiling my setter, and I don't believe in feeding him scraps from the table. When he's fresh off a perfect performance, however, and has had a particularly keen day in front of both myself and friends, I'll set a place for him at the head of the table. No steak is too prime nor is any sofa too new for the bird dog that delivers close-flushing game to the gun.

Great bird dogs, too, are more than game finders. They're the alibis we need to flee our domesticated lives for a few moments of sanity in the marshes, fields, and woods. A good bird dog also travels well. That means he doesn't mind long sojourns in a pickup, and he knows how to peek around corners and run for the door when sneaking him into a roadside motel in bird country.

The spirit of a great dog, like the fire of a champion fighter, never quits. By the end of several consecutive days of hunting in Wisconsin grouse coverts, prickly ash and blackberry thorns would shred my setter's ears and scar his muzzle. He'd be one scab from nose to tail tip but, come the fifth day, no matter the temperature nor what hour of the morning I might awake, would greet me with the eager thump of his tail against the floor, ready to hunt again.

Most of all, a great dog never stops teaching its owner. And if an owner is wise, he'll never stop learning. A synchrony exists between an old dog and its owner, a synergy that builds with time spent together communicating in voice tones and body language. Birds might have first drawn us to the sport of wingshooting, but it's likely that our dogs have kept us in brush pants and double guns.

Bird dogs also introduce us to new friends, for gun-dog owners often have much in common. My favorite bird hunting partners are people quick to notice even my setter's most remedial field successes and always offer a perfectly logical excuse when the dog appears a candidate for a lobotomy. Criticizing another's dog, on the other hand, has much in common with walking in a mine field, take one step too many and you may never come back.

No matter what our experiences with bird dogs have been, we will never forget them. Our memories of dogs past tend to age like fine wines. I even speak reverently about a friend's former hard-mouthed, deer-chasing, chicken-killing setter that used to hold a point until I was *almost* within shotgun range.

In spite of such regressions, is there a feeling so grand as sitting by a fire next to a tired bird dog that has hunted to exhaustion for you? To be certain, there is both a rhyme and a rhythm to hunting with a good gun dog. The melodic jingle of a dog's bell is the favorite tune of the upland gunner, for it reminds us of the age old question: Do we own dogs, or do they own us?

Robert F. Jones *was for many years a senior writer at* Time *and* Sports Illustrated. *His essays and short stories have appeared in thirteen previous anthologies and a host of magazines, including* Audubon, Gray's Sporting Journal, *and* Fly Rod & Reel. *He writes a bird-hunting column, "The Dawn Patrol," for* Shooting Sportsman. *Born in Wisconsin, where he learned his love of the outdoors, Jones has since hunted or fished on every continent but Antarctica. He is the author four works of nonfiction, including the award-winning* Upland Passage: A Field Dog's Education, Jake: A Labrador Puppy at Work & Play *(Farrar, Straus & Giroux, 1992), and a collection of his African hunting tales,* African Twilight, *published last fall.* Tie My Bones to Her Back, *his sixth and latest novel, is set on the Great Plains in the 1870s.*

RUSTY AND BELLE

by Robert F. Jones

A boy's father should teach him to hunt.

Mine liked to fish. He didn't care much for what they call the shooting sports, and my only hunting uncle happened to be in jail during my formative years. (That's another story.) So my education as a budding Nimrod took a different course. In fact, like Mowgli in Kipling's *Jungle Book*, I was taught how to hunt by the wolves.

Well, okay...so maybe they weren't wolves. But a pair of half-wild, hell-for-leather Irish setters is probably the next best thing.

How Rusty and Belle sniffed me out as a candidate for on-the-job training, I really don't know. I don't even know who actually owned them. And yet, during a single glorious, murderous, never-to-be-forgotten autumn just after World War II, I found myself hunting behind them, gradually learning the nuances of the chase, gunning my first game birds over them, and developing under their rude tutelage a lifelong love of upland shooting. First times, as they say, are always the best.

Ever since my family had moved, in the fall of 1941, to the far western reaches of Wauwatosa in southern Wisconsin, I'd been mesmerized by game birds. Across the road from our newly built home lay a broad belt of virgin tallgrass prairie, stretching nearly a mile down to the Menomonee River. That reach of the upper Middle West is part of what scientists call the Prairie Peninsula, islands of grassland studded across the great, dark-green sea of the northern forests. This configuration provides lots of "edge," and the region was therefore rich in wildlife. Bison had roamed those prairie islands, as far east as Pennsylvania and New York, but the last of Wisconsin's buffalo was killed in 1832. Game birds remained abundant, though. Ruffed grouse, sharptails and prairie chickens, woodcock and snipe, clouds of ducks, and later the newly introduced ringneck pheasant—all proliferated on or around these grassy islands. In those parts, it was almost inevitable that a boy should become an upland hunter.

◆

That first winter in the new house I began noticing clusters of large, brown, football-shaped birds scuttling around in the field across the road as they fed in the snow on grass seed knocked down by the wind. I was not yet seven years old, but something ignited in my heart. I wanted to hold one in my hands, maybe study its feathers up close, perhaps even pluck them out—though I knew the bird would have to be dead for me to do that. Okay, so I'd kill it first. And then when it was plucked...

And then what?

I'd eat it!

Yes, hunting is instinctive with us, despite the arguments of the antis. *I had to have one of those birds.*

"What are they, Dad?" I asked one afternoon as my father and I were shoveling snow in front of the house. He looked across the street. A dozen of the big birds were feeding busily in the field near the road.

"Prairie chickens," he said.

I stared longingly at them, less than a hundred feet away.

"They don't make good pets," he said.

"I don't want one as a pet," I said. "I want to kill one. We could cook it up for supper tonight."

He laughed.

"Don't let your mother hear you say that," he said. My mother was a notorious critter-lover, weeping quietly whenever a songbird snuffed itself against a storm window, or at the mere thought of a dead raccoon on the road.

One of the birds was feeding toward us, well away from the rest of the flock. "See if you can hit him with a snowball," my dad said.

I packed a good one, as small and heavy and tight and round as I could make it. I crossed the road directly toward the bird. Not even looking up, it scurried back to the flock. I kept going. With every step I gained on them, they edged away deeper into the wind-bent grass. I couldn't get within range this way. I sprinted toward them in nightmare slow motion, the metal clasps of my heavy galoshes rattling as I ran. They scuttled a bit faster. Finally, panting, I hurled the snowball. They avoided it with ease and kept on feeding. By the time I had had enough, I was a quarter of a mile into the prairie, knee-deep in snow, redfaced and slick with sweat, and my arm ached from futile throws at unhittable targets. I plodded back to my father, who was gentleman enough to hide the grin that was threatening to erupt into a boy-shattering guffaw.

"A snowball's no good," I said.

"Guess not."

"Dad, could I have a bow and some arrows?"

"We'll see," he said.

For Christmas that year I received a lemonwood longbow of fifteen pounds pull. I was a big kid for my age, but the bow was too strong for me at first. I persevered, shooting at snowmen in the backyard during the winter, or hay bales or bushel baskets or (when the grownups weren't looking) at the occasional pumpkin in the neighborhood's communal Victory Garden across the road the following summer, and by fall I felt I was ready. I wasn't. Oh, sure, I could shoot a Pound Sweet apple out of the neighbor's backyard tree, and once I grazed a fat robin tugging a worm from the earth after a rainstorm, but I couldn't hit a prairie chicken that first autumn to save my wretched soul. I lost arrow after arrow, shooting at birds on the ground, and never nicked a one. They dodged the arrows as readily as they had my first snowball, and the arrow inevitably slithered off beneath the matted grass, rarely to fly again.

I began making my own arrows out of the long pinewood rods my mom used to support leggy garden plants, fletching them with brightly dyed turkey feathers from a cheap Indian war bonnet that one of my aunts had given me for my eighth birthday. In hopes of saving arrows, I arrived independently at the principle of the flu-flu, in which the fletching is glued around the tail of the shaft in corkscrew fashion to slow down the final flight of the arrow, and learned how to stalk quite close to the flock before shooting—sometimes as close as thirty feet.

Finally I hit a prairie chicken, a young one, just as the flock was rising in panic from my best stalk ever. I broke her wing, and it took me half an hour of frantic chasing through tangles of the low-lying sawgrass we called "ripgut" before I finally batted her flat with the bow. I fell on her like a fumbled football and wrung her rubbery neck.

I sat there in the prairie, with the bluestem towering over my head, my hands and bare forearms stinging from sweat and innumerable grass cuts, with hard, sharp grass seeds stuck in the blood that seeped from the slashes, holding her at last in my hands. She was hot, dusty smelling, heavy, limp, and dead as a doornail. I ruffled the transverse chocolate and white bars on her breast again and again, as I later would the short, thick, soft hair of the first girl I ever loved. Never in my life had I been happier than I was at that moment.

But I knew there had to be a better way.

That way was with a dog and a gun.

◆

My grandfather, Frank Jones, had led a peripatetic life as a young man, before the turn of the twentieth century. Born in 1871, he'd run away from home in Chicago at the age of fourteen after smashing a slate over a schoolmaster's head when that man falsely accused him of whispering to a classmate. He'd bummed around the Midwest, working on farms, becoming a dab hand with horse teams. He drifted into the small towns occasionally, working as a shop clerk, a hackney driver, once as an assistant to an undertaker, among other odd jobs, but finally fetching up back in Chicago. There he became a foreman on the production line in a packing house. The company he worked for, maybe it was Swift or Armour, I can't remember, had developed a revolutionary new canning process, and a New York City packer pirated him away to steal the new technique. He went to New York in 1890 and remained there for nearly ten years. When his boss at the packing plant told him that all employees would be expected to vote for the Republican incumbent, Benjamin Harrison, over Grover Cleveland in the upcoming

1892 presidential election, my grandfather quit his job, though he was still a few months shy of twenty-one and couldn't have voted if he'd wanted to. He was damned if anyone would tell him how to vote.

Out of work, he and an unemployed partner pooled their resources, bought an old 12-bore W. W. Greener hammer gun, rented a team and a buckboard, and went across the Hudson River to the Jersey Palisades to hunt for the New York restaurant market. They brought along a stray dog they'd befriended, a lop-eared, curly coated, liver-colored pooch named Fred who may have been an American water spaniel.

"I didn't care what breed he was," my grandfather used to say. "Old Fred was good at his job and that's all I cared about."

"What did you hunt for?" I asked him.

"Bog-suckers, pa'tridges, and prairie hens," he told me. I later deciphered those names to mean woodcock, ruffed grouse, and—of all things—heath hens, the last-named being the eastern equivalent of my beloved Greater Prairie Chicken (*Tympanuchus cupido*). The heath hen died out in the early years of this century, of course, almost simultaneously with the last of the passenger pigeons which once darkened the skies of nineteenth-century America during their spring and fall migrations, both birds the victims of unbridled habitat destruction and wanton American blood lust.

But while it lasted the hunting was superb—too easy, the way my granddad told it. One of them would drive the wagon through the little pockets of open country back of the Palisades while the other walked ahead, with the dog and the gun, popping whatever got up. "We'd cross the river on a Friday night and come back Monday morning with the spring wagon groaning. We got two bits apiece for the bigger birds, and a nickel each for the little fellas."

To me, at the age of ten, it sounded like heaven on earth.

"Do you still have that shotgun?" I asked hopefully.

"No," my granddad said, rolling another cigarette. He was a lean, leathery old man already in his seventies, with hard gray eyes, a thin scar of a mouth, nicotine-stained fingers, and a great, gritty fund of stories. He would live to be eighty-seven, and rise up from his death bed on the final morning of his life to shave himself with his cut-throat straight razor, having reshingled his roof, unaided, only a few weeks before. "And even if I did still have that old iron," he added, "I'd dassent give it to you. Your ma would never forgive me."

◆

Clearly I would have to seek elsewhere for a shotgun, and when I'd found it, keep any knowledge of the gun or of my hunting adventures from my tender-hearted, gun-hating mother. The few birds and rabbits I'd killed so far with the bow, I'd cooked and eaten out in the fields where I shot them. My friends and I filched lard, salt, and matches from home, a little bit at a time, and kept them hidden in a "fort" we had dug on the prairie. We dug it into a side hill, roofed it over with scrap lumber we swiped from a nearby building project (already the prairie was being nibbled to death by post-war housing development), and laid thick slabs of bluestem sod over the boards. We salvaged a rusty old frying pan from the town dump, cleaned it up with bootlegged Brillo pads, added an old-fashioned stoneware coffee pot one of the gang found in his attic, hauled water-smoothed rocks up from the river to build a fireplace, and were snug as jolly plainsmen in our splendid hideaway. It had everything a boy could desire—including a huge stack of moldy comic books. Everything but a gun and a couple of bird-dogs.

Enter Rusty and Belle.

They came trotting up to the hidden entrance of our our fort one hot September Saturday when a couple of us were boiling some crayfish we'd caught in the river. Crayfish were called "crabs" in those parts, and they were a pretty big subspecies, some of them six or eight inches long. We caught them with a hunk of liver tied to a piece of butcher's string and dangled near their holes in the shallows, under the river rocks. You let them glom on, hoisted them gently up near the top of the water, then netted them with your baseball cap. We boiled them up in an old Maxwell House coffee can, after letting them soak for about an hour or so in clear, cold water to clean the mud out of their systems. When they were done, they turned red as lobsters. We cracked them open with stones, sprinkled salt on the pieces, and scoffed them down, sometimes with crackers and peanut butter for dessert.

Snuffle, snuffle, snuffle. We saw two big, square, wet noses poking into the doorway. Nostrils big as gun muzzles, flexing open and shut as they sniffed the delicious smells.

"Cripes, it's a couple of dogs."

"I know them," Danny said. "They're Rusty and Belle. I think they're called Irish setters."

My ears perked up. A setter was a hunting dog. I'd never seen the Irish variety, though.

"Hand me my bow and quiver," I said.

"You're not gonna shoot 'em, are you?"

"No, asshole. I'm gonna see if they know how to hunt."

I brought out some crabmeat and a handful of Saltines for the dogs. They accepted the snacks eagerly and looked up for more.

"You've got to earn it," I told them. I strung the bow—I'd graduated to a thirty-five pound Osage-orange long-bow by this time—nocked a homemade flu-flu arrow, and headed off at a trot toward where I'd seen a small family group of prairie chickens only about an hour ago. We were hunting into the wind, so the bird scent would blow back down to the dogs. The only trouble was that they stayed right at my heels. No good, I thought. I want them out in front. I stopped. Rusty stopped too, and looked up at me. His eyes held the big question. *What do you want, Boss?*

"Go ahead," I said, gesturing with my free hand. "Hunt 'em up!"

Belle responded first to my command, suddenly lighting up and hunting forward on a zigzag line with her head high, sucking in the hot autumn wind. Rusty took off after her, quartering in counterpoint to her course. Whenever they got more than fifteen yards ahead of me, I whistled them back, then sent them out again. I don't believe they had ever been trained to this, but they must have had at least a smidgen of hunting instinct left, though I've read since that the breed had gone almost exclusively to bench stock by then. The red gods were certainly feeling benevolent that day, to send me by sheerest chance these eager, alert, glossy-red bird dogs.

Suddenly Belle stopped. Her broad-feathered tail went up. Her head poised flat and rock-steady, almost snake-like, angling slightly downward and ahead of her. By God she was on point!

Foolishly, I ran in ahead of her in my eagerness, and the whole flock of chickens erupted at once, a great rattling blur of brown and white. I snapped an arrow after them but missed miserably. The birds flew on, fast and low, a few strong wingbeats, then a long gliding pause, then a few more wingbeats, until they were just dots at the far end of the prairie.

I couldn't bring myself to look at Belle, who I was sure must be furious at me for blowing the shot. But she wasn't. She looked delighted with herself, smirking and pirouetting like a wanton minx. She and Rusty hunted on. We pushed through the tall golden grass toward where the birds had pitched in.

About halfway there, Belle pointed again. This time I kept my head, walking in slowly ahead of her with the arrow nocked firmly and the bow held crosswise at waist height. A large, long-tailed bird suddenly scuttled ahead a few steps and took wing. A pheasant! A big, slow, greenheaded, white-necked, bronze gleaming cockbird, cackling metallically as he lifted off. I drew, fired, and hit him, and he tumbled end for end into the grass as feathers drifted off downwind. Rusty, who had been to one side, was on him like a crimson flash. I ran up quickly, not knowing if Rusty would run off with the bird to eat it, and while he was still wrestling with it, got it away from him and wrung its neck. I praised them both to the skies and they wagged their tails in doggy delight. It was my first ringneck ever, and only a lucky hit at the base of the left wing accounted for our bagging it. On the way back to the fort, Belle jumped a rabbit which I also managed to kill. A great day! I rewarded my newfound friends with a fair share of the rabbit meat when we fried it up that afternoon in our underground hideaway.

Later that fall, I arranged to buy a beat-up old single-barreled, 28-gauge Savage Model 220 from a kid in my grade at school. The gun was choked Improved Cylinder and had a 28-inch barrel. Ron's dad was a wealthy doctor who spoiled him rotten, and had just bought him a 16-gauge "Eagle Grade" L. C. Smith. I gave Ron eight dollars for the Savage—money I'd been paid by neighbors for mowing lawns and shoveling snow, hard-earned every penny of it. Ron threw in three boxes of low-base $7\frac{1}{2}$s and one of high-brass 6s, along with a can of Hoppe's nitro solvent and a cleaning rod. No contemporary gun deal in the streets of Miami or Harlem ever went down more surreptitiously.

I couldn't bring the gun home for fear my parents would discover it—my mom was an inveterate snoop, always poking around in my room while I was at school to see what I'd been up to. So I wrapped the Savage in oily rags and kept it, during the week, in the fort. That didn't work for long. Every minute of every day, I was afraid some tramp would wander up from the Milwaukee Road right-of-way just across the river and find the fort. He'd swipe my gun and hold up a bank, or something. It was driving me nuts. My schoolwork also suffered.

I had a friend named Harry who lived near the grade school, and I prevailed on him to let me hide the shotgun in his garage. There were fields across the road from the school, just like the ones across from my house, and I figured to do some hunting there after school or on the weekends. Rusty and Belle had taken to following me to school that fall, hanging out in the playground during class hours and playing "keep away" with us during recess or the noon hour. Once they saw, smelled, and heard the gun go off, they were even more strongly bonded to me. I've often wondered what their rightful owners thought they were up to during those long, long absences from home.

It took a lot of trial and error—more of the latter than the former—to perfect a decent shooting style with the Savage. But my experience in wingshooting with the bow stood me in good stead. The bow had taught me how to swing with a rising bird, and keep swinging as I released the shot. With the shotgun, I had a tendency to overlead birds—especially rising woodcock, which have a disconcerting habit of pausing at the top of the rise before zigzagging out on the level through the tops of a cover. Pheasants were easy—slow, loud, straightaway fliers. Ruffed grouse were harder, startling to the point of paralysis in the racket they made getting up, then lining out low or with a tree between them and the gun, denying me a shot either way.

I wouldn't shoot at a really low bird for fear of hitting one of the dogs. I also swore off rabbits for the same reason. I could never break Rusty and Belle of tear-assing off after every bunny they jumped, like greyhounds at a dogtrack. Once Belle ran a bunny into a long piece of drainage pipe, wide enough for the rabbit but not for the dog. Rusty figured out instantly what was happening and leaped to the far end of the pipe, just in time to intercept the panicky rabbit when it emerged a moment later, still at full gallop. The gluttonous mutts quickly ripped it apart and ate it. I figured this must be the way they hunted before they took up with me. Old habits die hard.

No, they weren't perfect gun dogs by any means. In addition to eating perhaps one in every five birds I killed, they had a tendency to take off suddenly for parts unknown in the middle of a hunt, sometimes not returning until the next day. Rusty was a car chaser, and Belle a cat chaser. They inevitably took on any skunk they happened across, with predictably malodorous results. Fortunately we lived too far south for porcupines. Once they tackled a big boar raccoon, and before they learned their lesson both of them had deep gashes in their noses, flanks, and bellies that put them out of action for the better part of a week.

But now and then they were splendid. I'll never forget a double point that occurred one November afternoon in the fields across the railroad tracks. We'd been puddle jumping mallards along the river, with only sporadic success, when Belle—who had the better nose—suddenly lit up. I followed her into the wind, away from the river, across the tracks, and into a low, damp swale that gave way to cattails before rising again to a farmer's planting of field corn. At the edge of the swale she froze on point. Rusty pussyfooted up behind her, then looked to his left. Sniffed a couple times. He angled over in that direction about ten yards and locked up.

Could be the same bird, I thought. A runner, moving ahead of Belle's point. But when I went in ahead of Belle, a woodcock got up right under her nose. As I mounted the gun, I heard and then saw from the corner of my eye a big cock pheasant vault skyward from Rusty's point— no doubt flushed by the piping of the woodcock's wing feathers. It was one of those bright, cold, cobalt-blue Wisconsin afternoons—no wind, sunlight gleaming on the dogs' rich mahogany-colored fur, the field corn pale yellow in the background, the cock pheasant resplendent in full flight.

"I'll kill 'em both!" I thought as the flight paths of woodcock and ringneck momentarily crossed. I shot in that instant. Both birds fell.

That's gunning at its best.

◆

Rusty and Belle disappeared from my life that winter, with the arrival of the first deep snows that put an end to the bird shooting. I have no idea what became of them. Maybe their owner moved away. Maybe they died—both of them were reckless enough. Whatever it was, I'm sure it had nothing to do with a loss of interest in hunting. I've never met a keener pair of gun dogs—nonstop, indefatigable. I'll always be grateful to them for infecting me with that enthusiasm when it counted the most.

My mother never learned of Rusty and Belle—not until I told her about them, years later, toward the end of her life.

"Where did you develop this unhealthy passion for blood sports?" she asked me one afternoon when I was visiting from my home in the East. "You never got it from me or your father."

I told her the story, just about the way I've told it here. Her eyes began to fill with tears, and suddenly I was sorry I'd confessed. I looked out the front window, across the street. It was wall-to-wall suburbia now, clear down to the river. Not an acre of native prairie left.

"If I'd known it meant so much to you, I would have allowed you to hunt," she said. "Better that than keep it hidden from me all those years."

Fat chance, I thought. Don't feel sorry for her, feel sorry for what's gone. She just doesn't get it. None of them do. They never will.

Thomas BeVier was raised on an Ohio farm in the 1950s, and it was there that he shot his first pheasant and woodcock in front of his first dog, a Brittany spaniel, with an old J. C. Higgins 12-gauge shotgun, which he still owns.

When barely out of his teens, he went to work for his first newspaper, The Lorain (Ohio) Journal. Later he worked for newspapers in Oklahoma, where he learned about shooting quail from horseback, in Tennessee, where he had a brief flirtation with pointers, and in Michigan, where he has renewed his association with Brittanies.

For the last decade he has covered the northern Lower Peninsula and the Upper Peninsula of Michigan for the Detroit Free Press and the Detroit News. He has also written for various magazines.

THIS IS WHAT IT'S ALL ABOUT, ALFIE

by Thomas Bevier

I am a modest man. Just ask anyone who knows me.

They will tell you, for instance, that only occasionally do they catch me boasting that my wife is the best cook north of Toledo. Nor do they hear me extolling the virtues of my two sons, although the boys have met all reasonable expectations for this day and time, having each served only one overnight jail term. My hubris is so contained that I usually resist informing fellow anglers that catching a muskie is not a big deal by reminding them that I got mine the first time out.

And so, with the understanding that braggadocio is a minor function of my character, I may be excused for stating that when it comes to dogs, I have few peers. I am confident my current Dog in Residence, a bonnie Brittany called Francie, would bear out the claim.

(A digression and an explanation for those who may wonder how I came up with a name like Francie for my dog: Francie is my wife's middle name. When things are rocky on the domestic front, I find it constructive to vent anger by simply calling my dog. "Come Francie, you bitch," I holler from the back stoop. Francie the dog doesn't mind, and Francie the spouse is always well out of earshot.)

My rationalization for an uncommon breach of modesty is that it is needed as a preamble to telling about Alfie, a pointer of refined bloodlines and noble bearing about whom it is difficult to compliment further. There will be more said about him in due time.

And there is this: Perhaps, by recognizing my considerable skills with dogs, others who have squandered their precious time and considerable sums of money because they believed, completely and unquestioningly as I did, in the general goodness of dogs, from the lowest mongrel even unto the Best of Westminster or Grand Junction, will find comfort from my experience with Alfie.

So my motive is pure when I say that dogs come when I call them, that they sit before me as willing vassals, wagging and never jumping up, and that rare is the one that doesn't quickly surrender to disciplined heeling with me on the other end of the lead. Also, that I easily calm puppy fervor, the stupidity of studs, or the raised hackles of a one of those barking monsters unleashed on visitors by a boorish owner. A raised hand, palm out, unthreateningly, or a sharp word is all it takes. Firm but friendly, that's my style. With dogs, I am the boss I have never personally had: kind and rewarding most of the time, charitable and constructive with criticism, patient and understanding in the face of failure.

Francie, I should note, is the ultimate benficiary of my gift, standing as she does at the head of a long line of canine friends who have enriched my life from puberty onward toward initiation into the American Association of Retired Persons. But much as I adore her, this story is not about Francie. That is because she is perfection, with a certain allowance for being firecracker-shy and thunderstorm-shy, as well as a bit gun-shy.

The first rule of journalism, my chosen trade, says that stories about perfection aren't worth printing. Alas, it's a waste of ink to write about the honest politician, the straight-arrow car dealer, or the understanding cop. "Give us good news," readers choir, but they don't mean it. What they really want is stories about blood and gore, malfeasance at all levels of government and finance, and the petty failures of their sports and entertainment heroes. Failing any of that, they'll settle for saccharine reports on the misfortunes of their neighbors.

I assume the general reader's crass appetite extends to stories about dogs. And for that, fortunately, I presume, I remember Alfie.

◆

"What's it all about, Alfie?" It was one of the pressing questions of the era, an era fulsome with questions both great and small. Dionne Warwich sang the song, and a previous wife had a crush on Michael Caine, who starred in the movie.

Alfie came to me as a puppy, like all the other dogs I've owned. As a matter of fact, I can reckon my life in puppies. There are other ways to take an accounting, of course. Children or jobs could serve as a basis. I read someplace that one's life can even be counted out in coffee spoons. I prefer puppies.

There are disappointments with children or jobs, and coffee is bitter. A puppy has never let me down, not even Alfie. That he failed me (Or—this essay's cosmic question—did I fail him?) in his adolescence and early manhood is beside the point. As a puppy he was great. All puppies are great.

When I bought Alfie, I was living in the deep South, land of barbecue, antebellum architecture and politics, and—best of all—coveys of very shootable quail. Growing up in Ohio, I had hunted pheasant, woodcock, and ducks, but only when I flushed my first quail did I experience a wingshooter's epiphany.

I was introduced to quail by the sheriff of a rural county, a gentle and thoughtful man, the likes of whom has so often been put to slander in films and commercials. It's true that his shotgun of choice in the field was the riot gun from his patrol car, a weapon several inches short of legal which threw a fearsomely broad pattern, but in all other regards he was a true sportsman.

"I'll tell you why I hunt," he drawled. "It's to watch the dogs work. I just love watching my dogs work."

What dogs they were—four pointers, two males and two bitches, as I recall, and all distantly related. I had never seen such dogs, honed to muscle and bone, conditioned beyond conditioning. They were houndlike in repose, lanquid as a Delta evening or their master's voice. But loose them from the cages on the pickup truck, and they were immediately transformed. They danced, almost feline in their grace, and then with a word from the sheriff they were off, running on the edge of control.

On the edge of control...but never out of control. With a whistle, but mostly with hand commands, the sheriff guided them in the hunt, moving them left and right to quarter the wind, motioning them back when they ranged too far. Ballets have been performed less artfully. And then they'd strike a scent, and sometimes a dog would be so eager to come to point that he'd tumble head over heels before freezing into the classic, shivering pose.

"Easy, easy," the sheriff would drone as we moved through the cover, and the dogs would hold. Then, in that whir of wing and motion that always surpasses expectation, the birds would flush. The guns would sound. Birds would drop. The dogs would fetch them.

"So sheriff," I said, "Where can I get a dog like yours?"

"Son, dogs like these are made not born. It takes a lot of work and patience to make a good dog. No offense intended, but I don't know if you're up to it."

I informed him that I had trained a half-dozen dogs, and that while only one of them had been a bird dog I was sure I wouldn't have any trouble with a pointer. Against his better judgment, I suppose, he gave me the name of his breeder. "Tell him I sent you, and, oh yeh, take money," he said.

I expected to pay maybe as much as $200. Forget it. Talk about sticker shock. "You get what you pay for," the breeder told me. To this day, I confess only to my closest friends how much I paid for Alfie. I never did tell my wife. Actually, I lied when she asked. We were later divorced. What can I say?

He was a fine looking dog, deep-chested, long in the leg and with head found only in the pure of breed. And energy. Even as a puppy, Alfie could tire five children at play. He'd go on point on a quail wing dangled from a string from the very beginning.

Friends dropped by. "Fine dog," they'd say. "How much did you pay for him? When are you going to start training him?"

I built him a house and pen. Alfie was not a pet, I told my brood. "He's a hunting dog," I advised them. He chewed his way out of the pen to chase them around the yard. Then he climbed the chain link fence and ran away. It took hours to find him.

Serious training started early, perhaps too early as I think back. He was a quick learner. Come. Sit. Heel. He learned easily, easier than any other dog I'd ever had. But the minute I'd take him off a lead he'd run away, hell bent for who knows where.

Leads became progressively longer until we were so strung out I felt foolish. Fifty feet of nylon cord is an unwieldy lot. I'd work him mornings and afternoons. He'd respond to voice commands, hand signals, and a whistle. He found birds. But each time I'd take him off the lead, he'd run off.

"My dog ran away," I'd explain to my boss when I was late to work. It happened so frequently that it became a joke around the office.

"Where's BeVier?" the city editor would ask.

"Chasing his dog," somebody would respond.

A year passed. Alfie was still running away. I was at my wit's end. I'd paid so much for him and invested so much time. I was beyond pride and into disappointment.

And so I gave him to my friend Charlie, with the proviso that he'd take me hunting when he got Alfie properly trained.

Charlie was confident. "I never saw a dog I couldn't train," he said. "The problem with you is that you coddle him. You've got to be firm."

I shrugged. I'd tried both coddling and firmness with the same results. Alfie always ran away.

A week passed. I called my friend.

"How's Alfie doing?" I asked.

"Fine. Fine."

"I'd like to drop by and see him."

"Well, not tonight."

"What's happened, Charlie? Did he run away?"

"Yeh, but I'll find him."

He never did and thereafter when Charlie and I and a bunch of the guys got to talking about hunting and such and the subject of dog training came up, Charlie and I would tell the tale of Alfie.

"I bet I could have trained him," somebody would invariably say.

But Charlie and I knew otherwise, having learned the ultimate lesson: that once in a while you run across a dog that's just too good to do your bidding. And that's the one that gets away.

Randy Lawrence made his first trip west for sharp-tailed grouse in 1991 and since then, divides his autumns between being on the prairies and wishing he were there. A close friend who manages his farm for quail and dog training introduced Lawrence to hunting off horseback. "I've always envied the pros who head for Saskatchewan to run bird dogs in the late summer through the early part of the season," says Lawrence, who has kept Tennessee walking horses as an important companion pleasure to his Longhunter setters and pointers. "It's everything I dream about the rest of the year: a steady pony, the dogs sailing across big country, pretty points, big covey rises, and elegant wingshooting. To me, it's the ultimate expression of the gun dog experience."

Closer to home, there are bobwhites, ruffed grouse, and woodcock within minutes of the Hocking College campus in Nelsonville, Ohio, where Randy is a teacher of writing. First published in The Drummer in 1986, his work has since appeared in Gray's Sporting Journal, Game and Gun, Shooting Sportsman, Quail Unlimited, and The Double Gun Journal. He is currently a field editor for Sporting Clays Magazine. Randy, his wife, Jacklyn, and their four children share a Lancaster, Ohio, home with three bird dogs, one yellow Labrador, and an insolent Jack Russell terrier.

RING THE BELL
FOR POPEYE

by Randy Lawrence

Old Popeye had gone down hard, and he wasn't getting up. Tom Roberts stared, slack-jawed, from the other side of the white board fence, the shotgun and bird dog forgotten.

Roberts had bustled through breakfast, thinking he would give the pointer a long hunt on the back edge of the farm. An ice-blue dawn promised the first bright weather in a week, and he meant to have all of it.

While he worked his feet into the scarred pair of birdshooters, he opened and closed his right eye, gravely testing the left. He was still suspicious, though only a tinge of blur remained. For Tom Roberts, most matters came down to trust, and that Judas eye had let him down. No body part should ever betray a fellow during the bird season.

In the back porch mudroom, Roberts spilled a handful of purple shells into one deep pocket of the faded canvas vest. While he fumbled for his whistle and reached the battered shotgun down off the wall pegs, he peeked out the storm door to see his "house covey" scuttling around a feeder set in the winter ruins of his garden. The quail melted off into tall weeds when Roberts popped open the porch door and stepped out into the morning.

He fetched Holly, fat from a season of inactivity, down from the kennels and was trudging past the barn when he noticed Popeye drowsing in the pale January sunlight. Roberts did not want to startle him, coming up on the horse's blind side that way, so he gestured for the pointer to hold and called softly to the ancient white gelding.

"Hey, Ol' Man. Hey, Popeye!"

As if he'd been hit by an electric prod, Popeye squealed, tossed his head, then leaped high, twisting and kicking. He piled into the frost-steeled paddock dirt, struggled to free his legs, then went limp. The thick white neck flopped, slamming the horse's head into the turf.

Roberts backed away, horrified. What had he done? Trying not to panic, he collected the tail-tucked Holly and huffed back up to the kennel shed. Tom penned the dog, leaned the empty shotgun in the corner next to the feed bin, and, from habit, dug the heavy calf's bell out of his vest pocket and hung it over a nail amid a dozen faded field trial ribbons. He felt light-headed, and stumbled back to the shed's doorway.

Slumped against the casing, Roberts could look down into the paddock. Popeye lay stretched and still, like the last mound of dirty snow left in a slow thaw. Tom closed his eyes and tried to catch his breath, tried to beat down the sick feeling roiling in his belly.

What else could happen this year? In October, he'd lost 'Lilah, the setter, to cancer. November brought problems with his own health, a bad cold that had sunk into pleurisy. The coughing came from so deep in Tom's chest that the retina tore loose in his left eye during one wrenching, hacking fit. There had been surgery, then another six weeks stolen from his shooting.

"'Tween that old horse and me, we ain't got but one head's worth of good eyes," he joked when his nephews came to visit. For the first time in his life, Tom Roberts had needed to ask a neighbor for help with his chores.

And now this. He stayed propped in the doorway until the queasiness ebbed, then walked down the hill again, this time to the tack room he'd made out of the barn's old milkhouse. Through the warm smells of harness and horses, he found the moldy, leather halter Popeye had worn lately only for his Amish farrier.

The horse was barely breathing, squeezing air in shallow, choking rasps. His head was flat to the ground, his left eye topside, brimming with hurt and blinking against the sunlight. Roberts knelt and gently worked the halter up and over Popeye's ears. The cheekpiece buckled easily.

Clucking quietly, as if urging him up a steep and slippery grade, Tom slid his hand around the noseband and leaned back in a steady pull.

"C'mon, Popeye. Get on up!"

The horse made no effort to move. Roberts let off for a moment, gathered himself, and dug his boot heels in for another try.

"Come *on*, goddammit! Get *up* !"

Popeye made a throaty moan, but only his head gave to Roberts's weight.

Tom dropped the halter and sank back on his haunches. A seizure? Some kind of stroke? Had Popeye just been startled, then hurt himself in the fall? He stroked the soft muzzle and felt warm breath on his palm.

A shiver rippled along the horse's ribs, and Roberts felt a chill climb his own neck. Popeye. Never sick. Never tired. Just old. Finally, just too damned old.

Tom had retired him from hunting the year before. He didn't know exactly how old Popeye was, but he had ridden him for over twenty years. Last season, Roberts had begun to notice him laboring up hills he'd always taken easily, stumbling over ground that didn't seem rough. The day Popeye tripped at the shallow creek ford and went to his knees, Tom had kicked himself out of the stirrups and made a clumsy vault into fast water.

Roberts had staggered back to fish for the reins, feeling the wet cold creep through his boots and brush pants while Popeye found his footing and shook himself like a giant white dog. Tom led him out of the creek, whistled for 'Lilah, then walked the long mile back to the barn. In a box stall deep with straw, he unsaddled Popeye and took an extra long time rubbing him down. There had been a month left in the quail season, but Tom pastured his horse and hunted February on foot.

The field trialer who had sold Popeye to Roberts swore the one-eyed gelding was out of a flashy, gaited mare by a registered Tennessee walking horse. But the squat build, the coarse head, the heavily-feathered fetlocks hinted at a less imperial ancestry, and Popeye had more bouncing rack to him than any kind of smooth, running walk.

That hadn't mattered to Roberts. He had been new to bird dogs and shooting ponies; the little horse was a calm, easy keeper. From Popeye's broad back, Tom Roberts went to school.

Late each summer, he would leave his farm implement dealership with a younger brother, load the pickup camper, and take ten weeks' vacation pulling a heavy trailer that fairly bowed at the axles: Popeye, a cache of gear, grain, and hay, and four bird dogs bound for the Canada prairies.

Some years, he hooked up with pro trainers he met at field trials, getting his own string worked in exchange for tending horses, scooping kennels, scouting, roading dogs into condition, whatever was needed.

Later on, he struck out on his own, finding farmers who would let him keep camp in the middle of good bird country. Alone with his horse and his dogs, Robert rode out after gray partridge and sharp-tailed grouse.

The Model 21 he'd shot since college stuffed in the saddle boot, Roberts would cast two dogs. His particular fancy was a mixed brace, setter and pointer, and he would whistle them into the wind before nudging Popeye into a nodding, plodding, all-day stride.

Sometimes, Tom sang to his dogs, calling, "Heeyy! Heeyyep! Yep, yep, heeyy!" to keep them hunting, to let them know where he was without their checking in.

Most days, though, he rode in silence, his eyes on white shapes tacking back and forth against the horizon's dark rim. Settled into his trooper saddle's deep seat, he daydreamed to the creak of oiled leather, and faint jingle of dog bells.

When one of the distant forms finally froze, Tom would squeeze Popeye into a slow canter and, if he could, wave the other dog around in position to back. He usually rode within twenty or thirty yards of the stand, dismounted, and let the reins fall to the ground. Popeye would stand as quietly as if he were staked out, head cocked so his left eye faced the action, ears pricking forward and back while Roberts pulled the shotgun and watched his dogs.

In the early part of the season, sharptails held tight, sometimes ripping out of the ground only when Roberts stepped into the flock. On the rise, they made frantic chortle-cackles, and Tom would measure his shooting in deliberate, clean strokes.

The dogs fetched the big grouse gently, gray feathers barely ruffled in easy mouths. Studying each bird as if he'd never held one in hand before, Roberts would give the dogs a blow, then carefully arrange the grouse, head to tail, in the mesh game bag tied behind the saddle.

Partridge were tougher to pin, harder to shoot. Roberts had permission to gun huge tracts of farmland, and during the grain harvest, he and the dogs started spooky Huns from yellow stubble. Later, Popeye would trail the dogs to abandoned farm sites where partridge loafed in the shadows of ruined sheds and leaning grain bins. From ghost barnyards, the birds lifted with cries like rusty shutter hinges on tumbled-in, homesteaders' shanties.

Often the covey would flush before Roberts could reach his dogs. Broke steady to partridge temptation, they stood tall and trembling, eyes wide, marking the birds' long flight. The younger dogs always had to be bullied in to heel at Tom's stirrups before he could lead them away from the flush, get them under control, then whistle them on again.

Roberts stayed on the prairie, hunting wheatfield edges, the deep fingers of brushy coulees veining down through broken country, thick creek bottoms dressed in rosehip and buffalo berry. At dusk, he burned wrist-sized sticks of carefully hoarded deadfall into shimmering orange coals, roasting game on a homemade spit he faithfully tended until the birds were done to a turn.

He would lie stretched by the fire, propped on one elbow, letting the meat cool a bit before savoring each bite of sweet, dark sharptail breast, still pink near the bone. Tired dogs lay curled by their tie-outs, snoring off the day's hunt and a full feed pan. Popeye would be picketed off from the camp, the sound of his yellow teeth snatching at dry prairie grass, loud in the chill night air.

As the nights turned colder, Roberts would need an extra blanket in the camper, and the dogs slept double in snug kennel boxes built into the trailer. The morning he had to break more than a skim of ice in the water buckets, Tom would know that time was running short.

On the last day of his hunt, Tom would run all four dogs together. The goal was to get one obliging pack of grouse to hunker down and treat Roberts to the spectacle of four hard-muscled gun dogs together on one stand. Some years, it happened just that way, one or two dogs pointing, the rest stacked behind, honoring. Then after Tom had made a photograph or two from the saddle, he'd deliberately ride up the birds.

Popeye would arch his heavy neck and dance a little through the cackle and chaos of sharptail wings, the dogs holding while grouse faded into distant specks, their flap-flap-glide, flap-flap-glide, stroking them over the edge of another prairie autumn.

Back home in Kentucky, quail was the quarry, and Roberts hunted his own farm, plus several thousand acres of his neighbors' ground. After each morning's chores, he would ride to where he wanted to hunt, two dogs trotting alongside.

November was spent prospecting for new coveys, getting reacquainted with bevies of birds that he had hunted for years. The Winchester still rode along in the scabbard, but Roberts shot just enough quail to keep the dogs keen and the occasional evening meal a delight. Most of the covies he flushed in front of staunch dogs were saluted with blank popper shells Tom loaded himself.

Saturdays and Sundays, Popeye's saddlebags toted sandwiches and a canteen of sweet cider, and on warm days he would noon in the sun. One pointer and a setter would sit attentively next to him, trying desperately to be still, drool oozing from the sides of their mouths while they watched Roberts eat quail breast and thin slices of Vidalia onion pressed between homemade wheat bread. Sometimes he wrapped himself in his rain slicker and capped lunch with a short nap.

Usually, the dogs' fidgeting woke him. During noon breaks, he always threw the stirrup leathers over the saddle seat to keep Popeye from getting tangled in them and to remind himself to tighten the cinch. While he fussed with the tack, the setter and pointer would whirl and wriggle and whine, begging to go.

Finally, Tom would "whoa" them, lead Popeye away, then swing into the saddle. When it seemed they would fairly burst, Roberts would growl, "All right now, hunt 'em up", and watch twin streaks of bird dog burn up a long fencerow or reach out for a cedar-studded knoll bristling over the fields...

Over two hours had passed, and Popeye had not moved. Tom's legs were cramped. He heaved himself to his feet, let the blood come back, and limped into the barn for an armload of choice timothy hay and a bucket of fresh water that he arranged close by the horse's head. Roberts tried not to hear the halting, ragged breathing that now came almost as a sob.

When he could bear his vigil no longer, Tom stumped back to the house, brewed a pot of coffee, then let it grow cold on the kitchen counter while he sat near the window and stared off toward the paddock.

He thought about a time right after he'd retired the old horse. A friend had come from town, and they'd headed out with 'Lilah just above the kennels. It was the shank end of February, and Roberts had released some of the feisty, pen-reared birds he kept to hunt closer to home when the season waned. Rounding the hill above the far pasture, the guest stopped suddenly and laughed. "Why, look at your ol' horse!"

Here came Popeye, head up, belly rolling over that jouncing, heavy gait of his. He chested up to the board fence, whickering a low chuckle.

"He's done that ever since I turned him out," Tom said, rubbing his mouth with the back of his hand. "All he needs to hear is the dog bell and no matter where he is or what he's doin', he comes runnin' like he's tellin' me to wait up."

"Ah, Tom, he's just nib-nosin'," the guest snorted. "You think a horse misses all the work you made him do any more than you and I would miss goin' in every day?"

Tom spotted 'Lilah scrambling over the hill and pushing upwind toward a long strip of red-topped sorghum. Roberts followed her, his back to where the white horse stood watching.

"The only one I know about is Popeye," he answered testily, "and I know he liked it. You could see the way he'd study those dogs, listenin' to the whistle. Got to be where I'd give two toots to hie the dog around, and Popeye'd already be headin' in that direction, even before the dog would turn."

'Lilah was making game now, head low, her tail working like a boat propeller. Roberts shifted the open gun to his left arm.

"When I'd ground tie that horse to walk up a point, he'd usually drop his head, scroungin' something to eat. But sometimes I'd look back when the birds'd go out, and he'd have his head as high as the dogs, watchin' them outa' one eye like he was watchin' us just now, like he was wondering how we'd shoot or where those birds were going."

'Lilah's orange-flecked body had gone hard two rows into the sorghum, her tail now flagging ever so slightly. Roberts motioned to his friend. "They're movin' on her some. Just step in there across her face and put 'em up."

The man looked to his gun, then egg-walked in front of the dog. When he was nearly even with 'Lilah's nose, Roberts swung around to look over the hill. Popeye was standing at the fence, ears pricked, when the covey broke and caught two quick shots...

The horse had now been down six hours. Tom tried to rouse him twice more, had sat beside the grizzled white head and talked to him, petted him, tried to help him manage a drink. Finally, he could hold off no longer: Popeye was suffering, and Roberts could not allow that. It was a matter of trust, a pact he had made with all the dogs who had shared his life, a deal he had cut with the horse, too. It was part of being fed and sheltered, worked, and respected.

He walked slowly back to the farmhouse and rooted around for the phone book.

Scott Sullivan was an out-of-work coal miner who kept his family fed doing custom butchering of steers and shoats. He was a practiced hand at dispatching big animals. Roberts was still rehearsing what he wanted to say when Sullivan's voice interrupted the ringing signal. He said "hello" twice before Tom could begin talking.

It was late afternoon when Roberts watched a grimy blue pickup slowly pick its way up the rutted lane. He pulled his denim work coat from the peg by the kitchen door and ducked into the stained, brown fedora he wore to town in the winter. When Scott Sullivan pulled up in front of the barn, Tom was waiting for him.

While they shook hands, Roberts glanced over the younger man's shoulder to see the silhouette of a rifle hanging upside down in the rear window rack. "I called Todd Holt, over t' Webb's Summit," Sullivan offered. "He said he'd have his digger here after a bit. We knew you'd wanna finish with this tonight if you could."

"I 'preciate it, Scott. I'm awful sorry to have to ask you to do this. I would have done it myself, but I just..." Roberts's voice trailed off, and Sullivan looked away for a long minute while his neighbor bowed his head and dug the toe of his boot into the driveway gravel.

"Tom, you got someplace you could go for awhile? Let me and Todd take care of it for you." The sound of the backhoe rig rumbling up the county road came to both of them, and Tom could feel his belly tighten and twist like it had when Popeye had gone down that morning.

He and Sullivan spoke for a short while longer, making certain of where Holt was to work, the talk finally breaking off when the orange machine drove into view at the far boundary to Tom's farm. "Go on, now," Sullivan urged. "Todd and me can handle this. Come back in a couple hours, and it'll be done."

Suddenly, Tom Roberts was very tired. His eyes roamed the barnyard, lighting everywhere but on the paddock or out toward the approaching engine noise. Finally they came to rest on the end kennel, where Holly stood on her hind legs, front paws hooked on the chain link, tail wagging tightly against her hocks.

"I wanted to get this dog some work this morning," Tom mumbled, more to himself than to Sullivan. "She's fat as I am, sittin' around most of this season." With that, he moved away from where the blue truck was parked, walked up the hill, and disappeared into the kennel shed to fetch the bell collar. Holly was leaping up and down at her gate when he came around to get her.

They walked as fast as Roberts could manage, on past the quail pens, beyond the pond, trying to outdistance the backhoe's menacing drone. When they made the second hill beyond the house, the one overlooking most of the ground he hunted, Tom paused to get his breath, remembering all the dogs he and Popeye had followed off that knoll: Billy, the gangling setter who'd accounted for the field trial ribbons nailed up in the kennel shed; Luke, the derby who'd been killed by a prairie rattler one hot morning on the plains; Cass, a tri-color Llewellin, and stylish Elhew Trudy, Holly's mother; the tiny setter Raggs, whom Roberts couldn't break of barking when a covey went out; bloody-tailed meat dog 'Lilah, resting now in the high pasture near where Tom had directed the backhoe to dig.

He bent and belled the pointer, ordering her to "hold" while he reached inside his coat and pulled the whistle out of his shirt pocket. Two harsh blasts, and she was gone.

Roberts turned to take a long look at the empty white line of pasture fence behind the barn, then angled off in the wake of the steel bell tolling Holly's cast across the fading afternoon.

The birds were where he knew they'd be, laid up in the rough between a wide, shaggy fencerow and four rows of soybeans left by Roberts's tenant farmer. Holly was steaming back along the fence's lee side when the stop came like a sharp blow, the pointer twisted into the light breeze.

Tom let her stand until he could sleeve away the blur in both of his eyes. The quail held tight while he scuffed through the thick weeds, a wild, late-winter covey blowing out the far side of the fencerow when a single gunshot echoed over the hills.

Gene Hill, an associate editor of Field & Stream, *is the author of eight books of essays on the out-of-doors. Prior to being with* Field & Stream *he was the executive director of* Sports Afield *and a vice president of J. Walter Thompson. He has trained and field trialed better-than-decent Labrador retrievers and a couple of middling English setters. He has hunted birds and big game in a long list of places and is an eager, if not notable, clay target shooter. Fly fishing takes up what time is left, especially in tarpon and bonefish water, unless there is a chance for Atlantic salmon.*

PLAIN DOGS, SPECIAL DAYS

by Gene Hill

I've got a very soft spot in my heart for the ordinary working dog. The bird dog or retriever that doubles as house guardian, walks the kids up to the school bus and waits for them to come home, goes along on trips to the hardware store, and does what can be done about keeping the squirrels out of the attic and the rabbits out of the kitchen garden. He doesn't get much in the way of bird hunting, and the man that owns him is just about the same. What with chores and making a living, the days in the field don't quite measure up to the hopes and dreams.

Just before the season they put in a little yard work and, with luck, an hour or so with a live pigeon or a quail or pheasant from the local game farm. Chances are that neither of them is sure they're going about this exactly the right way, but the smell of fall is in the air and there's a big red X on the calendar just a couple of weeks away.

We'll see them together on the back roads look-ing for just the place; the Brit or pointer or setter sitting up front making nose smears on the windshield, and himself, just as anxious, wishing he had a better gun, was a better shot, knew a perfect covert—wishing especially that he could offer old Duke all these things...all the time.

Whenever I see this pair of pilgrims I wish them their "day of days." I've been with this sort of team on a lot of occasions and much to my delight and surprise have had some honestly unforgettable days over what the usually apologetic owner calls "just your ordinary bird dog." One was in Texas and when I lavishly and honestly praised the little lemon-and-white pointer, her owner blushed and said, "I know you've seen lots and lots of better dogs and I know Dixie ain't much but she *will* find and hold birds if they're around." Well, that's all we really want 99 percent of the time anyway. Dixie had a nice gait for a walking gunner, a merry attitude, a good nose, and nice manners. She'd never make the cover of a dog book but she had more than enough style to suit me. Her owner admitted that she more or less broke herself since he didn't know much about fancy training but just needed a dog to find birds. He said that even though he had to work almost every day, he found time to put her into birds. I asked him how many birds had been shot over her and he grinned a little so I wouldn't make the mistake of thinking he was bragging, and said, "Well, maybe over a thousand." He said that this might have made up for her not having any "papers." I said I thought it might too. He asked me if I'd seen any of those big field trial dogs and I said I sure had. Then he asked, "What's wrong with my Dixie compared to them?" I told him that the only thing I could see wrong with Dixie was that she didn't have a twin sister looking for a good home.

A lot of us, probably most of us, don't have birds in that kind of number or the time or the places. We rely on faith, good luck, and hope, and often enough they come together and we can say that wonderful phrase, "If there're birds there, she'll find them," and know it's true.

The trouble with most bird dogs are the bird hunters who own them. One dog I wanted to own belonged to a man who had absolutely no good idea of what a dog ought to be doing. He wanted to run the show, regardless of wind direction, regardless of cover, regardless of common sense. He shouted, he threatened, he waved his arms in the air and missed no chance to confuse and intimidate the dog. He'd bought the dog because he liked the way it worked for its trainer, but in two weekends he had reduced the poor thing to a neurotic mess.

Like a bird dog that "just goes out and finds birds," all an ordinary hunting retriever has to do is learn to sit, stay, and mark fairly well. If you have such a dog, you'll be surprised at what he, or she, will learn to do on its own. I believe that a lot of otherwise fine dogs are ruined, or at least curbed, by overzealous and often ill-advised training—or better—overtraining. It takes an expert to draw the line between bringing a dog along at the pace of the dog's ability rather than at a pace the owner decides is right—regardless of evidence to the contrary. Dogs are like children. They come along in fits and starts, each different, each unique. Some dogs are superb markers and can early on handle triples. Some come along slowly, and others never can do it perfectly. I don't care how good a shot you are; I can find someone better. But you're probably good enough to enjoy yourself and occasionally have a day where you're superb. And now and then have a day that you don't want to talk about. But by now you know your limitations. Why should your dog be any different? Learn the difference between what he can't do and what he won't do and direct your handling along those lines; you'll both be happier and he might just surprise you, when given a little time and understanding.

I've had a lot of retrievers and they've all been a different study. My first one was instinctively good; a far better dog than I was a trainer. She just went out and did it, often to my great astonishment. She didn't really like schooling, it seemed to bore her and when she had had enough of it she just lay down and said "enough." Another loved it and would work until everyone was exhausted. In truth she was just too much dog for me, and I never developed her potential; she belonged to a professional and I wouldn't give her up and let that happen. Another was lovable and seemingly useless until she was two years old, and then she decided that she wanted to do what the other dogs were doing and became a fine field dog.

As a now and then field trial judge I've seen too many dogs that were either not ready or not capable of repeatedly doing advanced work: long and difficult marks, intricate handling to blind retrieves, and the like. Most dogs will do something remarkable from time to time, but that doesn't mean that they are on a particular level and will stay there.

A noncompetitive dog, the one you want to take in the field and be your pal, doesn't have to be a canine Ph.D. You have to enter into the picture as a partner as much as a schoolmaster. Correct annoying faults, surely, but don't ask a dog to do things it simply can't do, whether from breeding or brains or physical ability. Most bird dogs can't run at top speed for three hours like the national champions do. You wouldn't want them to. You want a dog to work at such and such a speed and at a given range. It's possible to alter this *somewhat* but that's all. A pickup is not an Indy car.

I hate to say this but it's true: too many bird hunters don't really know what they want their dog to do. They forget that it is the dog that's doing the hunting and they are the shooter. They don't give the dog the benefit of the doubt or acknowledge that the dog might know more about cover and wind and how to work this particular area better than they do. I can say this easily because I've made all the common mistakes often and some of the rare ones more than once. One of my faults, when I was younger, was to hunt a dog too fast. I kept pushing and pushing until the dog said, literally, well if he just wants me to run through all this, that's what I'll have to do. Or I'd poke around a cover like I was looking for a lost dime until the dog, who had long ago known there wasn't anything here, got bored and went off somewhere else or came in and hung around my feet wondering what the hell I was up to.

What most of us need and get in a dog are too often different things. Obviously, if you like to potter around in the grouse and woodcock covers you don't want a rib-sprung pointer that was born and bred to quarter quail country in front a man on good horse, with an outrider along for good measure. Obvious? Sure, but it doesn't work that way as often as you'd think. One of the best bird dogs I ever hunted over was sold to me by a man who *never* hunts on foot and he couldn't stand the thought of a dog ranging out there about forty yards, no matter how letter perfect she was. A black Lab I sold as a puppy grew into a one-hundred-pound rocket that was born for top-flight field-trial work. He was bred from fine trial stock and everything really came together, but he'd drive you crazy if all you wanted was a dog good with the kids or one able to bring back the odd duck from an occasional Saturday morning shoot.

If you only have time and room for one dog and you get one that isn't going to work, it's only fair that you do something about it and do it quickly. Some dogs require a firmer hand than most of us are willing or able to lay on.

Others turn out so timid that only the most patient and saintlike handler can bring them around. A good breeder will work with you on this, which is another good reason to be most thorough when you go shopping and make this arrangement in advance. I know it's hard to do but I also know, firsthand, that it's harder in the long run if you don't. I once had a Brittany that was a lot more than I could handle. She was top of the line and her field work was superb, but I just wasn't tough enough to make her work for me and hunt how and where I wanted. She belonged on the southwest prairies and knew it; I wanted a choirgirl, and she longed for bright lights and the fast lane.

If at all possible, both you and your dog will benefit from its living in the house as a member of the family. You don't need forty acres to teach the basics of obedience; "sit" and "stay" work just as well in the kitchen or the den. You'll develop a closer bond, that subliminal magic that defies explanation but exists nonetheless. I suppose I flatter myself but I feel better when I have Tippy or Ben around to comfort me and want to believe that this works both ways.

Like many of you, I wouldn't hunt without a dog. The enthusiasm and joy and the feeling of partnership come, in the main, from my being there with my pal. He understands the dream and plays the leading role in the drama. He consoles me when I'm blue and does his crazy little dance for me to show he's glad that I'm happy. I once wrote how I feel about all this and since I don't think I'll ever say it any better, I'll take the liberty of quoting myself: Nobody can fully understand the meaning of love unless he's owned a dog. He can show you more honest affection with a flick of his tail than a man can gather through a lifetime of handshakes. I can't think of anything that brings me closer to tears than when my old dog—completely exhausted from a full and hard day in the field—limps away from her nice spot in front of the fire and comes over to where I'm sitting and puts her head in my lap, a paw over my knee, and closes her eyes and goes back to sleep.

Thomas McIntyre is the long-time Hunting Editor of Sports Afield *magazine where he writes the "Hunting" and "A Hunter's View" columns. His hunting and fishing travels have carried him to five continents, from the High Arctic to Australia, Africa, and New Zealand, and from the Czech Republic to Hawaii. His essays and short stories have appeared in over a dozen anthologies, and he is the author, as well, of three works of non-fiction, the most recent being* Dreaming the Lion: Reflections on Hunting, Fishing, and a Search for the Wild *published in the fall of 1993 by Countrysport Press. Tom, his wife Elaine, their young son Bryan Ruark, and their two dogs, Bubba and Beckett, divide their time between southern California and northern Wyoming.*

BLANCA

by Thomas McIntyre

"Where's that dog?"

I stood in the shaft of cool February sunlight falling through the doorway, my eyes adjusting to the darkness within the adobe house. Pete sat on the three-legged sofa, a brick propping up the broken corner and a Navajo blanket concealing the holes in the upholstery. On the wall behind him hung a cane fly rod and a wicker creel, beneath it an A. H. Fox 16-gauge, displayed like heraldic devices. He laid the Badminton Library book on coursing he was reading beside him on the sofa, opened, on top of the pile of other old books, and stood. His boots kicked up small billows of dust as he crossed the carpet. I stepped into the overheated house, and Pete and I exchanged *abrazos* and backslaps. Sally came out of the kitchen dressed in a flannel shirt and faded jeans, and when I leaned down to kiss her I smelled in her hair the smoke of the cigarettes she'd been sneaking outside, the cancer that would kill her in less than a year already shadowing through her lungs.

"Let's see her," I said.

They led me to a doorway off the living room. The door had been removed from its hinges and set crosswise inside on the floor across the bottom of the door frame, making a two-and-a-half-foot-high barrier. The room had been emptied of furniture and through the single curtainless window I could see in the distance bare cottonwoods along a wash and a pickup moving down the highway toward El Paso. The floor of the room was covered with flattened cardboard boxes, covered with newspapers, rags, torn sheets, and feces, and wet with urine. A large pan of water and one of dry food sat in the far right corner of the room.

Jesse-Bell stood with her front paws on the edge of the door, barking with each breath as she had been since before I'd walked into the house. Pete moved forward, taking her head in his hands and shaking her playfully. "Hush, now, Jess honey," he insisted, and the liver-and-white springer began to grin at him, wriggling the four-inch stump of her tail.

Pete stepped over the door and into the room, and I followed, the bitch backing away from me and growling softly, showing me her front teeth. The six pups, liver-and-white and black-and-white, clustered in the far left quarter of the room, exhibiting a sort of Brownian motion as they fought and rolled and yipped and played. Pete waded into them and lifted a black-and-white one by its fat eight-week-old belly.

"Here you are," he said, handing the pup to me. Its tail was docked, and I lay it on its back in the crook of my arm and saw it was a female. At once she began to squirm and to yelp sharply.

"Pick of the litter," Pete said, smiling, slipping his hands into the front slash pockets of his Wranglers so he could not readily reach out again to accept the pup back from me. She was squirming too hard now to hold, so I squatted and placed her on the floor.

"Pick of the litter," I repeated.

"Set her aside especially," Pete replied.

I watched her as she began worrying the sheet. "How much you asking?"

For you—for Big Ed? Three hundred."

The pup had hunkered down to pee now. She had a wide saddle of white on her back. While Pete and I were in the nursery, Sally had gone to the kitchen and come back with two tall plastic picnic glasses half filled with ice and sour mash. Grinning, she handed the drinks over to us, and we each took a pull from them.

"She'll make him a good dog," Pete said, rocking gently on his heels, his left hand in his pocket and his drink held against his chest.

"What are you going to call her?" Sally asked, as if the deal were done. I looked at Sally's smiling face, and then Pete's, then at the pup's saddle of white. She was a dog meant to make all the difference in the world.

"Blanca," I said, raising my glass to Pete.

◆

In the driveway I sat with my hands on the wheel, the engine switched off and the heat ticking out of it. Beside my car was parked the Roadmaster on which, over the years, Big Ed had replaced every moving part with his own hands. As I sat I was letting the highway replay itself inside my head, first the high plateau in the dark, the green spark of a shooting star arcking across the sky, then the canyon at sunrise, the big hill down to the saguaros, and the long desert run through the day to the pass and the basin filled with fouled air at sunset. Eating while I drove, I'd stopped only for gas and every few hours at a rest area to let Blanca out of her carrier to walk around on the lead, starting to work with her on heeling while white-haired snowbirds stared at us over their tuna-fish sandwiches, wanting to make sure I wasn't going to let her shit next to their recreational vehicles. I'd traveled so quickly because I hadn't wanted to waste a minute getting her back.

Now Blanca was asleep in the carrier in the back seat of the Land Cruiser. I looked into the windows of the house, looking for any lights within. The house appeared abandoned, but I could see a faint blue glow coming from the living room. I sat for a minute more, then got out of the car.

I opened the rear door of the car and unlatched the gate on the carrier, lifting the sleeping pup out, tucking her under my left arm. Pulling open the screen door, I found the front door of the house unlocked and I entered, walking through to the living room. Dan Rather was just wishing everyone goodnight. On top of the set stood a dusty pair of mounted chukar.

Big Ed sat in his green leather armchair, looking shrunken in his clothes. For several seconds he did not notice me standing beside him. Then he lifted his head and stared at me through the tops of his bifocals, his eyes large and wet behind the lenses.

"I've got something for you," I said, offering the pup.

Big Ed blinked, recognition ebbing into his expression. His eyes moved from my face to the pup in my hands.

"Her name's Blanca," I said.

Big Ed now saw the little dog I was holding toward him, and for a moment he didn't seem to know what to do. Then he reached out his large hands for her, drawing her into his lap. He petted her gently and Blanca nestled back into her sleep.

I went into the kitchen and turned on the lights. In the wash rack by the sink were a plate, a knife, and a fork. I opened the refrigerator. Inside stood a carton of milk, a carton with two eggs left in it, half a stick of butter on a dish, a loaf of bread, a package of boiled ham, a squeeze-bottle of yellow mustard. I went outside and got the carrier, the lead, and the bag of puppy food I bought before leaving Pete and Sally's and brought them into the kitchen.

Walking back into the living room, I found that Big Ed had switched on the lamp beside his chair and was studying the sleeping Blanca as he softly stroked her, smiling to himself. On the stand was the framed twenty-five-year-old photograph of Big Ed and Joan and me, laid flat. On the TV set, beside the chukar, stood another framed photo of Big Ed, his hair still black in those days, showing him kneeling beside his old springer Bubba, Ed holding his Model 12, half-a-dozen Gambel's quail arranged on the rocky ground in front of him and the dog.

"Let me buy you supper," I said. Big Ed, still smiling and petting the pup, shook his head. "I've eaten."

"All right," I said. I reached into my shirt pocket and pulled out the folded sheet of yellow legal paper Pete had written out for me and lay it on the lamp stand, covering our photograph.

"Here are her feeding instructions," I said. "She's got enough food for a week, and I'll buy some more when she needs it. I'll take care of her papers for you, and I'll take her to the vet when her shots are due."

I hesitated, wondering if he'd heard me.

"They say she'll make a good dog," I said. "I'll help you work with her, if you want."

Big Ed nodded slowly, still smiling down at the curled up puppy.

"Don't worry," he said. "I can take care of her." He looked up at me. "We'll do just fine."

I wanted to reach out and put my hand on his shoulder, but instead I just nodded and turned to go.

When I reached the front door, I heard Big Ed's voice behind me in the living room. "Thank you," he said.

◆

The phone rang three times before I picked up the receiver.

"Hello," I said.

There was silence on the other end, but a silence tenanted by someone. I waited, not wanting to say hello again, wanting to let him have the time to find the words that seemed to be coming harder and harder every day.

"I'm having trouble with her," Big Ed finally said. "Blanca. I don't think I can handle her anymore."

"What kind of trouble?"

Big Ed did not answer. After more seconds of silence he said, "I think you'd better take her."

"I'll be over," I said, holding onto the receiver until, at last, Big Ed put down his.

When I crossed the bridge, the concrete bed of the river was dry, the steeply sloped banks tagged with spray-painted insignia. The spreading grounds still held rainwater, percolating down to the water table to be pumped out again; but all the sprigs that had swum on that water through the winter, as incongruous in the city as orchids on a fire hydrant, were gone now, only a few coots remaining. Just past the river I turned down a cul-de-sac and parked once more in Big Ed's driveway.

In the kitchen Big Ed was bracing himself up with one hand on the edge of the sink as he drank a glass of water from the tap. He looked at me over the rim of the glass as he finished, then turned and care-fully rinsed the glass, placing it in the empty wash rack. He turned nervously back to me, as if he were preparing to flinch. A six-month-old Blanca ran barking into the kitchen and looked at us both, then ran off again.

"I just don't know how to handle her anymore," Big Ed said.

"That's all right," I said. "We've talked about this."

"I just don't know," he said.

I walked into the living room and saw where Blanca had just peed on the carpet, other places that Big Ed had not cleaned up visible as well. One of the arms on the green chair had been chewed through, the stuffing showing. Blanca ran excitedly around the room, then turned and crouched at me to bark, before racing off again.

I managed to haze her into one of the corners of the room and scooped her up, struggling in my arms, strong as a piglet. I carried her back to the kitchen and pushed her into her carrier.

Big Ed still stood by the sink, looking neither at the carrier nor me, but out the window at his narrow backyard where a crow hopped on the lawn.

"It's time to take her to the trainer anyway," I said, Big Ed making no acknowledgement of my words. I picked up the dog box and carried it outside to the back seat of the Land Cruiser, Blanca barking continuously inside.

As I turned to go back into the house, Big Ed was standing behind the screen door, barring my entry.

"A few months with the trainer," I said to him through the screen, "and she'll be fine."

Big Ed didn't say anything, just stared at the Land Cruiser.

"A few months," I said, "and she'll be ready for us to take her hunting."

"I just don't know what to do with her," Big Ed said. Then he stepped back from the screen and closed the front door.

♦

The Mexican in the blue ball cap was hosing out one of the dog runs when I drove in and parked in front of the kennel's office. Inside, Corrigan sat behind his desk, fat and hung over, talking on the phone. He waved me to the chair across the desk from him.

"...the entire science of animal training's changed tremendously in the past twenty years since we've learned more about animal behavior," he was saying to a potential client. "Well, sure, you can find somebody who says he'll train your dog for less, but what kind of a dog do you get back? That's the question...No, you go ahead and think it over...Anytime. Glad to help." Replacing the receiver, he folded his arms and leaned forward on his desk, looking at the phone. "Assholes," he said. He looked at me, the veins webbed red across his cheeks. "Like I always say, The problem is never the dog, it's the fucking owner." Pushing himself to his feet, he walked around the desk and toward the front door. "Come on," he said as I stood, "let's see what that little bitch of yours can do."

We drove off the hill and out onto the flood plain. Corrigan opened the door on one of the compartments of the dog carrier that took up the back of his pickup and lifted Blanca out. He clipped a long white rope to her collar and handed the end to me. I could see how in only a few months she had changed from puppy to a dog. Corrigan opened another compartment and took out a pigeon, cupping its body in his hand, its head held between two of his fingers. Then, holding the pigeon next to his body, he got his over-and-under out from behind the seat of his pickup, breaking it open with one hand and laying it over the crook of his arm that held the pigeon. He slipped in a couple of No. 7½ loads and then took the rope end from me.

"We talked about making this dog into a slip retriever, didn't we?" he asked. "I just wanted to make sure."

As he walked out across the willow stubble I hung back. Blanca ranged off a few yards to his right and just slightly ahead of him, staying within the length of the rope. About fifty yards out, Corrigan dropped the rope and lifted the over-and-under off his arm, then threw the pigeon into the air. As the bird fluttered for a moment to get its bearing, Corrigan closed his shotgun and when the pigeon started to fly away, he dropped it thirty yards from him with his bottom barrel. Blanca had been watching this procedure curiously, and at the sound of the shot she stiffened, then turned and ran off to the right, making a large circle back to the pickup, crawling beneath it as Corrigan cursed.

The noon sunlight cast the shadow of Corrigan's brows over the red veins of his cheeks as he broke open his gun and stomped back toward the pickup, shouting, "You no-good piece of shit," as he came. I walked back to the pickup first and squatted down. Blanca stared out at me from underneath it. I snapped my fingers at her a few times and reluctantly she came out. I had her in my arms when Corrigan got to us.

"Give me that goddamn dog," he said, throwing his shotgun onto the seat of the pickup through the open door.

"No," I said.

"That dog wasn't much," he shouted, his red hands kneading the air in front of him, "but she was coming on. What screwed her up was you being here.

"It's you talking baby-talk to these damn dogs, then expecting me to train them, to make something real out of them. You don't have any idea what a real dog is supposed to be. You could take a stick and beat a pup every day and still make it a real dog. But all you want to do is talk baby-talk to these goddamn dogs, and all you end up with is a piece of shit like this."

He was starting to run out of steam as I put Blanca back into her compartment in the dog carrier and closed the door. His hands had dropped to his sides, heavy and limp, when I turned back to him.

"Let's go back to your office now and I'll settle my account with you."

"Useless piece of shit," he said, but by now he was saying it to himself.

◆

Blanca was barking when I got home from downtown. I took the Model 12 with the tag on the trigger guard and the manila envelope out of the Land Cruiser and carried them into the garage, laying them on the work table. I walked into the backyard and Blanca ran up to me, rolling onto her back at my feet as I reached down to pet her. I changed the water in her bowl and gave her two cups of dry food for her dinner.

In the garage I opened the manila envelope and removed the two items in it. One was the gold wedding band, the other the pair of bifocals marked with dried flecks of blood. I put the wedding band into my shirt pocket and dropped the glasses into the trash barrel beside the work table. No one had wanted the Roadmaster, so I sold it to a wrecking yard. I clamped the Model 12 into the vice on the table and got down the hacksaw.

As I sawed I could hear Blanca barking in the backyard, and in my mind I could see her standing rigid, the stump of her tail up, barking at nothing I could ever see. It was then I realized that, like Big Ed, I didn't know what to do with her any more than he had. She was as useless to me as she had been to him.

◆

It was late one night when Pete called. Sally had been dead for over two years. Pete was drunk.

"How's that dog of yours?" he shouted.

I told him that she was fine.

"Showed her many birds?"

No, not many birds at all, I said.

"You got to show her more birds," Pete insisted.

Yes, I agreed with him.

"But you have to be careful," Pete said. "You have to be careful she doesn't run away. If you're not, she'll be gone before you know it. And might never get her back."

◆

I wore my own wedding band now, and Blanca never did make a dog. She was nine and Owen was two. At night, after his bath, Owen would come out and stand beside me as I sat in my armchair, reading the paper. I would pretend for a moment not to notice him, and he would pretend that he did not notice me, intently watching his fingers as they played with one another. Then I would fold the paper and put it down and I would stare at Owen. In a little while, without really looking up, he would lift his arms to me and I would pull him up to me, hugging him to my chest and smelling the scent of his clean hair, of spices like cloves and nutmeg, feeling the coolness of his cheek against mine, and hearing the beginnings of his giggles. And wishing that I knew a way in this world for Big Ed to have done the same, if only once.

I never did learn what to do with Blanca. As she'd gotten older she'd just seemed to get crazier and more useless. I had to watch Owen when he was in the yard with her, because I had seen her snap at him more than once if he got too close. But I still could not find a reason to take that stick to her or to have her put down. There was still too much of unfinished business about her, too much of a gesture made that had gone somehow unseen. Or that had been the wrong gesture to begin with.

One day, when we were packing our household belongings into moving crates, Celeste came in and asked me if I'd looked at Blanca lately.

She lay on the carpet in her house, seeming very subdued, nearly depressed, and I noticed that she looked bloated, bigger than I had ever seen her. Not fat, but swollen. Then I saw the large tumor on one of her teats.

At the office, the veterinarian asked me to lift her onto the stainless-steel examination table, because he had long ago flagged her file jacket with a red sticker that read, "Bites." While I held her head, he felt her other nipples and said that the tumors had already spread to them. Then he did not speak for a few moments, before saying that there really was not much that could be done. I asked him if I could stay there with her, and he said, Of course.

I signed the release slip authorizing the euthanasia, then while I held her and stroked her softly, the vet felt on her leg for the vein. Strangely, Blanca didn't try to struggle at all, staying utterly quiet the entire time. The vet warned me that she might go into convulsions as the drug took effect, but she would feel no pain. Then he slipped the needle of the large syringe filled with the pink drug into her vein, drawing back a small plume of blood into the barrel, then slowly depressed the plunger.

Blanca didn't struggle or convulse at all, just held my eye in hers. As I felt her growing limp in my arms, I began to cry for the first time since I was a child—I hadn't even been able to cry for Big Ed, but now there were tears for such a sorry dog as this. I kept saying to her, "That's a good girl. That's a good girl." And at that moment, as perhaps at no other time in her life, she was a good girl.

As her heart was stopping, it was as if she wanted to show me her true heart after all.

I walked out of the office into the hazy sun of late afternoon, wrapping Blanca's lead and collar around my hand, wondering what "useless" really means. Is any dog completely useless, does any sign of love truly go unseen?

Jim Fergus is a freelance writer whose work has appeared in a variety of magazines and newspapers, including Newsweek, Newsday, Esquire, Outside, The Paris Review, Harrowsmith Country Life, The Denver Post, The Dallas Times-Herald, *and others. He is a field editor of* Outdoor Life *magazine, for which he writes a monthly column, "The Sporting Road." His book,* A Hunter's Road: A Journey With Gun and Dog Across the American Uplands, *published in 1992, was a selection of the Book-of-the-Month-Club and the Outdoor Life Book Club. Currently in its third hardcover printing,* A Hunter's Road *was recently published in a paperback edition.*

When not on the road researching, writing, hunting, fishing, and living in a 1972 Airstream trailer with his yellow Lab, Sweetzer (with whom he travels upwards of 20,000 miles a year), Fergus divides his time between his home in northern Colorado, Idaho, Arizona, Florida, and points between. Whenever possible he lives with his wife, Dillon, and two other dogs, neither of them with any potential whatsoever as hunters, but good dogs nevertheless.

A DOG'S LIFE

by Jim Fergus

A Rose by Any Other Name

Let's get this one thing out of the way right off: I have the dubious distinction of owning a yellow Lab that, by general consensus among hunting friends and companions all across America, has the stupidest name ever conceived for a hunting dog. Sweetzer, she is called—named after Sweetzer Summit in southern Idaho, as I am forever explaining apologetically to those who express their thinly (if at all) disguised contempt for the name. A columnist in one of the sporting magazines even complained about my dog's name in his review of a book Sweetz and I collaborated on a few seasons ago. Indeed, one of my very best friends loathes the name so much that he refuses to use it, has actually given her another name that she must go by at his house. The affrontery! The indignity!

So let me just say this in my defense, in Sweetz's defense, in my wife's defense (not to be unchivalrous about this but actually the dog belongs to her, *she*

169

named her Sweetzer): there are worse dog names. You don't believe me? O.K., for instance, a couple of seasons ago while bird hunting in eastern Montana, I was camped in an RV park when Sweetz and I ran into a retired gentleman from Oregon who was also out walking his dog—one of those little furry, yappy *foo-foo* dogs, which due to their compact size seem to be the dog of choice for retired couples traveling in RV's or living in condos in south Florida. (And who can blame them? Just try, as I have, to get a Lab into an RV or a condo in south Florida.) Anyway, we stopped to chat as dog people naturally will, and I quickly ascertained from our conversation and from one of many tattoos that ran up and down the man's ropy, muscular arms, that he was an ex-Marine, a drill sergeant, in fact, who from the look of him had clearly earned his living after he mustered out of the corps in some manner other than sitting behind a desk. He wore a white T-shirt and still had a Marine crewcut and though no longer young, he still possessed the strong, broad-chested physique of one who might have been lifting major appliances for the past thirty or forty years. Deciding to take the offensive and get the inevitable moment of ridicule over with, I asked the man what his dog's name was; it wasn't much of a dog, as far as I could tell, but I figured it to have a macho name—Rocky, or Buck, something along those lines. Suddenly, much to my astonishment, the ex-Marine got all bashful. "I'm almost ashamed to tell you," he mumbled.

Ashamed to tell *me*? "Hey, look," I said, "it can't be any worse than my dog's name."

"What's your dog's name?" He asked hopefully.

"My dog's name is Sweetzer," I said, steeling myself for the burst of disdainful laughter with which this information was generally greeted.

"Well, that's not such a bad name," he said, and he seemed kind of disappointed. "Mine's a lot worse than that."

"Really? Well go ahead and tell me. I promise not to laugh."

And then the tattooed ex-Marine drill sergeant, a man who I'll bet in his prime could have lifted a full-sized refrigerator/freezer all by himself, easy, actually blushed, turned downright crimson as he muttered his dog's name, barely discernible.

"I beg your pardon?" I asked, not certain I'd heard correctly.

He gathered himself up and glared at me defiantly, as I had done many times myself in defensive posture to queries about my dog's name. "Precious," he said clearly. "My dog's name is Precious, O.K.? The wife and I named him that because when he was just a little bitty puppy, he was so damn *precious*."

"Ha!" I exclaimed triumphantly, delighted to have finally found a wimpier, more insipid dog name than Sweetzer.

"I thought you said you weren't going to laugh," the man reminded me.

"I'm not laughing," I said, quickly adding, "It's a fine name. And, in my opinion, he's still precious!"

Unfortunately, it was quite clear that Precious had never been a hunter, so, as I am repeatedly reminded by friends and acquaintances alike, I still own the stupidest-named hunting dog in America.

The Things They Carry

One morning, only a few weeks after I brought the new puppy home, my wife woke up to discover that her wedding ring had disappeared off the bedside table. Being an extremely tidy and responsible person who hasn't lost or missplaced anything since maybe 1962, she immediately fingered our new family member as the likely thief. I tried to defend the defenseless little pup; she was hardly bigger at the time than, say, a plump throw-pillow with stumpy legs, and already could do no wrong in my eyes. "How could she possibly have taken your ring off the table?" I argued. "Even if she was standing on her back legs, she's hardly tall enough to reach up there. Besides," I added "we'd have heard her, and nothing else on the table is even disturbed." We searched the house all day long, from top to bottom, but the ring did not turn up.

In the wee hours of the following morning, long before dawn, I was awakened by the distinctive heaving sound that dog owners learn to dread, particularly when it occurs in the bedroom at 3:00 A.M. (Spoiled from the start, Sweetz slept in a dog bed at the foot of ours, working her way up quickly to a spot curled next to me on the human bed, until, the growth of Labs being what it is, she had eventually driven my wife to take up residency in the guest room.) I got up to see what was ailing the puppy just as the heaving reached its crescendo. There on the carpet, glittering in the moonlight, was the purloined wedding ring.

"I hope you're going to clean that mess up," my wife muttered sleepily, oblivious to the contents.

"I'll take care of it," I said, "Go back to sleep." I rinsed the ring off in the bathroom sink, dried it, and gently slid it back on the bedside table, as if the mysterious thief of the night had had an attack of conscience and returned the stolen goods. The next morning my wife slipped it on her finger without a word.

The wedding ring had to be secured now, because, although Sweetz would never again mistake it as edible, once discovered as a desirable *objet*, a collectible if you will, it would also never again be entirely safe from her burgeoning carrying fetish, its scent forever imprinted in her mind as definitively as if it had wings. And she took a similar interest in other items. Soon her bed filled with an eclectic collection of stuff: empty toilet paper rolls (which fit perfectly in her little mouth and must have seemed like small retriever dummies even before she knew about retriever dummies) would be recycled from the bathroom trash to be paraded proudly around the house for all to see. One earmark common to the canine carrier/collector is the pride they take in their hobby, the desire they seem to have for everyone to admire their stuff. Empty Dove soapboxes were another favorite to be pilfered from the trash. These she carried slipped over her lower jaw like a sheath before depositing them on the bed with her other stuff. She became particularly fond of the little fabric covered elastic bands that my wife used to pull her hair back in a ponytail. They must have felt soft and springy in the puppy's mouth and she devised a special way of pilfering them off the dressing table. She would sit casually against the table, arc her head backwards and daintily snatch the hairbands in her teeth, then stealthily make off with her booty. Soon her collection included bands in all the assorted colors, and, of course, my wife had none. "Tell that dog of yours to give me back my hairbands," my wife would demand periodically. Actually, as I mentioned, the dog was supposed to belong to her, but my secret intentions to appropriate her as a hunting dog had already been made clear. For my part, I had either read somewhere, or possibly just decided in my own mind, that retrievers are never to be punished, nor even reprimanded for carrying things in their mouths lest they begin to think that this is not a good thing for them to do. So, admittedly, I wasn't much of a disciplinarian around the house.

Soon no item even vaguely cylindrical, and in size between a chapstick tube and a small fireplace log, was safe from Sweetz's burgeoning interest in carrying and collecting. Indeed, if we happened to be looking for the former, we would be as likely to find one on her bed as in the medicine chest. And that winter when the firewood supply by the hearth became depleted and it was cold outside and we didn't feel like going out for more, we could usually count on finding among Sweetz's cache at least one log with which to stoke the dying embers.

Of course, she collected the more banal stuff as well—the obligatory shoes and socks, and the underwear pilfered from the laundry hamper. There were occasional recurrences of that awkward stage signified by the wedding ring incident—the inevitable puppy transitional period when the distinction between the activities of carrying, chewing, and swallowing are sometimes blurred. This is a stage that the bird hunter desperately hopes the dog will outgrow, and in Sweetzer's case, on one occasion it would prove nearly fatal.

We were on the road for a magazine assignment and had left the puppy in the motel room while we went out for a quick bite to eat. We returned to a grisly scene. Sweetz had gone into my wife's suitcase, removed a ziplock bag full of toiletries, opened the bag, and removed from it a full bottle of estrogen pills. Under normal circumstances this would have been nothing to worry about because pill bottles, which also have a pleasingly cylindrical shape to them, were another favorite carrying object. Unfortunately, in this case, the frustration of being left alone in a strange room had been too much for the still young dog. Somehow she managed to open the childproof bottle (putting her, I guess, on an intellectual par with a seven-year-old human), and had consumed nearly the entire bottle of pills; the remaining few were scattered on the bed, along with the bottle and the violated cap—it looked like nothing so much as the scene of a suicide attempt. We phoned the local vet and arranged to meet him at the clinic, where he gave Sweetz a shot to induce vomiting. Fortunately the pills had been ingested recently enough that only the sugar coating had dissolved from them, and no harm was done to her.

Having survived it, thankfully, the swallowing stage didn't last long and soon the carry became an end in itself. She enjoyed concealing smaller items altogether in her mouth, parading around the house with a pleased, platypus-like expression, until someone finally took notice. "You're dog has something in her mouth," my wife would remark, and I'd call Sweetz over and ask her to deposit whatever she held in my hand. Sometimes she would give up a mechanical pencil stolen from my desk and held, not crosswise, but lengthwise in her mouth, just the point peaking out from between her teeth. At other times, she might produce a single grape, taken from a bowl on the kitchen table, dropping it lightly into my palm as if offering up a precious gift. Corn-on-the-cob waiting to go on the grill was another favorite. So delicate was her grasp that she would barely dent the kernels with her teeth. Apples and oranges and even melon quarters became highly prized, and if one wasn't too squeamish about a little bit of Lab drool, they could still be rinsed off and eaten. Then one day that first spring while running with my wife on a dirt road up a canyon near our home in Idaho, Sweetz brought back a rattlesnake; fortunately it was dead, but this seemed nevertheless to augur another inauspicious, and potentially dangerous, new turn in her hobby. It also marked a whole new wildlife phase in her collecting, a phase that coincided with our retrieving work on live birds that first summer.

"Your dog has something in her mouth," my wife said one day, barely looking up from her book. Indeed, Sweetz had come in from outside and was now promenading around the room, wagging her tail, jowls compressed in their goofy platypus expression.

"Bring that here," I said. She came over to me coyly; she liked to make a bit of a game out of it. "What have you got there?" Proudly, though somewhat reluctantly, she deposited a live hummingbird in my hand. I'd held them before; cupped gently in hand (and presumably in the mouth), the impossibly delicate little birds will usually remain perfectly motionless, perhaps feigning death. I didn't know how she had caught the humming-bird—who knows, maybe she snagged it right out of the air—but in any case, it seemed to me an interesting retrieve. I took the hummer outside and opened my fist. A bit damp from Sweetz's mouth, which must have seemed like Jonah's stomach to the tiny bird, it looked around as if startled, shook itself off like a wet dog, and buzzed indignantly up out of my open palm. Sweetz and I watched it away, our first, although not our last, experience with catch-and-release hunting.

"You're dog has something in her mouth," remarked my wife on yet another day.

"Bring that here," I commanded. She obeyed. "Open up and let's see what you've got there." Inside her mouth was a tiny, hairless, newborn cottontail rabbit, evidently stolen from the den; it was alive, unharmed. "I'll be damned," I said, "It's a bunny. She's got a baby bunny in her mouth!"

My wife looked at me strangely and shook her head, a look and a gesture I've grown rather accustomed to over the years. "Tell her to put the bunny back where she got it," she said.

Of course Sweetz is all grown up now, entering middle age, but she still hasn't lost her interest in collecting. For instance, I'm looking at her right now; she lies snoozing on the bed in my office, surrounded by some of her prized possessions—an eclectic collection of stuff. Her head rests on one of my shoes, which also has a sock, a tennis ball, and a chapstick secreted in it (she's learned to collect several items in one mouthful, filling a shoe for instance with smaller things). By her chin is an empty cardboard toilet paper roll, an empty Dove soapbox, and one of my wife's elastic hairbands—all perennial favorites. Against her stomach, she has deposited one of her retrieving dummies, and tucked up under her haunch is another tennis ball. Right by the tip of her nose is my old sweat-stained orange hunting cap, sun-faded to a kind of peach color—it must certainly remind Sweetz of past days afield, and of those to come.

And now as I watch her on the bed, surrounded by her booty, her nose begins working back and forth, her eyes rolling in REM, her feet and legs twitching spasmodically. Probably she's hunting in her dreams, and maybe, if I'm lucky, I'm hunting with her.

True Love

One time late in a dinner party of old bird hunting cronies who had known each other for many years, and who had seen each other through sundry personal difficulties that included marital discord, divorce, separation, illness, death, bankruptcy, and all the rest of what is frequently referred to as "real life," after everyone at the table had consumed rather too much wine, and the conversation had turned, as it naturally will, to bird dogs, someone suddenly posed the incredibly imma-ture (even by bird hunters' standards) query: "Everyone present who prefers the company of your favorite bird dog to that of your spouse, raise your hand." Snap shots all, a unanimity of hands fired up around the table— a stunningly naked group confession. Hands aloft the hunters looked at one another with growing sheepishness, as if they had all accidently fired both barrels on a covey rise of ground doves. And then, all at once, everyone roared with laughter.

Of course, it was all in fun, and it wasn't strictly true, nor was it necessarily a question that only hunters would so answer. Ask the same question of any table full of drunken dog lovers (or even sober ones) and one might expect the same response. Still, I can't help but feel that we sportsmen love our dogs *more* than does the average pet owner. And if this last statement is likely to elicit howls of protest from the toy poodle devotee, then let me qualify it, let me put it another way, and as bluntly as possible: the *quality* of the sportsman's love for his dogs is superior to that of the average dog owner. Now I can literally feel myself being pummeled about the head and shoulders by a mob of angry pooper-scooper wielding Central Park dog lovers: *We love our dogs just as much as you do!* they protest, *and what's more we love them every bit as well!*

Well, maybe so, but I still think that the quality of the sportsman's love for his dog is superior for the simple reason that the sporting dog itself is superior. (More outraged howls: *Elitist swine! Hunting dog chauvinist!*, and now the incensed mob of garden-variety house dog owners are wielding their pooper scoopers like lacrosse sticks, pelting the retreating author with their cargo of unmentionables.)

But listen, it isn't such a hard argument to make. Let me give you a real-life example: two Lab puppies from the same litter, one male, one female, go to two different owners who also happen to be old friends. The owner of the female is a nonhunter, let's say he's a poet. The owner of the male is a lifelong bird hunter, say, a novelist. Now the novelist immediately begins training his puppy as a bird dog, both for flushing and retrieving upland birds and as a retriever of waterfowl. Said novelist is a consumate hunter, and the training process, although quite specific, is at the same time rather casual and completely natural; by putting his dog in hunting situations, he is, in fact, simply reinforcing, heightening, and refining centuries of genetic selection that has resulted in his dog's instinctual predisposition to find and retrieve birds. And right from the start, there is no mistaking the fact that the hunter's dog while growing daily in confidence and competence, is having a whole lot of fun in the bargain.

Now the poet, on the other hand, provides no training for his puppy, formal or otherwise, though he does take her on long daily walks through the woods and on long drives in the car. These excursions are also lots of fun for the dog, but they are without structure, specific purpose, or real challenge. Not incidentally, every day the poet also recites his morning's output of poems to his dog. This is, arguably, a somewhat less compelling activity for canines, but then who am *I* to say so? And don't get me wrong, the guy is a wonderful poet, who, I'm sure, loves his dog as much as it is possible for a nonhunter to love a dog.

Yet I still maintain that the novelist's dog is a superior creature—smarter and more imaginative, capable of more intuitive thought processes; his wits have been tested and expanded, his instincts focused and honed, his intellect heightened by use—by being required to *think*. And in the bargain he has also become a superior athlete. He has, in short, benefited from a very well-rounded education. At the same time, he and the novelist are partners in a mutual passion, not simply owner and pet, but full partners in an activity that they both love to do, were both born to do, and at which they are both quite good. This provides an incredibly strong bond between them, a bond deeper and fuller than that between the poet and his dog, who's relationship is based on...what?...a mutual love of iambic pentameter? And so it follows by this line of reasoning that the hunter loves his dog with a more informed love, a love more focused and specific and equal, in short, if one dares to qualify love—a greater, fuller, superior love. *Voila!* Now the author is finally out of range of the pooper-scooper brigade, their missiles falling hopelessly short of their intended target.

A Codicil

Here is what I mean to say, finally, about our sporting dogs: They are far more than just pets, companions, and pals; they are full-time collaborators, the too-short decade or so of their lives a perfect mirror image of that same period in our own. Through the medium of our dogs we can take a surprisingly accurate measure, not only of birds killed, missed, retrieved, but also of the day-to-day events—the changes, advances, and reverses of our lives, the sheer mileage—not to even mention the less tangible measure of dreams, regrets, joys, and sorrows. And each dog that passes by becomes another white cross along the side of the road, one more milestone marking our own "lonely march toward doom" as another poet once put it so well.

Gary Marek lives in the Boardman River valley south of Traverse City, Michigan, a few miles from the stretch of river where Len Halliday created the Adams dry fly. The Boardman is still a good home to the Adams, pockets of grouse, and woodcock with a taste for tag alder. Marek resides with his wife, Arta, and a teenage daughter, Brooklynne, in a questionable house that nevertheless sits within a few hundred feet of swamp-edge woodcock and grouse. He has written for a variety of publications, including Fly Rod & Reel, Gray's Sporting Journal, *and* Audubon. *He continues to believe that fishing and bird hunting are his best means of discovering essential truths.*

IN PRAISE OF PORCUPINES AND OTHER MEN'S DOGS

by Gary Marek

I felt the needle seek deeper territory. "So, is yours steady to wing and shot?" the orthopedic surgeon asked with genuine interest. I was off guard in every way. I hadn't even thought about such an irrelevant and rarified subject in years. Hell, *I'm* not steady to wing and shot, I reminded myself. I managed a meditative groan and felt some of the prepatory swab liquid run from my shoulder down the back of my arm. It began to drip off the point of my elbow.

"Yeah, hang in there now. Here—let me clean that up a bit." I had just noticed that the rivulet felt a bit heavy and slow. "Sometimes there's a little blood with one of these, but it won't be too much longer now," he added.

Finally, my head cleared itself away from the area where pain and cortisone simultaneously rushed deep into my entire shoulder. My favorite shoulder, where right-side movements of great physical impor-tance were controlled and carried out, like fly casting and handling a 20-gauge shotgun.

"She's steady to wing" (a lie) "but not to shot," I said as casually as I could. It was my second visit to this young surgeon and what we shared in common besides an interest in the storms of pain brewing within my right shoulder and upper arm was ownership of German shorthaired pointers. Mine was nine years old, an aging if not old hunter. His was a two-year-old adolescent, a carefully trained but "unfinished" sporting dog with lots of potential. I had recently come to see myself as a bird dog realist; the surgeon was still an optimist pursuing cherished images and the creation of a canine laser with all of its sophisticated energies precisely aligned. A focused and empowered individual, as people of the nineties like to say.

The needle was out, the wound swabbed and bandaged, and I felt anything but empowered. "Actually, now I just go hunting when I can. I let her run and hope for the best," I added. This could get touchy. I wasn't in the mood for debate, swagger, or poignant testimonials, and to avoid the treachery of different field theologies I decided to play commoner to his erudite skills and membership in elite professional societies. And it was true that I still hadn't returned his two expensive dog-training videos. The starring dogs were automatons of perfection.

Sometimes I'm amazed that I even have a bird dog, I went on to say. We finished our cortisone encounter with a second and almost evil shot into the top of the right elbow. My shooting hand and forearm would be lubed in no time. I drove home left-handed to my shorthair and gun-shy vizsla and, perhaps because blood was still in the air, spent the rest of the afternoon reflecting about the mysterious personae of hunting dogs and the humans they tolerate or love or dominate.

♦

I did not understand the long vowels and mournful language of the new beagle next door. While I loved the pounding rhythms of Eddie Cochran and Buddy Holly by day, the midnight wailing of this, this *hound dog*, was annoying even to an essentially brainless kid whose greatest concern in 1958 involved the quantity of frogs he was going to spear in Indian Mill Creek near Farmer Pete's slaughterhouse. During that long and very hot summer, I was introduced to blood sport (I now prefer the term food gathering) and the sporting breeds.

My best friend lived a few blocks away and while hanging around my house one night after we'd picked some nightcrawlers he took note of our neighbor's howling beagle. "We've got one near us, too. They're *hunting dogs*, you know. They're different." My friend is a psychologist now and still believes they're different. He has acquired a new golden retriever that (I refuse to invoke the personal pronoun who) receives occasional foot massages from his wife to reduce the energy field the dog carries with it every waking moment. If the golden's behavior doesn't come around I expect the burgeoning dog chiropractic movement might reach my friend's house someday as well.

I lost track of hunting dogs for nearly two decades after the beagle and frog summer but developed a sideways-glance interest again when I turned from a bird-watching anti-hunter (I could snap my Bushnells on target as fast as anyone in the woods) into a tag-a-long hunting agnostic. I even thought it might be interesting to acquire a bird dog someday so I could walk along and take pictures while friends tried to shoot birds. I had heard watching a good dog at work in the woods was a little like fly fishing—aesthetically pleasing.

Springer spaniels appealed to me and I finally decided to surprise my wife with a ten-week-old male as an early anniversary present. As she petted and cooed at him I felt his obvious intelligence measure us through slightly enigmatic eyes. Not many weeks later and well before he reached his physique of steel, he vaulted into the air and sank his small teeth into my wife's midriff. Apparently, she was not supposed to enter the room at that moment. I was thankful that he was unable to spring a bit higher.

"The best thing you can do is hunt him. Repetition and the smell of birds. Get him out there as often as you can," an avid bird hunting friend from Leelanau County advised. The reactions to his behavior problems were consistent: bird dogs are high-spirited creatures that need to hunt. "But remember—he's a flusher so you aren't going to see any points. Then again, that's not so terrible. Springers work close and get all wiggly when they're onto a bird. Just take him to birds and he'll end up tired and happy."

After many years of quiet opposition to hunting, I still wasn't ready to begin wielding a shotgun, but I did have another close friend who grew up with a springer ("Heidi, the greatest mouser in the history of the world!" he would brag) and wanted to convert me to the brotherhood of the long gun. He would be glad to give my dog some work.

◆

"Gary, you don't need to do that, honest!" My friend seemed a little exasperated. I was only trying to be safety conscious by instantly dropping to my knees when a bird flushed within range. It was the inverse of the soldier's "incoming!" When there were outgoing flights, I hit the dirt. In future outings I began to do much better and decided my partner wasn't going to cooly swing on a woodcock and accidently ventilate me. Unfortunately, after a promising outing or two my young springer began to act erratically and even stopped working periodically to sulk. I am certain my air-raid behavior had nothing to do with it. Then one day in Ghidra's Cover (named after a huge woodcock reminiscent of those Japanese film monsters) he decided to stage a real sit-down strike. I quickly tired of dragging a 60-pound dog through thick aspen and carried him most of the way back to my cabin. He was not tired. His eyes were both distant and demonic.

I soon retired as a bird-hunting sidekick and our bird dog continued to alternate between affection so touching that he was "almost like another person" as all dog owners say sooner or later, and a rabid Cerberus.

On the eve of my wife's thirty-second birthday and in the fifth month of her pregnancy with our only child, he did us a great favor: he drew real blood. This time he attacked my wife with full Jekyll-and-Hyde fury. Persona lifted, anima revealed. Serious injury was averted only through luck and a frantically slammed bedroom door. In the morning we drove him into town in the front seat of our pickup while he licked our faces and remained oblivious to the psychotic episode of the evening before.

At the vet's I put his favorite blanket with him, stroked his soft feathers, and whispered I was sorry. Two hours later he was dead by lethal injection. I am certain that if he had lived he would have tried to kill our baby daughter. Years later I was fortunate enough to learn from a magazine article and eventually other sources that he undoubtedly suffered from what some dog experts call Springer Rage. It was a relief but an anticlimax.

My bird dog ownership days were over.

◆

And my hunting days suddenly began. Heidi's owner sold me his old Italian side-by-side 20-gauge and took me back into the woods, this time without the camera. That same autumn another good trout fishing friend invited me to join him and his dog Meg, a somewhat cerebral but still pleasant vizsla. Among a small circle of friends and relatives, Meg's reputation for understanding the full importance of bird hunting inspired reverential tones.

This was in the Dark Ages Before Electronic Collars and Training Videos. However, according to Meg's owner, Ted, she was as enthusiastic as a "two-peckered billygoat" in the presence of birds and had developed a precise lifestyle. That is, she rested during winter and spring, went on commando vegetable raids and grasshopper pointing sorties in the family garden during summer, and then centered herself on bird business as autumn arrived. Apparently it had taken some mistakes and a few years of mutual alignment, but she and Ted had made it official: they were man and bird dog.

The first precept that these two friends (I quickly perceived that Meg wasn't aloof but simply a focused professional) destroyed for me was the myth that hunting grouse and woodcock was difficult or complicated. Sure, learning how to shoot properly and especially hitting canon-fired grouse or those diurnal bats with long bills that whistle up from underfoot is always difficult, but the rest was quite simple. We followed Meg until she shifted into a slow-motion creep or froze on point. Ted moved up to flush the bird, or if one of us happened to be closer we followed his quick, traffic-cop commands and "walked up" the bird ourselves. If one of us hit the bird, the red dog would find it and take it to Ted. He is a superior shot with gunslinger quickness, which means that the bird more often than not belongs in his vest. But if it were downed by a partner, the bird was quickly removed from Meg's grinning chops and handed over. That was that. Simple. Almost a system, as the technocrats would say.

Never was the ease of bird hunting more clear to me than during my second season of hunting. I had rationalized the shame and depressive effects of going zero for fifty during a preseason warm-up skeet shoot with Ted and two other close friends at an abandoned prison camp softball field. I could still hear the sympathetic voices assuring me that "you nicked that one for sure I think," but a year had passed, I had logged a fair amount of hours in the woods alone, and I'd killed a few birds. I also sensed acceptance; my three bird hunting friends were now of the opinion that I wasn't going to trim off an ear or mangle a shoulder with careless excitement if a bird happened to fly between us. And perhaps just as important, Ted deduced that I wasn't going to shoot Meg. Therefore, he wouldn't have to worry about shooting me and damaging our friendship.

The light of an early October dawn charged me with energy. Hoarfrost surrounded my cabin. With the overripe peach smell of freshly split red oak in my hands, I rekindled the fire and slipped into my almost furry nylon-faced hunting pants. Hunting without dogs tears at skin and frays clothing with an unrefined kind of violence. I would need a new pair, maybe one with Cordura armor, next year. October bird mornings are crisp but they are also uncomplicated and full of assurance. With just a little effort, the cold air becomes warm, the fall woods become artistic blends, and the day is ours.

Only minutes later Meg reached my cabin door well before Ted and his brother Bill. Once again she was convinced this would be the best day of her life.

A short drive put us in the woods listening to the high jingling of a working dog's bell. Meg's breath appeared and disappeared like puffs of sentinel smoke. Wet with the softening frost dripping from still green ferns, she gleamed with an aura of antiquity like a burnished cello.

As sudden as a released breath, the sound of a grouse halted us. But it vanished. Then another, also out of range and made only of faint reverberations deflected by motionless shafts of maple and aspen.

"She's creeping! Could be a covey!" Ted strained to mute his voice. Pressing a shutter and pulling a trigger do not create equal amounts of passion and concentration. I was more conscious than I had been in a very long time. "She's on. Over here Bill—Gary go ahead! Walk up to Meg. Meggy you stay!" But nothing happened as I thoroughly moved around the frozen dog. I felt as if I could hear a spider take a step from one leaf to another. Suddenly she broke twenty feet toward Ted and his brother Bill, then stopped on point again. Ted thought a running grouse might be in front of us, but after some wandering around, he explained for my benefit that she probably was pointing where the birds had been walking moments earlier. We were beginning one of those impromptu breaks during which the hunters try to calm down and reconcile a nearly ideal and lost opportunity (*If only I'd walked around that windfall, I would've had a clear...*).

I listened to droplets of water fall from trees and strike the lemon and vermillion forest floor as if it were fabric. Air now bright with morning sun moved slightly through the tall grasses of the large field behind my cabin. The open land hadn't been disturbed by anything but deer hooves for over sixty years. Ted tried to call Meg back to us and Bill laughed at her staunch devotion to an evaporating scent. I tried to imagine the field defined by the giant white pines of a century ago, but hunting is a vital counterpoint to thinking and I couldn't organize thought and emotion. I decided that on this day I was a part of the forest and the field in the same way colossal trees once had been.

Ted swung and fired so quickly that for a heartbeat, the entire woods filled with movement. The roar of grouse and shotgun converged and almost as quickly were joined by a red dog weaving toward us with a large grouse. Ted giggled through glee and crooned *good girl* repeatedly. Apparently sane dogs enjoy baby talk. This is pretty nice, I was thinking. Real bird dogs even find and send you birds out of trees. I wondered if woodcock ever spent much time in trees but didn't want to interrupt the effusive dog praise with a question. Bill repeated *unbelievable* enough to bore the dog and drive her into a slink toward cover. I wore out *awesome* and began to look at hemlocks with new perspective. Like all great dogs she could smell a thought if it involved the birds of passion.

The tree grouse set off a bird pointing seminar that ended with the three of us washed with the earthen aroma of spent shells, a good number of birds against the small of our backs, and a dog that had gone from a high-stepping, allegro pace through the ferns and trees to a posture that seemed to say, I'll hunt until I die but I wouldn't turn up my snout at an intermission right now.

A long rain fell that night and in the morning the autumn woods dripped a cold gloom. I didn't really want to leave my fireplace. Radiant heat permeates October strains and I was sore.

"I think we should try the pines and higher ground by the ski lodge. What do you think, Meg?" asked Ted. Meg squealed and shimmied. He had arrived recharged and damn near full of glee again.

"O.K. but I can't hunt seven hours like yesterday." I tried not to seem jaded or in need of analgesics.

"No, no. I want to get home this afternoon and try a cover out by Lake Michigan. Might be some early flight birds there after this weather." These redheads were dangerous I noted to myself.

I wasn't sure what we were up to, but the idea of hunting in the almost arid terrain of red pines seemed simultaneously hopeful and stupid. Even I knew woodcock and grouse didn't care for the sterility and public atmosphere of red pine plantations. We started in a fringe of tall aspen buffered by an uneven strip of hemlock, maple, and oak. In a blur Meg pointed three woodcock and Ted and Bill each made good shots. It is one of the special pleasures of bird hunting to be unable to see number 8 or 9 shot leave your gun—or someone else's—and travel toward a target. The Borgeld brothers will never know that I missed the third woodcock flying through the powerline opening by, shall we say, the better part of an acre.

We hadn't quite reached the pines when Meg's bell abruptly fell silent to my left. I easily located her bent into a crooked L-shape. She was looking directly toward me. Those amber vizsla eyes glared right through me, almost in disgust! What had I done wrong? "Where's the bird, Meg, where's the bird?" I chattered stupidly. The intolerance of a bird dog's eyes is a wonderful sight.

Then I saw it move. That terrestrial cousin of the echinoderms, the giant land urchin, stood its ground a few feet beyond Meg. I was going to see something now, I was sure.

"Ooh, a flash point!" Ted arrived only slightly concerned, making a pickle face. "Meg doesn't like these guys, do you Meg? A lot of hunters shoot porcupines but I don't know…"

"Why would anyone do that?" I snapped back. "Hell, they belong out here more than we do." My habit of instant sanctimony came back to me faster than a porky's step.

"I agree, let's go Meg—find us a bird!" Ted commanded his lieutenant. The porcupine was now knee-high up a red maple trunk; its cream and black quills appeared to be the stuff of which very bad dreams are made.

I finished that outing and that season as a tourist of two worlds: hunting calmly behind another man's experienced dog, and thrashing, poking, and slogging through every kind of tangled, aspenish, bushy covert (I was proud of my bloodied hands and forearms—Red Badges of birding courage only a few good men would understand) northern Michigan has to offer.

It was a life.

◆

In September I met the Egg. It was probably just in time. Without the Egg, changes in weather, fluctuations in woodcock populations, and the ever-mysterious Grouse Cycle—always at its very nadir according to local biologists and sages—might not have been enough to save me from concluding that bird hunting wasn't much of a challenge for real sportsmen. Could insouciance and upland smugness have been far behind? And wouldn't the deepest of disillusionment have followed when reality came to call?

The Egg was real. An unlikely nickname for a Brittainy spaniel, to be sure, but nonetheless another man's dog that taught me powerful—if incomplete—lessons about grouse behavior, days in the field, and the demons of the human mind.

The Egg did not like to touch her lips to dead woodcock, did not care to listen to her master's commands even if he was about to lose his voice to permanent laryngeal hemorrhaging by screaming, and cooly disdained hunting within the same bioregion as her owner. What the Egg did love was running to daylight. To cover, through cover, and to the point. And holding woodcock until the next month if they agreed to stay. They didn't.

Sure the owner was a friend of mine and Ted's brother Bill, and sure it was great to get together in the crisp autumn air suffused with summer and winter and eternity, and sure the Egg earned a bird here and there, but damn it, all this yelling, this dog hunting, and this busting of precious grouse into the great beyond was wearing on me. It wasn't sporting.

Hunting behind Meg had always been so predictable, so Pavlovian that the world seemed inhuman, organized, and sensible. Now a roly-poly agent of chaos was turning the hunt into a frenetic chamber of dark thoughts, missed opportunities, and frayed psyches. I just wanted to greedily shoot a few birds behind a reliable dog, the Egg's owner simply wanted his dog to do anything that would prevent his emotional breakdown and estrangement from friends and family, and the Egg yearned to be released to the glorious and uncontrolled pursuit of certain scents.

I was upset with being upset. I was thinking of trying to point birds myself—then maybe I'd have a shot. I'm sure the Egg's owner knew I selfishly resented his dog's juvenile behavior and his bellowing at her to come back to the same hemisphere we were hunting, but I didn't know what to do or say. So I damned the Egg with faint praise, told myself that she must just be an exception to the rule, and promised that I would not fall victim to the ownership of such a confused animal. I made an oath to never indulge in pleadful ranting while afield should I ever own another bird dog. I hunted alone near home even more and developed a secret smugness about finishing the latter part of the season as the star in *The Loneliness of the Long Distance Hunter.*

◆

Oh, I'd like to tie that little ghost to a tree so she'd have to helplessly listen to me blaze away at grouse, I mumbled to myself. My partner, the owner of the dog (a thirty-five-pound comet of an English setter named Ginger) blowing toward the next county on the hot wind of desire, didn't seem to be the proper audience for sharing this thought. This was yet another angling friendship that had pleasantly evolved afield.

Then again, I couldn't hold back forever and finally broached the dreaded subject of so much interest to so many hunters: the behavior of someone else's dog—*your* dog—in the field. Actually, that's a euphemistic phrasing isn't it? What I really mean to say is the incompetent, impulsive, juvenile, stupid, inexplicable, and maniacal mistakes your dog has committed that helped to ruin what could have been a perfectly wonderful hunt.

"She's just far-ranging. That's the way setters like to work. It's their style," my partner and at this point still my friend replied, emphasizing the last word. I concluded that our friendship was much more valuable than any number of prematurely flushed grouse, and was relieved that he had not taken offense. I don't believe there's a single bird hunter of any substance who hasn't witnessed or at least heard of a friendship or family relationship that was strained or somehow turned into a stew of resentment because of a bird dog.

"Doesn't your dog work that way?" he asked evenly. My new dog, a German shorthair named Claire, was of course another subject altogether.

"She's got a lot to learn," I said with absolutely no sense of irony. In the setter I had met yet another culture. And I was struggling with intolerance. This white flash was not a nose-to-the-ground relative of the hound, not a Versatile that works close to its master, but rather a high-prancing speed merchant searching the air for the shadow of a scent. We would have to follow, not direct her. Where we, or at least I—myopically of course—wanted to look was based on the limitation of sight and held no significance. My friend mentioned something tongue-in-cheek about the setter being a Refined Breed.

That may explain how something—a prehistoric odor rising from pasty black soil or huge aspens leaning at dangerous angles over bushes and burdock taller than we were—in the narrow cover along the Sturgeon River that day seemed very wrong for a fleet English setter and two professional types to be hunting. We had been exploring a sunny ridge and followed a grouse through an opening down into a darkened theater of swift river, wind-thrown trees, and foreboding. Instead of shafts of sunlight illuminating the surroundings, the autumn light only heightened the dark bars of shadow everywhere around us. There are dead people in here from long ago, I told myself. "Something bad happened down in there" my friend offered later while still wiping his dog's blood off his hands. Like unpretentious boys and with no deliberation, we named the site the Valley of Death.

But there were grouse that day—thunderous, old gray birds that disappeared into shawls of Virginia creeper or vanished among fallen timber and black root masses the size of abandoned cabins. While my partner pressed on toward the general location of a flushed bird but especially toward the old railroad tracks and open daylight, I pulled and pushed my way through the webs of creeper and looked for a glimpse of Ginger. She moved like a pale fox through the Valley and disappeared for what seemed to me to be inappropriate periods of time. I yelled to the tracks that I had no idea of her location and then had to gulp a breath to correct myself. I saw movement in the waist-high weeds and bushes just forty feet or so to my right. I even heard the bell. Then more muffled ringing and more rustling. "She's hot!" I yelled and kicked my way forward as quickly as I could. "Are you coming in?"

I was told to take the bird myself. I accepted but was still a little confused by the movements in front of me. This dog held points with smooth determination; she was not a creeper.

I shouted that she must have a running grouse and then broke through the final fence of vines to reach the point. The dog was either guarding or regarding a porcupine that looked to be the size of a bear cub. I did not have time to invoke déjà vu: this dog took a big bite.

In a burst of hysteria I wailed descriptions from the edge of the Valley and lunged into the fray. The round dark mammal wasn't in a hurry. The lithe white mammal squealed ever so faintly, began to show portions of red, and hopped unnaturally on three legs. One front leg was cushioned with quills. I think I feared for her eyes but I can't remember for sure. An unwelcome memory returned to me: the dazed, lost, and I believe dying bird dog wandering along a county road one day as I drove home from fishing the Sturgeon River. For miles I thought about turning around to help but continued on toward home. I grasped Ginger by the collar and pulled her through obstacles and up the eight feet of ballast onto the tracks. Her muzzle and throat were darted with quills. I was in a terrible state of mind.

What happened next was simple, instructive, and invaluable. My friend calmly (under the circumstances) reached into his vest, pulled out a hemostat, and proceeded to remove whole clumps of porcupine from his dog's face, leg, mouth, and throat. Within a few minutes the bleeding subsided nicely, I began to compose myself, and Ginger seemed to be looking back toward the Valley for more.

"No, that's it for today, buddy," he said and began to wipe the blood from his hands. "I wouldn't go anywhere without a pair of these," he added as he wiped the surgical tool clean. For once I hardly had anything to say except that I was amazed the dog's eyes were unharmed and her behavior nearly normal except for a distinct limp.

We turned our backs to the Valley and walked to the trestle near our car. My responsibility—family, financial, emotional—and involvement in this crisis was over. And I felt completely drained.

"They're tough, they're different," he added as he picked up his dog and carried her across the river trestle.

"This was not an easy hunt," I said to no one in particular.

◆

Life, as I was indicating to the surgeon not long ago, is an evolving history. My shorthair shows great potential but is still unfinished. I am still unfinished. Yet the seasons and our dogs, young and old, press on.

I seem to recall that Ortega y Gasset observed that hunting dogs are like arrows, living extensions of the hunter. The grouse and bird dog fanatic from Leelanau County called one day in early March to ask if I would like a German shorthair. My friend knew my springer, knew about a particularly black birthday five years earlier, and I think even knew that on that day I was called back by my veterinarian's office an hour after our dog had been killed. The vet was running late with appointments and since I wanted a lab analysis—some kind of an explanation for the psychotic episodes—could I please take the specimen to the airport in time for the flight to Lansing and Michigan State University? I somehow agreed and rode the box on the seat next to me as if it were strontium 90. It was my dog's head.

"I don't know, you've taken me by surprise."

"That's the idea. You've seen Cochise."

Indeed I had seem him hunt on a couple of occasions in the hilly thickets near Lake Leelanau. What I saw was a fierce, animate arrow. He was sometimes a garbage-stealing, boneheaded whiner at home, but in the field Cochise was a sagacious incarnation of his master's hands. The litter had been sired by a dog with heart and power. I knew nothing of the female, except her owners once lived in Australia, and I didn't care.

"Thanks, I'll come and take a look."

Grouse and woodcock hunting are too enjoyable and the aroma of grilling woodcock (rare please) and lemon-butter grouse is far too medicinal to be sacrificed for check-cords, whistles, and backyard training regimens. In other words my shorthair, Claire, didn't get any time afield until her second fall.

During the bleak days of her first winter I watched the dog and our young daughter warm each other and our home. I reminded myself not to be harsh or punitive with either one. Positive reinforcement. No yelling.

Claire hit her first season running and showed great interest in ferns, popple thickets, vine-strewn windfall entanglements, and extending the distance between her heat-seeking course and me. She was on a mission but disdained her orders. Still, she handled some woodcock quite nicely and brought in a crippled grouse one day. I only exhorted her to hunt with me a couple of dozen times and slapped her with *No!* a few more.

Much to her dismay, I left her behind on hunts with friends and other dogs. It just didn't seem to be good form to subject them to our developing relationship. And I'd be damned if I was going to be the one to obliterate a good hunt with a goddamned lunatic of a dog. There was another problem. My friends' dogs knew the significance of wire; but Claire did not regard it at all. Wire is thick cobweb, wire is to run through. In lower Michigan nearly all public land meets the barbed wire of private property. I was certain that she would destroy an eye (*Daddy, what did you do to Claire!*) or at least require zipper-length stitches if I ran her with the other dogs.

The leaves of that autumn turned brown and ocher and suddenly dense woods revealed long views of steely light. Snow propelled the last woodcock south and some days my dog ran with them. She apparently delighted in flushing grouse before I could see them, although I really don't know since I wasn't open to delight. Some people "put up" their antique cars, farm machinery, and various boats for the winter. I put up my dog and hunted the last woodcock and late grouse season alone again.

In the ensuing years it became obvious that weather isn't the only natural force that is unpredictable. Some hunts were marvels of blue sky, good dog work, and clean shooting. Later the house would fill with steam saturated with Worcestershire sauce, butter and acorn squash. Woodcock and Merlot. Grouse and a fine Riesling.

Other trips—near home or seventy-five miles away, it didn't seem to matter—were wicked mixtures of grey-hound imitations, obscene epithets, and sulkathons in which the winner was the first one to discover a bird to chase. Alone.

All of the great pine and hardwood forests of Michigan have been gone for a century. Some of the cleared land is still partially open and, of course, bordered by second and third-generation trees. I hunt a piece of state-owned land near my home that is remarkably large, interspersed with grassy, wild cherry openings, and punctuated with bird cover. For some reason—possibly because were are always alone—my dog often behaves herself and hunts with some of the purchase of her father.

We entered some misshapen circles of blackberry, aspen, and witch hazel after a good one-hour hunt in a different cover that I ended by throwing a temper tantrum and screaming myself hoarse. Claire had found and held three woodcock, two of which I shot as if I had handled a shotgun since puberty. The third bird I missed because it rose into a ceiling of bigtooth aspen leaves and disappeared. Not to worry. My dog followed up on the bird—or was it another?—again and again, and yes, probably again. Order surrendered to chaos and reason to rage.

I pursued the dog, my voice failing and croaking, for a heated distance. After a passionate reunion and simpering contrition, we rode together to another portion of the state land in silence.

I pulled off a two-track and parked in the edge of a field. I left her in the car while I retied my boots, combed the sweat out of my hair, and adjusted my sodden shirt and vest. If I were wearing a tie, I would have retied the knot.

I finally opened the door and commanded the dog to heel. She stopped nearby and looked up at me. Good enough. Trying to hone my voice into a flashing razor, I again confided my deepest desire: I want you to hunt *with me*.

She worked the first aspen and berry island thoroughly, checking back with me a couple of times, but there were only old splashes. She crossed an opening and faded into some birdy-looking bushes and trees. I had to let her range a little, but in less than a minute an uneasy near-silence stopped me. Claire's bell was quiet but when I closed the distance between her approximate location to my west, I immediately saw that she had ranged into maple and large timber. If there were any birds in there, they were chickadees and crows.

Her screams were not blood-curdling but instead muffled with blood. I don't know if she had sampled the porcupine from various angles or simply opened once wide and hard. I was a half-mile from my truck and many miles from the nearest people. Claire's keening shocked me in a way I had never known: this pain was mine, my dog was wounded.

I barely glanced at the porcupine as I rushed her out of the darkening woods into the light of open land. Her throat and muzzle gleamed red. My hands were already slippery with blood.

Her eyes were unharmed. I reached into my vest pocket and grasped the hemostat. I worked frantically on the quills under the chin, in her muzzle, and ominously protruding from her chest. Only a few had speared her legs and they were especially easy to remove, but why wasn't she calming down? Her jaws rattled together and deep whimpering poured from her throat. I pried open her mouth and would have run away through the field if I could. Blood spit from her tongue and the roof of her mouth was not visible through the dozens of stout quills. My forearms were red as I fought off panic. By the time I finished removing what I could, she had suddenly calmed down and stopped crying. Her bleeding almost disappeared and on my rush back to the truck she veered toward a little aspen island to start hunting again!

I drove back dirt roads at improper speeds and thought of what I had once told an acquaintance who was thinking of bringing a bird dog into the family. "If I were to give you one, which was once done for me, I'd say this: 'There's a little bit of blood with one of these but they're almost as wonderful as daughters and sons.'"

Now, fairly drenched in the family dog's blood, I wasn't so sure of anything. I poured on the speed and turned up the radio. "To All the Girls I've Loved Before" reverberated in the cab and suddenly flashing past my eyes was more than a blur of northern maple, aspen, and pine. All of the easy, carefree hours behind Meg,

Ginger, and Chelsea the Egg rushed through my blood and then focused. I owed them and my friends everything. So it's to those white and porky and auburn canine girls who gave me more pleasure than I was capable of realizing that I dedicate this long song.

Dave Meisner is the publisher and editor-in-chief of The Pointing Dog Journal. *He's the founder and original publisher of* Gun Dog *magazine, which he sold in 1985. Dave and his wife, Barb, live in Des Moines, but Dave spends the bulk of his time pretending to be at work at his farmhouse-office on the edge of a 1,000-acre shooting preserve near Adel, Iowa. He is currently owned by a young Elhew pointer named Gilly, who is working hard to break Dave of fifty years of bad habits.*

IN THE HEART
OF HER MASTER

by Dave Meisner

"Yes, sir, if you have never had a hunting dog, then you have missed out on a great part of life. It is as though you had been born without sight or hearing, or only half a heart. Once you have had a dog, you will have many more. Though some may hunt better than others, or do this and that, there will never be but one first dog. He will be with you always, in a special place, where no other dog or person can intrude. A little place which no one knows about and sometimes you are afraid to go there yourself because you cannot control the tears."

—Excerpted from "First Dog" in *Backtrack*
by Charlie Dickey

It's always cold in central Iowa in the middle of February, and it was especially so on this windy morning as I toiled in pre-dawn light. Still, a clammy sweat covered my forehead and glued my shirt to my back. I was in a sparse stand of timber and it had been difficult to clear even a small area of packed-tight frozen leaves, brush and branches, and especially to bust through two inches of frost with a pick axe in order to reach the softer dirt below.

It was not a good day, or a particularly good place to bury a dog...as if there could be either.

◆

I bloomed late as a bird hunter, already married and in my twenties before I felt the urge to buy a hunting dog. I had started to read Hill and Evans and Spiller and Babcock and others who painted fascinating word pictures of bird dogs standing as stiff as brass cannons before proud masters. Somehow, for whatever reason, the till-then dormant hunter's gene within me awoke, and I found myself wanting to be in their stead.

The ad in the Green Bay paper simply read "English setter pups; $35. Call after 5:00." I had read that English setters were hunting dogs—what more mattered?

The next day Barb and I made the thirty-minute trip to Green Bay. We found the pups in an affluent neighborhood in the home of a dentist and his family. The dam was there and she was huge, with a massive head and floppy ears and jowls. She was white with orange ticking and she was, to be kind, *animated*. She yipped and panted and slobbered all over the good doctor's floors and furniture while he, oblivious to her lack of manners, showed us first one pup, then another. For what now are unfathomable reasons, we selected an active male who very much resembled his hyperactive mom. I offered $25; we settled on $30, and we headed home with my first "bird dog"...or so I thought.

I'd never owned nor attempted to train a dog before; I only knew what the books in my small collection told me, and the more I read—and experienced—the more I began to understand that Rusty, though a bird-dog breed, was definitely not a bird dog.

Rusty was from "show stock," the product of generations of breeding for looks and conformation, without regard for hunting ability. He had not an ounce of pointing instinct within him. Still, he was my dog, and in my blind and ignorant enthusiasm, I tackled the impossible task of making a bird dog out of him.

I took Rusty out frequently his first fall, and I'm sure we were quite a sight as we pushed aimlessly through the grouse woods near our home, a matched set: I had no idea what I was doing, and Rusty had no idea what I was trying to teach him to do.

I'd turn him loose and spend the next couple of hours totally frustrated as Rusty crashed through the woodlands, terrifying the creatures whose quiet domain we had invaded. He was a demon possessed, four-legged whirlwind—an orange belton Tasmanian devil!

When at last I would manage to collar him, Rusty showed no remorse, and no greater understanding of my pleadings than he had of my screamings. He'd just look at me quizzically, with his droopy, bloodshot eyes, and shake his head so drool from his big, sloppy jowls sprayed a half-dozen feet in either direction. He was a totally hopeless cause—living, breathing proof that breeding is more important than breed.

Eventually, I gave up and advertised Rusty "free to a good home," and though it was the last time I ever saw him, I didn't shed a tear when a local farmer packed him off to his new home in the country. I hoped Rusty lived happily ever after.

◆

My search for a bird dog continued, and the next ad that caught my eye was in a Milwaukee paper. It hit hard on the one thing I had learned from my experience with Rusty: breeding is all-important. Just because a dog happens to be a bird dog breed, doesn't necessarily make it a bird dog. I had learned that, as a result of generations of breeding for conformation and the show ring, many pointing breeds simply don't point and won't hunt, just as many show-bred Labradors won't retrieve and can't swim.

Where Rusty would point nothing whatsoever, Samantha—at only eight weeks—pointed *everything*: meadow larks, grasshoppers, and frogs included. This pup, I quickly concluded, had the makings of a *real* bird dog.

Sam was a Brittany, and the dogs in her pedigree came from outstanding field-trial bloodlines. Her ancestors included, among others, Dual Ch. Pacolet's Sam, Dual Ch. Albedo Valley Dingo, Dual Ch. Pacolet's Cheyenne Sam, Dual Ch. Pontac's Dingo, Dual Ch. Tex of Richmond...a virtual "Who's Who" in the world of Brittany field trialing.

On exactly her forty-ninth day of life, Sam drove with me to her new home. She was to become "Mei-Stylish Samantha," and I thought that I had made the perfect choice in both breed and breeding. What I did not yet realize was that, while that breeding practically assured me of a dog possessed of great hunting desire and point, it also practically assured me of one with great range—a dog that would run, and run big...and how she did.

In 1971, at about Sam's first birthday, I packed up my family and we moved from our home in northeastern Wisconsin to bird-rich central Iowa. It was a career move, but one motivated in no small part by tales of Iowa's vast numbers of wild roosters and thirty-bird coveys of quail. Up to this point, I'd never shot a wild rooster—only the "put and take" variety—and I'd never so much as seen a quail except in books. I was not disappointed in Iowa.

In the early 1970s, even the public hunting areas near Des Moines held an abund6ance of birds, and Sam and I went after them with a primitive passion. Being new to Iowa, I hunted *alone*—and I do mean alone. Straight out of the dog box, Sam would head for the distant horizon to hunt birds; I hunted Sam. Most often the only clue I'd have as to her whereabouts was the distant cackling of flighted pheasants with a flash of white and orange in hot pursuit—oblivious to the screams and whistles of her would-be handler—shades of Rusty! But there were other scenes too, those that kept me coming back. In those early days especially, finding Sam locked on a quivering point was an adrenalin rush of monumental proportions.

She hooked me, and made a bird hunter out of me. Though I was frequently frustrated by her extreme range and uncontrollable desire to find birds, she gave me special moments that bonded us in a way only another dog-owning bird hunter can understand. We became the best kind of friends—forgiving of each other's faults— and the more we hunted together, the more I began to realize that it wasn't killing birds that mattered; it was the pursuit, and that undefinable element of "being there," but more, being there with my dog, with Sam. It was she who had addicted me to bird hunting, not the guns or the birds, or killing them. I knew after that first full season in Iowa that if I had to choose between hunting without a gun or hunting without my dog, the gun would lose, hands down, every time.

Sam was a big, old-school Brittany, with just enough of a mean streak in her to be a great watchdog. She didn't like kids, or people in general. Her world revolved around me. She slept at the foot of our bed and every night, right after I settled in, she'd walk over to my side and push her head under my hand. She had taught me that this action meant I was to scratch her head and ears, and it was she who would determine for how long. Some nights she might allow me this privilege for as long as two or three minutes before she'd pull away and retreat to the foot of the bed. Other nights, the scratching might last only twenty or thirty seconds—an obligatory scratch, if you will, because she needed to be consistent in her training of me. And she was; so far as I can remember, there was not a single night she did not initiate this ritual.

During our second year in Iowa, a new element was added to our now-favorite pastime—neighbor Norm Beattie was to become my close friend and constant hunting companion. Though dogless, he shared my enthusiasm for bird hunting, and he demonstrated his friendship in a profound way—in that he never, in a dozen years of hunting together, criticized my dogs. Such friends are hard to find.

We hunted often, and hard; we were intense students of the sport, becoming very good at what we did, and in Sam we had an efficient bird-finding machine.

Others will argue in favor of their dog, but I doubt the world has ever seen a dog that lived to hunt as much as Sam. When we'd turn off pavement onto gravel or dirt roads, she knew we were close to where we were going to hunt and she'd begin to claw at her crate and whine and howl, almost hysterically. There was nothing we could do to quiet her until at last we stopped and turned her loose.

There was nothing dainty or delicate about Sam. She barreled recklessly into the brushy draws of the farms we hunted, oblivious to multiflora rose and the piercing thorns of honey locust. It was rare that she wasn't bleeding from one place or another, or that something wasn't sticking in or out of her.

A Saturday morning in the mid-1970s found Norm, Sam, and me just north of the Missouri border on a day we shouldn't have been there. Though skies were bright, the real temperature was near zero and the wind chill was twenty below. I know better than to hunt quail on days like that now. On sub-zero days, quail need the warmth of a covey to survive. If a covey is busted by a predator— or a foolish hunter—the scattered singles may die of exposure before they can covey back up.

We hunted a few favorite draws without moving a bird. What had been slush the day before had fast-frozen into sharp and jagged ice floes that caused us to slip and Sam's pads to tear. Neither Norm nor I wanted to admit to each other how much we wanted to quit, while Sam seemed immune to the cold and was unrelenting in her search for birds. Blood from her pads splattered her underbelly and froze around her paws until it looked like she wore four red socks.

Norm and I seized Sam's bloody condition as our excuse to quit. We nearly raced back to my Bronco, loaded Sam into her crate, and turned the heater on full-blast—then lied to each other about how bad we felt about quitting as we jockeyed with the vents to send more heat our way.

Warm, welcome heat flowed into the Bronco as we pulled out of the farmyard onto gravel and headed home. We hadn't gone a quarter of a mile when, as luck would have it, Norm spotted a huge covey hunkered in a ditch beside the road. We drove 100 or 150 yards past it, stopped, got out, and quickly uncased and loaded guns. "There's no need for Sam," I told Norm, "her pads are too torn up—she's bleeding too bad—we can do this dogless."

That was my idea; Sam had others. As Norm and I started cautiously back in the direction of the birds, Sam began to howl and scratch at her crate like a wild animal caged for the very first time. She knew we'd spotted birds and she was having none of this stay-behind-and-wait-in-the-truck business.

Norm and I had already traveled thirty or forty yards down the road toward the tight-sitting covey before we concluded that we were kidding ourselves to think that Sam would let us do this alone. We knew from her desperate howls that she might kill herself, or at least do serious damage, if we didn't let her out and let her come along.

We hurried back to the truck and, after we opened her crate, she hit the ground with all four bloody feet flying. She'd waited long enough; now, there was no waiting for me and Norm. Full tilt and flat out, she made a perfect beeline in the direction of the unseen covey.

When she hit scent twenty yards from the birds, she was going too fast to do much about it. She tried to put on the brakes, but when she did, her legs slipped out from under her and she skidded on her side a half-dozen feet to the road edge, rolled once, and righted herself into a magnificent point. She stood like a statue with her head high and one leg up, blood forming a pool beneath it. It was an awesome sight!

By now the covey was understandably unnerved, and the thirty or more birds flushed just before Norm and I got into shooting range. Perhaps because of the extreme cold—and unlike a typical southern Iowa covey rise—the birds held tight together and sailed downhill, with us watching the entire flight, landing in a field of knee-high grasses. It was a quail hunter's dream come true; we knew exactly where they had landed.

We collared Sam, sat down, and waited. We knew where the birds were, but they were air-washed and we were looking for shots over points, so we waited for them to settle in, move a little, and give off some scent.

During the ten to fifteen minutes we strained to hold ourselves back, the blood flow from Sam's pads increased, and when we finally turned her loose, her red socks had turned to red britches. She was orange and white on top and red on the bottom, and in this quail shooter's eyes, beautiful, as she slashed downhill and through that grassy field, pointing one bird after another.

During the next half-hour, Norm and I took four birds each over points and missed as many, maybe a few more. It was below zero, but it might have been sixty degrees for all we knew. Sam pointed and held and retrieved, and pointed and held and retrieved, and kept doing it. Norm and I were imperfect that day; we shouldn't even have been there, but Sam was flawless, and of such hunts— though marred by our fallibility—are memories made.

◆

On July 15, 1974, I bred Sam to one of the winningest field trial Brittanys in the Midwest, Field Champion DeMadison King, owned by Walt Chapman of Des Moines, Iowa. Eight beautiful pups arrived sixty-three days later and I named the tailless bitch I kept "Lucky." She was not nearly as bold or aggressive as her mom— much more a lady, quieter, easier to train, more biddable. And while I admired the orneriness and aggressiveness of Sam, I knew I had something very special in Lucky. She was a lover, not a fighter, but she would have fought to the death for me, and she was a certain hunt- ress, with the blood of generations of bird-finders cours- ing through her veins.

Lucky was loyal, both to me and to Sam, her mom. She was literally a trailer, following Sam wherever she went. She was most often the dog backing, seldom the dog on point, but it didn't matter to her—she accepted her role as second-string quarterback unquestioningly. Sam was the boss, period. And, this was true in our home—which they usually had the run of—in the kennel, in the yard, and in the field when we were hunting.

But while Sam was the leader of this two-dog pack, my allegiance slowly began to shift in Lucky's direction. Sam was my first real dog, to be sure, and nothing could ever change that. She was also a better bird-finder, had more desire, more stamina, better style, and more heart. But because of her enormous desire, Sam tended to self-hunt, not hunt for me. When I hunted Lucky with Sam, Lucky ran with Sam, but as I began to hunt her more and more often alone, she gradually developed into a very comfortable, medium-range shooting dog; hunting for me, not just with me or for herself.

As the years passed, the bond between me and both dogs grew. Each was special to me in her own way. And, as my knowledge of bird dogs increased, and I came to more fully understand the role of a class bird dog, I was finally able to appreciate Sam's range and desire. Seeing her cutting an edge a half mile to the front no longer bothered me, but instead, brought a smile, and even goose bumps.

While I admired Sam's special qualities and loved to watch her bust the horizons of the pheasant and quail country we hunted in central and southern Iowa, I turned to Lucky when I needed a reliable and steady shooting dog. It was she alone who went with Norm and me to our grouse and woodcock coverts in northeast Iowa; she who shared a sleeping bag with me on one particularly cold night in Yellow River State Forest when it was still primitive. The real temperature dropped to ten below that night, and the only heat we had in our tent was a Coleman lantern.

The next day the temperature rose to an almost-warm twenty above; the sun was shining and the skies were blue, as Norm, Lucky, and I strolled beautiful snow-covered logging roads through a soundless woodland.

That morning we experienced a sight most grouse gunners have read about, but only the fortunate have experienced. The night before—to escape from the bitter cold—a grouse had burrowed deep into the soft snow in the middle of the trail that now lay before us. I'll always remember the fantastic explosion of white as the grouse blasted out not a dozen feet in front of us, scaring two grown men and a now-experienced bird dog half to death.

He went my way, and I recovered from the shock of his exit just in time to shoulder a little 20-gauge, punch the trigger, and watch the bird fold. Lucky made a fine retrieve across the glistening white landscape, and the three of us sat for a long time, wishing we had it all to do over again.

◆

I live today with many memories of days afield with those two dogs, almost all good memories, because—as it should be—the bad ones have faded into obscurity.

Sam and Lucky were my constant companions, not just during the bird season, but all year long. They were well-trained and listened to me, and that, in part, is why it's so very hard to explain what happened to them.

In early 1980, we lived in a home well out in the country, at the end of a nearly mile-long gravel road. There was a lot of wildlife in the area, including deer. A fateful February afternoon Barb returned home from taking both dogs to the vet. She opened the station wagon doors and released them each from their crates. The slamming of the tailgate spooked a doe standing at the edge of the woods not far away, and both dogs took off in reckless pursuit, Lucky on Sam's heels, as usual. They didn't come back that night.

This dilemma was complicated by that fact that I was scheduled to go out of town on business the next day and Barb was going with me. This meant no one would be around our home when and if the dogs came back. It was impossible to cancel the trip, so I did the only thing I could do—I notified the closest neighbors, our vet, and the local sheriff's department, asking all of them to keep an eye out for the dogs while we were gone. Of course, we never had any way of knowing whether they returned to the house or not during the three days and two nights that we were gone. I strongly suspect they did, and had we been there, I believe this story would have a different ending.

I searched hard for the dogs after we got back from our trip, spending many anxious hours driving what seemed like hundreds of miles on the county trunks and gravel roads around our home. I had everyone I knew looking, and I posted notices in the convenience stores and gas stations in the area.

At midnight, eight days after their disappearance, the phone rang. It was the voice of a young man.

"Sir, on my way home from work tonight I spotted a dead dog lying on the side of the road. It was an orange and white dog. I took its collar off; I have it with me, and it has your name and number on it."

Barb was watching me, hoping the call was good news. She knew it wasn't as I fought to respond to the caller through the growing lump in my throat.

"The dog's name is on the collar," I said, "Tell me what it is, please."

"Sam."

I swallowed hard as my lips tightened and eyes glazed. Barb looked at me and asked in a whisper, "Which one?"

"Sam is dead," I answered. She lowered her head and left the room so I wouldn't see her tears.

The caller was patient and understanding, and waited through a long and awkward pause for my next question. "I lost two dogs," I finally continued, "did you see another one in the area?"

"No."

Knowing that I had lost Sam was heartbreaking, but now finding Lucky took precedence over all else.

"How do I get to your house? I'd like to have the collar back, I want to pick up my dog to bring her back here to bury her, and I have to look for my other dog."

"Come to my house first; I'll give you the collar and I'll sketch out a map that will show you how to find your dog."

He gave me his address, which was in a small town a few miles from where the dogs had run off. When I got there he was courteous and sympathetic, gave me the collar and the map, and assured me again that he'd seen only one dog.

As I drove alone to the spot on the map—a desolate stretch of a county trunk—a horribly strange mixed emotion tormented me. I was in a hurry to get there because I wanted to find Lucky, but at the same time I dreaded getting there, because I knew I'd find Sam.

The outer glow of the headlights fell on her, and I eased the car onto the shoulder of the road. And then I saw the other form—not ten feet away. To my horror, there was not one dead dog, but two. I couldn't move; I just sat there—stunned, motionless—with my mouth open and my eyes fixed in a helpless glaze.

I wondered at first how the caller could have missed two dogs that close together, but then, when I finally approached Lucky and touched her lifeless form, the awful suspicion that had raced through my numbing mind was confirmed: She was still warm, and the blood that trickled from her nose and mouth was still moist; Lucky had been hit only a short time before I got there. I sat on the cold road surface, with Lucky cradled in my arms, and cried.

I will never know, this side of eternity, what happened that terribly sad night, but knowing both dogs as I did, I can speculate. Sam was probably killed early on, perhaps the first night or two; otherwise, she would have come home. I suspect Lucky, because of her fierce loyalty to

Sam, refused to leave her body—staying instead for those many days and nights to guard it from the monster cars and trucks that infrequently roared past. I see her to this day, in my mind's eye, spending the endless hours standing vigilantly at her mom's side, boldly and protectively, yet scared, and surely confused. Sam had always been there with her, every day of her life. How could Lucky understand the cold stare in the old dog's eyes and the unresponsiveness of death?

When the caller drove by, perhaps Lucky was off foraging for food, or perhaps she was hunkered in a nearby ditch. If only I had traveled that stretch of road during the hours I searched, if only the caller had spotted her a day earlier—an hour earlier. If only...

◆

No, it was not a particularly good day—that cold, February morning in 1980—to bury a dog...or two. But I know now, a dozen plus years later, that I buried them in the right place. I learned of it from Ben Hur Lampman and his famous essay, "Where to Bury a Dog." After considering numerous plausible burial sites, Lampman sagely concludes that there is but one best place to bury a dog, and that is in the heart of its master.

There now reside Sam and Lucky.

As George Bird Evans wrote in *The Bird Dog Book*, "The death of a dog is the price of a priceless experience, having had them."

And so it was.

Charles F. Waterman says he quit honest work shortly after World War II and has been a freelance outdoor writer for nearly fifty years. Before that war he was a newspaper writer and photographer and during it he skippered a Steichen combat photo team with the Navy in the Pacific. He was raised on a Kansas farm, wrote his first outdoor column in 1934, and has written seventeen hunting and fishing books, some of which, he says, disappeared without a ripple. His two latest releases, Gun Dogs & Bird Guns *and* Field Days, *were published in 1995 by Countrysport Press. He says that at one point when he and his wife, Debie, were faced with starvation he taught literature for a year at Stetson University. Their home is in Florida but for more than thirty years they have spent summer and part of the fall in Montana.*

POINTING WEST

by Charles F. Waterman

These western pointing dogs generally have a special look, as if they know things ordinary field trial champions and woodcock wizards haven't heard of. It is a secretive, conniving look that comes from listening for the soft cackle of chukars from distant rimrock and catching the rising scent of sage hens from far down the deep draws, with pronghorns watching from the ridges.

The man at the door had a sleek little pointer under his arm and she did not have the Wild West look. She was confused.

"This is a wonderful little dog," he said. "She came from back East and she has great papers, but she won't point Huns or sharptails and she looks funny when they fly."

I know all about that business.

"Just give her time," I said. "Come in and have some coffee."

The little pointer performed well before the Hun season was over, and for years she ran the canyon edges for chukars, grinned craftily at the aspen patches where the ruffed grouse lived, and watched the flight of wild-flushing western pheasants she hoped to catch up to when they had found a tight coulee. But I had made an educated guess. Not all pointing dogs can adapt to enormous stubble fields and the brush-choked foothill creek bottoms. For that matter, there are prosperous corporation lawyers who might not excel in defending the winner of a barroom fight.

I have a special qualification in the western dog business, even though I am a poor dog trainer and gave away a big-time field trial winner because I couldn't see his potential. My qualification is that in a goofy, self-imposed project I once shot all of the species of pointable North American upland birds over a single Brittany named Kelly. Although he was never really steady to wing and shot, he came through the list with a superior attitude toward other dogs and the aforementioned conniving look when the dog box opened. Now the project took no particular skill on my part, but I have found that mentioning it in the beginning of any dog tirade such as this gives me a protective pad of authenticity. My friends—and possibly my few scattered readers—are sick and tired of hearing of it. But some dog experts have never shot ptarmigan on Alaska's Donnelly's Dome or Mearns quail on the Mexican border. See?

There are western traditions concerning horses, hats, and boots, but somehow the list of upland birds has been left out, possibly because prairie chickens seemed trivial when they lived near elk and grizzly bears. Only a few years back, it was hard to buy much of anything but duck and goose loads in the smaller sporting good stores and youngsters thought "Full Choke" was part of a shotgun's trade name. That was when Huns were "little chickens" or "quail" and the rancher said there were no real grouse (meaning blues) on the mountain, although there were some of those little "ruffled grouse" down in the creek bottoms.

But even then there were specialists like Mac (a Brittany named for the trout fly, Rat-faced MacDougall), who followed ruffed grouse pedestrians into the willows and thatched brush along ice-edged little trout streams. When the grouse fluttered up into low limbs to inspect and cluck at the strangely spotted coyote, Mac would climb the tree after it with gutteral canine profanity. If you could get down in there without breaking a leg you might get an impossible shot at the disgusted bird as it bored off through the branches.

A Pennsylvania grouse lover observed Mac's procedure with distaste and explained to me that it was a different species of bird from the king of eastern coverts. I agreed, saving his day, although ardent study of grouse biology had shown the birds in the deep-cut creek bottoms were clinically indistinguishable from their more refined relatives.

For years there was the Big Field—an enormous flat of wheatgrass, some three miles across and with the ever-present backdrop of a great mountain, generally white on top. It was many miles to the mountain but it seemed to begin at the edge of the field where it began to break into draws and benches. Perhaps the Big Field was a bench itself, as it seemed a part of the big mountain.

Below the field on the side opposite the mountain was a pattern of steep-sided sage brush draws, leading down to more flats and more draws that led down to creeks that fed a river miles away. When I first saw the Big Field I put a big rawboned English pointer down from the truck and watched her catch the wind and fly—for once with all the running room she wanted. For a moment I had the familiar helpless feeling of watching a dog seemingly out of control, but I watched her bend a cast more sharply and turn to a high-tailed point at the head of one of the sage arroyos.

I hurried and panted and muttered instructions that the dog could not possibly hear, and when I came alongside her, shaky and panting, the covey of sharptail grouse went up with their monotonal "cuk, cuk, cuk" to swing down the sage-lined arroyo. I atoned for a shaky miss to get one bird.

She was a young pointer then, and it was years later when she pointed her last birds at the head of the draw—Hungarian partridge that time. In other years she had found burly sage grouse there—a natural exit from sage to grass.

It must have been in places like the Big Field that big-going pointing dogs were developed. The pointer who found those first birds at the tip of the coulee rejoiced in those square miles of open grass and would be a streaking white speck so far away there was no place for the word "control." I and any companion I might have would trudge along with our eyes watering a little from strain and wind and watch the speeding speck with its backdrop of snowy mountain. Now I am sure we must have faced the other way much of the time but I always think of Duchess before the mountain. Her full name was Duchess of Doonesbury.

When the white speck stopped we took deep breaths and started toward her, walking at flank speed, and grumbling when we saw our white marker move again to stop once more, for birds of the wide open will walk and run, and only the right dog can follow them at the proper distance and keep them on the ground.

So when we came close to Dutch we'd come up alongside her, getting an impatient glance from an eye that moved slightly sidewise in an unmoving head, and we would walk forward with her as she cat-footed in starts and stops, altering direction slightly as the unseen birds changed course. It would be Huns, sharptails, or sage grouse, and when they finally flew I always wanted to shoot too soon, before I was really on. Such pointing tactics are not followed by trial winners but it was Dutch's field and she ran the show.

When Spike, the engaging, leggy Brittany, appeared in our kennel, he accepted Dutch as the Big Field autocrat that she was, and although he could cast almost as widely as she did, he willingly gave up his points to her. In other covers Dutch might be as polite as a self-centered sixty-two-pound barn burner could be, but when the dog box opened and she hit the ground in *her* field, lesser individuals were only assistants at best. If Spike found birds and pointed, Dutch might turn away as if assuming he had a meadowlark or, if the scent was strong, she would simply soft-foot ahead of him and assume her dramatic pointing stance, which implied the entire world was about to erupt in squawks and feathers.

Once, when a covey of Huns seemed to be zigzagging up ahead, Spike happened to maneuver so that he was nearest to them, a situation Dutch evidently considered the matter of a child doing an adult's work. In silence, except for the soft thumps of her feet on the ground and the whip of wheatgrass about her legs, she charged the unsuspecting Spike, striking him just back of the shoulders with her broad chest, and he was knocked into kicking impotence while Dutch assumed her postcard pointing stance. Instead of showing rage or surprise, Spike simply rolled to his feet, took a backing position, and appeared apologetic. Sorry about that.

When I recall sage grouse, I think of the giant world they live in, the occasional pickup trails that may once have been wagon trails, the coyote shadow I am not quite sure I saw, and the sky with wind-torn clouds the way Charlie Russell painted them. I think too of old Tex, the big-shouldered Brittany, who was never quite convinced that sage hens should be handled as other birds. I think Tex had given them considerable thought while catching shreds of scent at the heads of sage-filled coulees and believed that with the right approach an enterprising bird dog could catch one.

Tex, who had impeccable ancestry along with the paper name of Tip Top Texican, was simply a burly Brittany who overstepped the Brittany specifications a little when it came to fighting weight. Willing to do a perfect job of pointing a scattered covey of five-pound sage hens after soft-footing upwind for hundreds of yards, Tex felt that fulfilled his obligation to me. But after the first bird was in the air and I was groping for it with a shotgun, Tex would try to catch the rest. Sage grouse are often a bit scattered and there are numerous sleepers, each of which Tex would charge with abandon. I always thought he wanted to bark at them but felt it was beneath his dignity. He maintained more decorum with other plains birds and even did fairly well on ruffed grouse in late fall aspen patches.

I have heard that pointing dogs cannot work well in sage because it kills their scenting abilities, an observation on the same level as the report that gunpowder in their food makes them run faster. I once said that I felt a flock of sage hens probably put out roughly the same amount of scent as a battalion of infantry after a week's maneuvers. I love to see a canny old western campaigner catch the scent of sage hens, especially when he's at the high end of a draw and the air is rising. He quarters cautiously and gradually begins to narrow his beat until he begins to roll his eyes in anticipation and I check the location of the safety repeatedly and keep telling myself that if I get a couple of shots I should reload quickly for the sleepers.

But sometimes sage hens run. Well, maybe we should call it "power walking," as the physical education experts say. A sage grouse takes pretty big steps and there are times when it appears as a moving dark spot on a distant slope since it is the color of sage and only its dark shadow gives it away. A birdy dog once stuck to a long sage hen trail followed by my friend with a Model 12 Winchester and by me with a truck. The trail was a mile long and only one bird put up out of range. We knew it had been a covey but the other birds had peeled off and the dog had to make a choice. In that mile he had pointed many times but sensed his targets were moving on. I don't know how many decisions he had to make as his covey melted away on both sides.

But while field trial judges shake their heads and squirm in their saddles, it must be said that many of the Wild West birds do not play the game quite fairly, and although "Gentleman Bob" is a common term for bobwhite quail, I have never heard of a gentleman sage grouse. In dealing with such game it is necessary to abandon some of the procedures that work smoothly for birds that hold tightly and fly hard when you wave a thirty dollar flushing whip over them.

So some of the dog work becomes trailing and one visitor asked me why a pair of setters didn't bay like coon hounds since they seemed engaged in long-distance tracking. In truth, the point-and-move program is not classic but is pretty exciting stuff and at least once it ended very strangely. A male Brittany named Kelly was involved, called that simply because the name Murphy had already been put to use, and at the time I was sticking to Irish nomenclature.

Kelly caught the scent and went birdy high on a slope that plunged steeply downward into a little network of draws that carried wet-weather creeks. Kelly was a dramatist who could approach a single bird as if the world had momentarily stopped turning, and after viewing his histrionics for a hundred yards or so veteran gunners have been known to fire wildly into the air when the bird finally flew. In this case I followed him through scraggly sage bushes and past some barren erosions. Some of the dry cuts were several feet deep and only a yard or so wide. Bad washes, as ranchers say.

Finally, Kelly pointed and gave me his look that always said,"Man, they're here and you better be ready!"

So I limped forward, trying to keep my left foot ahead of my right, a very difficult bit of gymnastics, but I figured you could never be too ready, even for big birds that take gravity very seriously and don't get up to flank speed for the first thirty yards. No birds flew and I noted that one of those deep and narrow ditches was immediately ahead of me. In preparing to jump it, I looked down and noted a flock of sage hens wedged into the narrow bottom of the ditch and looking up at me with resignation. They had no room to spread their wings so they had no way to fly out of the ditch, and whoever was in charge of that bunch had really blown it.

Now I may be as bloodthirsty as the next shotgunner, but I am not an executioner and fair is fair, so I turned and walked away, dragging a disgusted Kelly with me. To this day, long since, I wish I had simply retired a few yards and watched all those sage turkeys climb out of that ditch. I wonder if they flew when they had climbed out or if they just walked away with their heads down. Kelly didn't hunt very well the rest of that afternoon and several times I found him watching me with a mixture of disapproval and pity. After all these years he had cornered a covey of birds I could catch with a landing net and I had walked away from them.

I am unhappy to see chukars behaving on game preserves like ordinary birds. Chukars are supposed to be up there where the sage thins out a little and there are long strips of rimrock and great flat boulders that once were rimrock and have crumbled down through the ages. In India, they use chukars as fighting cocks, domesticate them, and carry them around in wicker baskets, according to an authority on the subject. I don't like that either. I want wild chukars where they are hard to get at and I want chukar dogs who listen to their ventriloquistic calls and help me get above them so they'll fly when they're pointed.

I do not believe you train dogs to be chukar experts. It is something that grows in the backs of their scheming minds. Kelly, who regarded bobwhite whistles the same as he regarded meadowlark calls or distant auto horns, would prick his ears and roll his eyes at the first wisp of wind-blown cackle from up there somewhere in any one of the several chukar states. Chukar mountains are not tourist mountains. They are tired, ragged old mountains that go with desert and near-desert lands and often they are above valley quail and their relatives, who sometimes live in the creek bottoms. They have interfered badly with my quail hunting. I took my friend quail hunting, preparing him with glowing terms about Kelly's quail expertise. Let us put in here that you should beware of anyone who promises specific things from a dog. You are consorting with a fool.

It was a brushy Idaho creek and the quail lived there all right. We began moving upstream along the bottom and Kelly worked diligently. He pointed once and the birds moved on him, but the next time he held them and my friend killed a bird that skirted the heavy brush.

It was shortly after that when Kelly stopped on the high side of the creek brush, stood stock still for several seconds, and cocked his head toward the steep slope with its scattered boulders, cheat grass, and shabby little sage bushes. It was not long after that when I could no longer hear his bell and I told my friend to get ready because we had birds ahead. We found nothing and I apprehensively forced myself to stare up the mountainside. Far up there was a little brindle spot moving cautiously among the boulders.

And then I caught a problem sound, coming with a little twist of breeze. It was the chukars' muted cackle from up where Kelly was moving. I got up there and brought him back to the quail hunt, but after he was out of sight ahead of us he went back to the mountain. Once a chukar dog, always a chukar dog. Kelly could not understand why we fooled with the quail. My friend suggested we go in. He said chasing chukars was too much work.

Mike was apparently the result of philandering by a male setter and a Brittany dam, and it is a little vague as to how we came to acquire him. My associate in bird dog matters was always reluctant to compliment "Iron Mike" on his hunting qualities but often said old Mike could whip anything short of a pit bull. This came from an early career as an alley dog and garbage barrel connoisseur, which occurred before we recognized Mike for his sterling stubble-field qualities and attached him to our little string. Mike could find Huns in stubble fields, and the bigger the stubble field the greater his enthusiasm. He'd hold them until dark.

But Mike had never hunted chukars and his hard driving style seemed like a natural so I took him to Nevada, where I heard chukars calling along a great strip of rimrock, high above a valley jeep trail. It was a long way up but there were a lot of chukars so I started climbing, forcibly holding Mike alongside as much as possible. It was much later that I reached the rimrock objective, loaded my scarred chukar gun, and mentioned to Mike that he could go on and hunt.

It developed that Mike felt chukars were to be caught and not pointed so he ran up a quarter mile of them. I saw them as specks that shot out from the rocks and dived into the valley. Then Mike came back, grinning and lolling his tongue, and evidently feeling he had accomplished the mission. He spent the rest of his chukar career in a dog box.

If the sage hen presents a scent that fills a brushy coulee, the Mearns quail is the opposite, and there was the Mearns veteran who told me to sniff a Gambel's quail and then a Mearns. It's true that with my nose an inch from the Gambel's I really could smell something but I smelled nothing when I tried the Mearns bird—an explanation of why good Mearns dogs often perform as if hunting mice.

I took old hard-charging Dutch to Arizona Mearns country on the Mexican border and put her in perfect cover— little draws that sloped up from a really wide one, and there were the scrub oaks that have been everywhere I've seen Mearns quail. She found birds, her broad snout inches from the ground and her eyes big with the realization she was almost on top of game. I was sure then that my adaptable old friend was a super Mearns dog but an hour later Dutch decided this close-order drill was foolishness and started chasing quail. I took her back to her beloved Huns, sharptails, prairie chicken, and sage grouse.

Let me tell you some time about bird dogs and ptarmigan.

John Holt lives in Whitefish, Montana, and writes regularly for publications that include Fly Fisherman, Men's Journal, Big Sky Journal, and The Denver Post. He has a number of books in print including Chasing Fish Tales: A Freewheeling Year in the Life of an Angler *(Countrysport, 1993) and* Kicking Up Trouble—Upland Bird Hunting In The West *(Wilderness Adventures, 1994). Holt can be found fishing anywhere or bird hunting with good friends in the middle of nowhere.*

SOYBEAN, PHEASANTS, AND CRAWLING GORDONS

by John Holt

"The Damn Dog is on his knees again."

There was not much to see, just the black-and-tan wriggling rear end of the creature as he burrowed into a thick tangle of dried soybean stems, vines, leaves, and dead flowers. The Gordon was soon out of sight but we knew where he was. The slight undulations and quiverings of the cover, like a mouse cruising beneath soft, powdery snow in January, was a dead giveaway.

Early October anywhere is a fine time. This is especially so in southern Wisconsin. The muted golden, often crystalline light cast a surreal glow on the countryside. The gray of the soybean field seemed illuminated from within. So did the nearby fields of corn stubble. The overgrown drainage ditches that ran with the merest suggestion of an agrarian master plan also resonated to their own soft intensity. The land had gone electric in a gentle way.

Losing sight of the dog, Toby, was common for us by now. Trudging and pushing through the thick growth took effort and concentration. We were several days into a promising season. A routine was casually established. The dog was happy with his work and we were already sweating, only fifteen minutes along so far. We had not covered much ground and were some distance from late season conditioning. Our old farmhouse and ragged out-buildings were still visible on the oak-covered rise behind us.

The brush ahead was silent.

"Toby. Toby. Dammit where are you," my friend yelled. He loved dogs but hated whistles. They sound like Rush Street during rush hour he always groused. Still no dog. "Toby."

Then thirty feet ahead of us the brush began to bulge and grow towards the sky. Branches popped and cracked. I caught sight of a tail, an ear, perhaps a two-toned flank. Then madness, the kind that draws us out here to begin with, flashed full force in our faces. A cock pheasant blew straight up into the air in a riot of colors—emeralds, scarlets, browns, whites—wing beats, cackles. Toby was right behind the bird. Though moving quickly, the setter was a still life, sparkling eyes clearly focused on the game at hand.

This was not a flush, it was a full-tilt explosion.

The pheasant was maybe seven, eight feet high and starting to beat down and away from us. Then it crumpled to the ground.

"Christ, Holt, I didn't even get my gun up."

I do not remember anything about shooting the bird except for the vision of all that feathered color falling to earth. I'll never forget that or the sight of that wonderful Gordon setter sounding from the depths of the matted soybean world.

"Meyer. How are we ever going to find the bird."

"Hell, I can't even find the damn dog again."

We looked at each other and laughed. This was the Age of Aquarius. Why should bird hunting make any more sense than anything else, including that sophomoric musical? The media was still trying to explain Woodstock, Jefferson Airplane, communes, and Oaxacan pot. We were trying to stay sane amid the psychedelic confusion and the not so far-off terror of Vietnam. My number in the draft lottery was seventy-seven. My friend's was just over one hundred. A couple of my friends had already been blown away over there. One came home maimed only to discover his wife long gone with a buddy of his. This could well be our last autumn together. We did not know what was waiting for us. The uncertainty and fear lent an intensity to the days in the field.

After a few seconds, Toby appeared from nowhere almost riding on top of the choking growth. In his mouth was the limp pheasant. Even with the life gone from them, ringnecks are spectacular sights. The setter brought the bird to my friend and dropped it with a barely audible thump at his feet. Meyer picked it up, held it to the light, and then tossed the pheasant my way. Still warm and feeling heavy, a bit of blood curled from the bird's beak. I wiped it away, licking the residue from my forefinger. Slight taste of salt-copper. The sun was still shining, but the air was slightly cool on my face.

Toby glided over, totally at ease with the cover now. He looked at the pheasant and then at me and he was laughing, too. "We're living now, boss," he seemed to say. I was already addicted to fly fishing so spring and summer were shot for productive activities. I had always enjoyed birds, and now thanks to a fine dog it appeared that I was about to lose my autumns to upland shooting. In an uncommon flash of insight I realized, but not with alarm, that making a living was going to be a sporting proposition.

Meyer and I rented the farmhouse somewhat west of a factory town called Beloit above the Wisconsin-Illinois line. The farmer still worked the 640 acres, rotating between corn, beans, and resting land. The farm was remote, perfect for a couple of clowns who liked loud music, whiskey, and a bit of nighttime gunfire. There was no one for miles and we were easily amused. This was not a gig grounded in responsibility. Meyer had already graduated from Ripon College and was working for the Milwaukee Railroad. I watched Toby, or he watched me, while my friend rode the rails. I was going to Beloit College studying creative writing and little else.

I don't think anyone would have considered us productive members of society. Not the types you invite to polite functions. That was fine with us. We were happy sitting around the farmhouse kitchen sipping whiskey from a couple of beer glasses that had found their way home from the Turtle Tap. A well-worn MEC reloader was bolted to a formica-topped table. Reloaded 12-gauge shells were stacked and scattered about in prodigious numbers. If the revolution was coming, and the Beatles said it was, we were ready.

Actually our objectives were more conventional. In addition to hunting the fields four or five times a week, we also staged regular live-pigeon shoots. The decrepit barn still held countless bales of old straw. Nearby rusty bins were filled to overflowing with tons of field-dried corn. Word about this accessible grain spread to better pigeon circles in the Beloit area. There were hundreds of the gray birds perched in the barn. Our farmer hated the damage they wreaked on his corn, which he fed to beef cattle on another operation he owned down the road. We were encouraged to cull the pigeon flock to the extent that powder, shot, plastic wads, primers, and occasionally wrapped chunks of prime beef appeared regularly on our crumbling cement doorstep.

The farm was a wondrous thing to behold when pulling into the yard late at night in Meyer's old but highly polished black Eldorado after another evening unsuccessfully trying to pick up girls in Beloit. Meyer was over seven feet tall. I was over six. The farm had a reputation for gunfire. We usually drove home alone.

The three of us would head out to the barn, normally in the early afternoon. A dysfunctional silo—metaphor everywhere we looked it seemed—opened into the barn. We had sealed all openings between the barn and the silo and hammered boards over the most obvious openings in the barn. In other words, the only easy way out of the structure during moments of avian panic was through a wide opening in the silo's metal cap.

One of us would work his way to the upper level of the barn and begin raising hell. The flappings of seriously upset birds would soon build to a tumultuous uproar. Then the pigeons would go crazy and take flight. A steady stream of them would burst from the silo—our own personal high tower. We'd shoot forever, trading places every so often. Toby truly enjoyed himself retrieving the fallen birds and dropping them into what quickly became an impressive pile. The setter went crazy whenever we grabbed our guns, whenever we started shooting. His square snout would work the air, sucking in deep draughts of air perfumed with gunsmoke. He was one of us. Meyer and I knew that there was top-notch bird dog lurking just below the surface in Toby. Time would prove the acuity of our assessment.

We breasted a number of the pigeons, sauteing them in butter, garlic, and white wine. But even Toby grew tired of the meat after a while. We turned to other methods of disposal. They loved our weekly pigeon drops at the county dump.

"You boys ever do anythin' sides blast dem pigeons?"

"Do you think we should?"

"Naw. You two look to be stretched pretty tight already."

And life rolled on toward somewhere.

We never tired of this sport and actually became fair shooters. The farmer was grateful. But if there is a hell, I'm sure there will be pigeons waiting for me. I hope Meyer can make the trip.

That is what I meant about not remembering the shot that dropped the pheasant. The hunting by this time was instinctive. The 870 came up only slightly behind the flush, quickly making up the disparity; most of the time the bird crumpled. The stalking and anticipation, especially with Toby digging through the soybeans or traversing the corn stubble, was always keen. The shooting became predatory and that developed into its own type of satisfaction. The same pleasure exists when I fish for weeks on end. The mind instantly measures the water and the cast needed, and the body executes the commands with dispatch. The sight of a wild brown trout hammering an Elk Hair caddis is the rush, like watching the pheasant tumble from the sky.

◆

Meyer took a lot of grief from his father, a confirmed golden Lab man, after he drove out to a farm near Madison and picked up the Gordon puppy one spring day.

"The breed is too slow."

"You can't teach them anything. All they ever do is follow their nose."

"Nobody hunts with them anymore."

"You'll never see the dog with all that black coat."

And on and on.

Meyer was not fazed. This was the kind of dog he wanted and now he had one. The first autumn, before we had the farm, most of our hunting was spent with Meyer yelling "Toby, god-dammit. Come back here. Dammit." And we'd watch the setter romp to his heart's content, pheasants flying everywhere, well out of range. We spent hours working with the eager dog who never seemed to tire of a game that he instinctively understood on a level far more basic than we did. His enthusiasm and willingness to please taught me a good deal about bird hunting. Toby would never "knock 'em dead" at a trial, but then neither Meyer nor I would ever make an Olympic shooting team. None of this mattered to the dog or to us, really. Toby led the way down the meandering path of that freeform autumn, a time where we became friends as one, sharing moments in the field beyond words. The sight of that Gordon charging about the thick cover, tail wagging, coat shining in subdued light was glorious. Even without all of the pheasants, we would have been satisfied.

Then one day Meyer came in from the field, flushed, wired. Something had changed. You could see it in his eyes.

"Holt, I told ya Toby'd catch on. Just needed time. He works right in front now. Perfect pace. Back and forth. Thorough. Tomorrow you'll see."

And I did. We hunted the land surrounding the farm. Toby stayed in tight picking up the scent that drifted on complicated seams of air. Or he exhibited that first embryonic down-on-his-knees, whatever-it-takes-to-move-the-bird intensity. He moved steadily with an air of confidence and he kicked up birds. We each shot our limit and the dog retrieved them without a hitch.

"Meyer. This ain't the same dog."

"Tell me something new. All the yelling. Maybe he even learned from watching me pick up so many pheasants. I haven't a clue. It's just there. Holto, I got a bird dog."

Meyer always called me Holto when he was pleased with himself and he was grinning brightly right now. It was a fine sight that still makes me laugh a little whenever I recall the moment. This is not to say that Toby had miraculously turned perfect. None of us ever do, and there were days when that dog would romp so far off in the field that we thought about filing a missing persons report. But for all of this, he had pretty much turned abruptly into an excellent bird dog. There were even times when he would come to point, a difficult task on the springy carpet of dead bean vines. The pheasants knew they were safe holding down deep in the cover. Eventually Toby would forsake the purity of his breed and dive into the brush in a pell-mell maelstrom of paws, legs, and vibrating tail. Soon enough the colorful birds would explode once again from the sere tangle with Toby close behind. Anticipating where the pheasants and that wild dog would surface was exciting sport.

We were in heaven, the three of us, and even Meyer's dad admitted, barely, that Toby had turned out to be a good dog in the field. We had things made. Meyer made good money from the railroad; I brought in enough from a bartending job. Toby had the land to roam and all those birds to chase. Life was sweet that fall.

We hunted almost every day of the season. The land was rich, filled with birds. There were so many hens that a couple of hundred cocks would be needed to handle the procreational responsibilities. Or so it seemed. A biologist told Meyer that the fields of soybeans were a magnet for pheasants throughout the valley. Trying to estimate populations was futile. Unrealistic. Unnecessary. The fact that we had all of these birds was sufficient. For every male flushed, a dozen females broke cover, bursting quickly in small brown-gray groups that cackled and squawked in demure imitation of their flashier companions. At first Toby could not understand why we did not shoot the hens. After all, to a dog's nose a pheasant is a pheasant. But he soon learned, though I am convinced that on those rare afternoons when cocks were rare finds, Toby would have liked one of us to drop a hen. I know how he felt.

Regardless, that autumn at the farm was, by a long shot, the best season of bird hunting I've ever experienced. Meyer moved to Washington and I moved to Montana. Toby is, of course, long gone.

◆

A couple of decades and some bar change have passed by since those intense times. Still, while walking the nearly unimaginable openness of central Montana hunting sharptails or working a ridge chasing blues, those days on that Wisconsin farm come to mind. Particularly the one where Toby first crawled after a bird and showed me what his kind of dog was about.

After that first bursting shot, the outing was filled with hens that I swung through but never shot and several more brightly colored cocks that Meyer and I did shoot. The sun moved into a western bank of clouds. We decided to head back up hill to the warm kitchen.

"Holto, we've still got a virgin bottle of Jim Beam rye. You mix a few cocktails and we'll sip them like civilized folks while I fry up the birds in a little butter, some sage, a little brandy..."

"Right Meyer. You want yours in a mug or a tumbler."

"Don't forget the ice."

"One cube or two?"

We were nearing the yard and Toby had vanished. We pushed on in silence.

Twenty yards from the barn the cover tore apart and a cock broke free with Toby in pursuit. We both raised our guns. Neither of us fired a shot. Toby stopped. The three of us watched the pheasant flash downwind in the last golden light of sunset.

Dan O'Brien lives in the Black Hills of South Dakota with his wife, Kris, where they hunt birds with shotguns and falcons over pointing dogs. He has received awards for his writing, including the Iowa Short Fiction Award, Western Writer's Best First Novel Award, an honorary Ph.D. in literature, and two NEA Fellowships for fiction. His books are, Spirit of the Hills *and* Center of the Nation, *both novels,* The Rites of Autumn: A Falconer's Journey Across the American West, *non-fiction, and* Eminent Domain, *short stories.*

JAKE

by Dan O'Brien

Since my wife and I have been together there have been several dogs in our household and Kris has loved them all. When we first met, her attraction for dogs was indiscriminate, embracing schizophrenic Pomeranians as passionately as finely focused English pointers. This, I felt sure, had to do with the fact that she had never seen a dog doing what a dog does best, hunting. I'd like to think it was my influence that created in Kris an understanding and love for hunting dogs, what they do, and how they can enrich your life. But, in fact, I was only a minor player in Kris's discovery. The real credit goes to Jake, who knew her long before I was on the scene.

You see, Kris was raised in southern California. She'd never been hunting, never fired a gun, never seen a well-trained dog locate, point, or retrieve a bird. But despite this disadvantage she was naturally drawn to dogs. One of the first things that attracted me to her was the eighty-pound black Lab golden retriever cross that had been her companion through four years of medical school. One of the first serious things she ever said to me was that she wouldn't have made it through school if it hadn't been for Jake.

He was with her the whole way, bounced around from city to city, keeping her company when she was studying, and sometimes waiting inside sixteen hours at a stretch until she could get home to walk him. She went to school at Dartmouth and told me that some nights, when she got home, the combination of long hours and subzero temperatures conspired to depress her to the point of tears. But Jake was always there to greet her and they walked every night and that's what gave her the strength to get up the next morning and do it again. The fact that she had learned the restorative powers of a relationship with a dog made me know she was special. And the fact that Jake had been the one to teach her made him special too. They got me thinking that my dream of finding a woman who would enjoy life afield with me and a dog might not be completely farfetched.

◆

Jake got his looks from his Lab side. Except for slightly longer hair you'd have never known he wasn't pure Lab. He was one of those blocky dogs with a head like chiseled granite and had that gentle way of looking at you—like he felt vaguely sorry for you, being human and all. Like so many of the really good dogs, Jake seemed to know how he could best support the people with whom he lived. After Kris moved on to her internship and residency, where she had even less time, and I started hanging around, Jake shifted a portion of his allegiance to me. I'm sure he knew it was what Kris wanted and I was grateful to be included.

Kris was doing a two-year residency in Denver and I took to spending a lot of time there. I was used to sleeping alone and while sharing a bed with Kris was a welcome change, sharing a bed with Kris and Jake was not exactly what I had in mind. I remember coming face to face with Jake one of those first nights, when I pulled the covers back to get into bed, and thinking that I should throw him out. But he stared at me unflinchingly and I realized that this was not my call. I was the interloper here and was infringing on the unity of a serious, well-functioning team. I never saw anyone work as hard as Kris. Except for Jake, she had been alone in a seven-year battle to make something special of her life. Jake stayed on the bed.

I tried to understand what they had both been through. I found that Kris was gone a great deal, fourteen-hour days and on all-night call every third night. Jake and I were thrown together and it was good for both of us. Her house was on a busy street. The traffic was confining—something I was not used to. For good reason, Jake had seldom been off a leash and I seized this deprivation as an excuse for us to escape the city.

We began going on extended walks in more remote places than Jake was used to. Kris was a little protective of him—suggesting that he wouldn't eat dog food without cooking oil over it and that November water was too cold for him to retrieve sticks from. She made it sound a little like Jake preferred tofu to T-bones but after I started taking him to my home on a South Dakota ranch, inhabited by a new English setter puppy named Idaho Spud and an ancient basset hound named Morgan, I came to know something for sure about Jake that I had suspected all along.

Morgan had run rabbits every day since his retirement several years before. He was like an old demented pensioner returning to the office out of habit. He got up early, had a little drink of water, and usually struck a trail about seven thirty. He'd run rabbits until the heat of the day. Then he'd come into the barn for another drink and snooze until four o'clock when he'd go back at it for another couple hours. A little after dark he'd come in to eat and sleep, and it would start all over again about seven the next morning. He was slow and inefficient. But he took his work seriously and didn't pay much attention to this big, black city dog who stayed in the house. But I noticed that Jake watched Morgan from the kitchen window. I caught him several times studying the old timer as he snooped through the grown-over farm equipment, and it wasn't long before the big head stiffened and the black ears came up at the sound of Morgan's strike.

Jake was aloof when it came to my hunting dogs but he couldn't help keeping an eye on Spud as we went through yard training and limited recall quail work. This whole scene, with its cacophony of new smells, made him a little nervous and he disdained close contact with these dogs. But he was interested. When Kris came out to the ranch and made a fuss over these two ruffians, it threw Jake into a tailspin. It was about that time that Kris began to take an interest herself. In me, I suppose, but more in the elements of my life. She asked about the roading harness, the electronic collar, the dog boxes in the back of the pickup. She inspected the kennel, and though I knew she had a hard time understanding the reasoning behind this way of keeping dogs, she never made any judgments. She had seen Spud pointing a wing and was fascinated by the way this little moron puppy went so deadly serious over a game. She watched steady old Morgan going about his chores and began to see how important all this was to me.

After about the third visit she wondered if, the next time we went to the ranch, she couldn't try shooting a shotgun and I, of course, bent over backwards to comply. I planned to let her shoot my side-by-side twenty but my hired hand and comrade of twenty years shook his head. "That's a mistake," he said. "She won't hit anything and that little thing will kick her silly." When Kris arrived at the ranch for her first shooting lesson we had a brand new Remington 1100 12-gauge with a shortened stock and butt pad waiting for her. She broke the first three clay pigeons she ever saw.

But, before there was any shooting, we had to put Jake in the basement. Though he had never seen a gun before, he was shy of explosions. Apparently Fourth of July fireworks had rattled him. Kris told me every year he spent most of the Fourth trying to get under the refrigerator. I had a hard time believing it. With little Spud pistoning in his kennel and poor old blind Morgan limping out to investigate every dead clay pigeon, it was hard to imagine that a dog like Jake wouldn't be clambering to get in on the fun. But he sure wasn't.

Kris and I came into the house full of good thoughts about the possibility of Kris going pheasant hunting. The season was half over by then but there might be a way to do some late season hunting. She was delighted with the shotgun and the shooting. I was delighted that she was delighted. She even mentioned the idea that Jake might go with us on the pheasant hunt. I knew that notion made sense to her but I tried to gently discourage it. I restated my theory that house dogs don't make good bird dogs and bird dogs don't make good house dogs. She looked at me oddly and said simply that I underestimated dogs. I know now she spoke from a native understanding, but then, I suppose, I only smiled.

When we went down into the basement we found Jake quaking in a corner. It was a terrible sight and Kris was upset so I didn't say anything like "I told you so." When she put her arms around him and apologized for shooting I knew the plans for a pheasant hunt were in jeopardy. I felt my dream of having a woman to share my days in the field slipping away. But it was a dream worth dreaming and—theories be damned—I made myself a promise to fight for it.

Thank God Jake loved cheese more than he feared anything.

Kris was skeptical, but after Jake figured out that the sound of the cap gun wrapped in a towel meant cheddar, it wasn't long until the towel was discarded. Another week and you didn't want to be between him and the kitchen when the starter's pistol went off. Finally he'd come full bore across any field for a 12-gauge—and a quarter pound of gouda.

So I figured we at least had a chance. Dog over his gun shyness, new shotgun, first-time hunter, this had the potential to be fun. Kris was very excited about the possibility of bagging a few pheasants. She had recipes she wanted to try and the idea of Jake becoming a focused bird dog, though I downplayed it, thrilled her.

◆

But there was another catch. On a picnic, during a rare medical school break, when Jake was just a puppy, he had wandered off and been caught in a chicken coop, knee deep in fresh plucked chickens. Kris said it was the first time he had ever seen birds up close but the owner of the chickens was not in a forgiving mood and whacked Jake across the nose. "He hasn't shown much interest in birds since," Kris said.

She swore the punishment had only been one crisp thump across the muzzle so I assured her that there was no problem. Jake didn't mind gunfire now and he loved to retrieve. His natural instincts would take over and he'd do fine. That's what I told her. But I'd gotten to know Jake pretty well by then and knew he learned lessons for keeps. I was worried that his desire to do what people wanted him to do might very well extend to that New Hampshire farmer. In an attempt to avoid a bad day in the field, when we did finally take Jake out, I dug a Hungarian partridge out of the freezer—partridge caddis can be a hot trout fly in the Black Hills—and thawed it one morning when Kris was at work. That afternoon I went into the backyard where Jake and I normally played fetch with tennis balls and sticks.

He leaped and twisted with joy when I held the stick over his head but sat, trembling with anticipation, when I gave the command. I threw the stick twice and he pounded after it, delivering it to hand when I asked. The third time I surreptitiously substituted the partridge from my pocket for the stick and sent him off after it with an encouraging "fetch." He bore down on it like a goshawk but never laid a tooth on it. As soon as he recognized it as a bird he pulled up like it was a cow pie and trotted quickly back to my side. He looked up at me like I'd pulled the dirtiest trick in the book and I knew I had a problem.

But by this time Kris was counting on a pheasant hunt so I reassured Jake by putting my arm around him. But that didn't help much. The nervous look in his eye told me that I'd better quickly get him back into retrieving or I'd have an even bigger problem on my hands. I went back to the house for his favorite toy—a green Day-Glo Frisbee—and this snapped him out of his paranoia. He did the happy dog dance complete with leaps and yips and I sailed the Frisbee out for him to chase. He was a pro—a veteran of San Diego beaches and Ivy League campuses—and made a long graceful lunge, picking the Frisbee neatly out of midair. It dawned on me that this might be the key.

I found a roll of duct tape under the seat of my pickup and, out of Jake's sight, taped the partridge to the top of the Frisbee. Then, in my most affected, excited voice, I encouraged Jake in his own excitement. I held the Frisbee above him—with the partridge safely on top and out of sight—and he again leaped and yipped. And when I sent it wobbling out into the yard he charged after it as usual. But when he came close, he jumped back like he'd found a rattlesnake. Still, he knew the Frisbee was there and wanted badly to bring it back. He didn't return to my side but sat down looking at the problem. Finally he reached out and, with his lips curled delicately back, took the very edge of the Frisbee in his teeth and drug the whole works back to lay at my feet. Never did he, in any way, come in contact with a feather.

We had to start with a single tail feather taped to the Frisbee and work up through two feathers, one wing, two wings, and eventually a whole bird. But in a week he was over his dread of dead birds. It took another two weeks and a very tolerant pigeon to get him to put a moving feathered object into his mouth. But once he caught on, he was a natural. In no time, he was making seventy-five-yard blind retrieves and doing it with extreme enthusiasm.

◆

While all this was going on I was working with Spud, getting him ready for his first exposure to pheasants. I didn't expect much from such a pup but figured him to put a few birds up. I ran the two dogs together on a route that included several stock dams and, of course, Jake would dive headlong into each dam as we came to it. If it was a hot day, he'd swim around for five or ten minutes and Spud, who was still only a year old, got so he'd follow Jake right on in. To this day Spud is the swimmingest setter I've ever seen and I attribute that to Jake.

In a lot of ways Jake was Spud's hero during that first summer and fall of life, but I wondered what Spud would think of his idol if he failed to retrieve a shot bird or, worse yet, just stuck close to Kris and didn't hunt. Spud has always been a go-getting bird dog and I had no worries that he wouldn't hunt hard. His problem, if anything, would be overzealousness and that is a good kind of problem to have. Jake, on the other hand, might decide he didn't go for this rowdy life and quit. I was afraid that he might influence Kris to do the same.

In the days before our pheasant hunt I got worried that Jake and Kris would have a bad day. Experienced hunters know that bad days happen and that you should just forget them. If the dog screws up or you can't shoot well, put it behind you—things will be better next time. But a bad day could be fatal for a thirty-year-old with high expectations of hunting with her faithful old house dog—both for the first time. And I didn't want Kris's interest to die. I knew if it did, my life would veer from its ideal path and I'd find myself hunting mostly solo.

So the importance of the pheasant hunt began to take on cosmic proportions and by the time the day arrived I was a worried wreck, and Jake must have been getting tired of retrieving that same duct-taped pigeon—with one wing left loose to flap. I had done everything I could but still I was not confident. I worried about Jake drawing a tough old rooster with only a broken wing for his first retrieve, I worried about Kris's shooting, I worried that I wouldn't be able to resist kibitzing.

By the time everything was ready it was late in the season and the wild birds had been worked over pretty hard. In an effort to control some of the variables, I chose a hunting preserve owned by a friend as the venue for our outing. Twenty dollars a bird seemed awfully high but my friend guaranteed there would be birds out there, and I reasoned that the team I was bringing—Kris, Jake, Spud, and myself—was not exactly a well-oiled hunting machine that could run up a huge bill.

The day dawned gray and overcast and low, flat clouds threatened rain. It was not the kind of day I'd hoped for but the weather report was for clearing with a light, warm breeze. I offered up a little prayer to Orion as I loaded Spud into his dog box. Jake had had only a few lessons in kenneling into a dog box, but he loaded all right and we were on the road by eight o'clock.

Kris was nearing the end of her residency and we had begun to talk about what would happen the next year. There were job opportunities in California, Chicago, about any big city, but she didn't want to go there. She had come to like South Dakota and thought she liked the kinds of things we were doing that day. I looked at the sky as we pulled into my friend's shooting reserve. There was a faint streak of blue directly overhead, but the horizons were still caulk and snow was still not out of the question.

My friend pointed us down the road to a half section of thick brome grass and old weedy milo fields along the edge of standing corn. There was a marshy spot there too, and cattails grew thick below a large stock dam from which we could hear the sounds of geese and mallards. We unloaded near the standing corn but, when we started out, I pointed Spud in the other direction. I knew there would be birds in the corn and if he got in there all we'd see would be roosters spiraling up like distant missiles.

I carried a gun but wasn't out to shoot. I hoped Spud would find a few birds and maybe flash point one or two. What I was really there for was to see to it that Kris had a good time. But it started out poorly. A rooster jumped at her feet before we were thirty yards from the truck and she fired twice before the stock had even touched her shoulder. She probably fired fifteen feet over the bird. Jake didn't flinch at the shots but didn't pay much attention to the bird either. Spud chased it out of sight.

While we waited for the little imp to return—which he did in fifteen minutes with his tongue nearly dragging—I tried to keep Kris's mood light. She's a competitive person and was used to breaking clay pigeons. She was instantly mad at herself for missing—the beginner's mistake—and I was afraid it would affect her whole day. I seldom care if a bird comes to bag, but that day it seemed crucial. I laughed it off, "Everybody misses, forget it. Take your time. You got lots of time." And the more I talked the more I knew it was the wrong thing to do. I had to force myself to shut up. We waited in silence and Jake laid down at Kris's feet. When Spud finally returned, Jake got up and sniffed the huffing Spud as if to ask what the big deal was.

We set off again, walking along the edge of the cattails and the sky began to clear. The winter browns went rich with shadow and we both praised the changing weather. Suddenly it was pleasant just walking there with Kris. This was more like my dream. Spud was somewhere in the next county but I wasn't going to let that spoil the day. Jake had begun to potter ahead of us and it was possible he might stumble onto a pheasant. Kris and I were both beginning to stop trying so hard and enjoy the day when Spud angled in from somewhere and flushed a pheasant twenty-five yards to our left.

I didn't even pull up on it. It was out a good ways and one of those tough crossing shots. But Kris brought her gun up and poked a shot at it. I winced when I saw the gun barrel stop just before she shot. The bird was going forty miles an hour by then. She missed it by a mile. "You got to keep the gun moving," I said before I thought to say it diplomatically.

Kris frowned. "I don't know about this," she said. It was in the tone of voice I had dreaded for weeks and I felt a touch of panic. It was me. I was making her crazy.

"Look," I said. "Spud is running amok. I'm going to take him up in that brome grass where I can keep an eye on him. You take Jake and walk up to the dam, then back through the cattails. There should be birds in the cattails for sure."

I gathered Spud up and headed out. I figured the only chance was to leave her alone and hope the improving weather would work its magic. As I started uphill toward the brome bench I saw Jake watching me. He looked from me to Kris and back again. At the time I thought he was just confused about our splitting up. But now, I think he had sensed the tension in the air. I believe he was evaluating things—trying to understand what was at stake.

◆

The day won me over. As soon as I started to concentrate on Spud, everything mellowed. He was wearing down and I stayed on him until he was quartering in front of me fairly well. We worked up through the brome for a quarter mile and he bumped a pheasant. I whoaed him and got in to where I could praise him. After we made the turn and started back he hit another one and held it until I was in range. When it came up, I shot and killed Spud's first bird.

We celebrated with a good petting in the dry grass and for an instant I forgot about Kris and Jake. But when we got walking again, there was still a nagging feeling in the back of my head and when we came to where we could look down on the cattail slough I was holding my breath, hoping Kris and Jake were not back at the pickup.

They were still hunting the cattails and I resisted going down to join them. Spud and I sat down in the golden grass above them and watched. They didn't really know where to look for birds and they wandered to areas that seldom hold them. It was all I could do not to shout directions from my hill. But Jake was out front and quartering within range and they looked happy enough. I had Spud on a lead and we settled in to enjoy watching the woman I loved work her first cattail slough with her pet retriever. I was afraid it would look like Abbott and Costello on a hunt. But they didn't look too bad. Their demeanor had changed since I'd last seen them. They were concentrating on what they were doing yet casual and relaxed. Something magic had happened in my absence and I saw an ease in Kris's walk that I'd never seen before, but have seen a thousand times since.

They were certainly pushing birds in front of them and, the way they were working the slough, they might just run into a herd of them at the end where they'd have to fly or run across a dirt road. There was a particular corner of firebush that looked great and Jake was leading Kris right to it.

I sat up a little as they approached the firebush. It looked like Jake's gait picked up. His tail was ringing! He began to bounce and up came a bird. Bang—and it folded. I couldn't believe it. It was beautiful. Jake charged into the brush and brought the bird to Kris. I could hear her squeal with delight.

But Jake just spit it into her hand and dove back into the bush. Up came another pheasant. Bang. Another perfect retrieve. Back into the bushes. Two birds. Bang, bang! and Kris stopped to reload while Jake searched out the birds.

Then birds were coming up everywhere. Bang! Bang! Kris had two more down before the rocketing pheasants turned into twenty-dollar bills in my mind. I struggled to my feet. "Wait." But Jake was still working the brush and I hustled toward them with Spud straining at the leash.

When I got there, Kris had six birds lined up at her feet. The gun was empty and she was kneeling with her arms around a panting, very happy retriever. She beamed up at me and I beamed back.

For weeks afterward all she could talk about was how great the hunt had been. Winter set in with a vengeance then and we didn't get a chance to go hunting again that year. But she was hooked deep. We lived off that day for months and it became part of our history, part of what makes us what we are.

Old Morgan died not long after and, though you always take the death of a good dog hard, we knew it was his time and he'd lived a full life. The real shock came early that spring, just after Kris and I decided to make our desire to spend the rest of our lives together official. It was the spring of Kris's last year of residency and we planned to get married and live in South Dakota where the whole bunch of us could enjoy a little more freedom than most people are used to.

Jake had not seemed his old self for a couple days and we took him to the vet's for a checkup. The vet wanted to keep him overnight for some tests and we really didn't think too much of it. But early in the morning—it was a Sunday because Kris was home—he called to say that Jake had died. Kris was speechless and handed the phone to me.

I listened dumbfounded while this perfectly nice young vet tried to explain. He was terribly upset and obviously had no idea what had really happened. I listened to him rattle on, searching for the explanation he never found. The cause of death was unknown. But I knew why Jake was dead. It all fell into place for me that morning and the knowledge changed my life.

Jake died because his job was done. He'd seen Kris through medical school, her internship, and her residency—been there through some rough and lonely times. He'd brought her from a college girl to a woman aware of so much more. He led her through important stages of her life and he led her through that cattail slough and into that flock of pheasants. He'd eased her gently into a new, more vital life and he was counting on me to take it from there.

It was a terribly sad time in our lives and most of the day I held Kris, and rocked her, and tried my best to make her see what Jake had given her. But his gifts were not only for Kris. I've come to know that he gave a great deal to me too. He made a dream come true.

Now Kris and I gun for pheasant, and grouse and woodcock and quail and partridge. We do it with joy and reverence. And we do it with good birds dogs that live like Jake always did. Idaho Spud is older now and has been joined by Old Hemlock Melville who is learning the trade and promises to carry on a tradition. They both live in the house. They sleep on our bed with us, and some nights, when Spud is hard beside me and Mel is pressing against Kris and they are both rolling the blanket under them and shrink-wrapping Kris and me closer and closer, I think this is the way Jake wanted it all along. His big square head with the deep, dark eyes floats through my dreams. His wisdom haunts me.

Paul Carson is a former newspaper reporter and columnist who is now editor of RGS, the magazine of the Ruffed
Grouse Society. He learned to hunt behind hounds and still
believes the baying of a pack of blueticks on hot scent should be
considered classical music. But it took just one trip to a grouse
covert with an old English setter to make him a bird dog
convert. Ever since, flushers and pointers—some with only a
vague notion of how to hunt grouse—have been part of his
immediate family.

TWO TO REMEMBER

by Paul Carson

The Dog That Mourned

Hunting season is winding down for another year. To tell you the truth, I won't be sorry to see it go. Oh, I got a few birds, had some fun, communed with nature—all that stuff. But you know what was missing? Competition.

I know, I know, it's sacrilege to mention competition and hunting in the same breath. But I've got to call it what it was—the thrill and joy of being out there with the greatest competitor of them all, Ripthorn's Coverbuster.

Even now it's hard to believe that Rip was a joy. If you could dip back a dozen years to ask me what I thought of him then, I would have said, "He's a crybaby that will be the cause of me never showing my face around my former hunting buddies again."

Rip checked out just before the beginning of this past hunting season. Back in August, while the rest of us were wallowing along through a heat wave, he started ignoring the prevailing conditions. He began perking old ears and gazing expectantly at far horizons. I thought everything was going to be okay with him. He knew October was out there somewhere, and he was getting psyched for it.

His attitude was contagious, and I began to feel vibrations of excitement tickling my nerve ends. Then, on the first actually chilly morning in September, I went down to the basement, to the box of cedar chips where Rip slept, and found the black-and-white English springer curled up stiff and cold. He had died in his sleep.

The full impact of what I had lost didn't strike me all at once. It sort of crept up on me through this past hunting season as I came to realize just how much Rip's hatred of my shooting a bird contributed to the splendid times we'd shared.

There were some really glorious hunts as I would outwit Rip and get shots at ruffed grouse. Rip, of course, would become enraged each time it happened, sit down right where he was and howl for a good two minutes. But that only kindled to a deeper glow my satisfaction—it was a lot like the opposing quarterback stomping in rage if your team were to pick off a pass and run it back for a touchdown.

What I felt, however, the first time Rip went into one of his acts was far from satisfaction. I'm several light years away from being wealthy, and after manipulating the family budget to where the kids wouldn't have to go shoeless, at least in the colder months, I took the plunge and bought my first bird dog, Rip. We spent the first summer yard training. But up until pheasant season opened that year none of the gunfire he had heard was aimed at birds.

Then on opening day, Rip and I, along with a couple of my hunting buddies, were sweeping through the swampy back pasture of a friend's dairy farm. A big cackling rooster flushed skyward like a dancing flame, Rip doing his darndest to climb up after him. A crack from the nearest gun brought the bird to earth.

Rip hesitantly walked over and sniffed the pheasant while I toyed with visions of him lifting it gingerly and fetching. Instead he crouched over the bird and sent a spine-chilling howl into the autumn day. He seemed to be mourning the pheasant.

The rest of the day he sulked at my heels and whimpered. My hunting partners tried to be sympathetic, but after a while the thought of a bird dog mourning the birds got to be too much. They started off with a few hand-muffled snickers but before long were themselves cackling, with glee.

The longest day of my life finally ended and I took Rip home and shut him in the basement. During the next few days my family avoided me as if I had hydrophobia. I will admit, I was a bit testy.

Finally, I couldn't stand sulking in the house and driving to work down back alleys to avoid people who might have heard about Rip. I had to go hunting.

I was ready to start out alone for my favorite grouse covers when the gentle-voiced mother of my children showed the considerable iron deposits in her character. She said I wasn't going hunting without Rip because the investment in him had cost her the chance for a microwave anytime in the near future. And, by golly, I was going to give him more than one chance to prove he was a hunter.

So I found myself in grouse cover with Rip. He was in his glory, quartering just ahead of me with his merry, stubby tail a wiggling blur.

We came to a ruined cabin, the walls lying about on the ground and the roof sort of rotting into a tangled mess atop the stone foundation.

Rip clambered up on the pile of timbers, stuck his head down a hole, and barked once. From beneath the pile came a scrambling rush and then a grouse burst out of a hole in the foundation's wall.

I snapped up my shotgun, but Rip was way ahead of me. He used the tumbled pile of cabin as a launching ramp and shot out into space after the climbing bird. With legs windmilling, the airborne dog rammed the laboring grouse and brought it back to the ground.

He came back with his head high and his short tail stiff out behind him to gently drop the limp form of the grouse at my feet. There was, I swear, a gloating grin spread across his face.

From then on, it was a pure and simple competition that grew fiercer and more subtle throughout the years.

He was sporting about it, I'll give him that. He hunted close, no doubt because he craved an audience for his feats. But I had to watch him like a hawk to get any indication he was making game. Usually I could tell when he'd scented a bird; he would suddenly assume an air of nonchalance as he tried to fake me out and work his way into a position where he would have the best run at his quarry.

If I could guess in which bit of cover he had pinpointed the bird, chances were pretty good I'd get there ahead of him, flushing the bird and shooting. Or I could get in position and wait until he had his try at the bird, and, if he missed, then take the shot.

But there were times I never got a chance to shoot, for Rip was out there to collect his own game, which he did often enough to make it meaningful when I got the bird instead of him. Then he would shriek and howl before going to look for another bird.

I came to learn he never held a serious grudge, at least he never bit me, and his fits of pique made my victory all the sweeter.

The Con Artist

Con artists in front of the Claysville Post Office are rare. At least I'd never encountered one there before.

But when I pulled up to mail a letter at the drive-by box one frigid February Saturday there he was limping across the sidewalk toward the car. As he hobbled along he muttered pathetically, giving me the impression someone had sent him inside to buy stamps and then as a cruel joke had driven off to let him walk 489 miles home on his three good legs. At the time, of course, I didn't know he was a con artist.

He was very well groomed, if somewhat genteelly overweight, and wore a new collar with a current tag. I wasn't quite sure what his actual predicament was because I couldn't speak Brittany, not the way he was speaking it, at any rate.

With his orange-and-white coat brushed soft and giving off the aroma of a good shampoo, I figured he hadn't roughed it enough to score very high in street smarts. And because Claysville is a little southwestern Pennsylvania town bisected by U.S. Route 40—with the post office's Stars and Stripes snapping almost directly above the eastbound lane—I decided this was no place for him to start learning about fast-moving cars.

After checking around the neighborhood to see if anyone was missing a Brittany with a bum front leg, I called the state police and got a telephone number from the dog license information they keep on file. The first hitch developed when I dialed the number and a recording informed me that particular number didn't belong to anyone.

I began to feel a tad uneasy, as if I'd surfaced in the middle of that old joke where the parents pack up and leave while the kid is away from home. In this case, substitute a Brittany named Buddy Boy for the kid. At least that's the name the police gave me from his license information.

But Buddy was no kid. As he gazed intently through the windshield from the front passenger's seat as we headed into the country, I glanced his way and saw where the gray was starting to frost his muzzle.

Everyone was a little surprised, and some more delighted than others, when we got home. Nick, our aging springer, whom I had shut in my basement office before bringing Buddy indoors, moaned in agony—which might have been because he was trying to squeeze his bulk through the crack under the office door.

Kate, the eight-month-old setter pup, almost whooped for joy. Here was another something that, figuratively speaking, wore pants.

I have a feeling, judging by the way she's been carrying on around Nick since she was a furry butterball, she would like to take up a life of wantonness. And Nick, who lost some primary parts and primal urges when the vet nipped and tucked some of his internal workings a few years ago, doesn't give her much encouragement.

For Kate, Buddy was fresh game. He hobbled into the basement, gave the pup some rigmarole about getting serious in a few months when she was older, and then homed in on Laurie with uncanny instincts. Our five-year-old will take people or leave them, but she'll take any dog, no questions asked, if it throws a sloppy kiss in her direction.

Within moments Buddy had a home for life, if he wanted it. He plopped his ample haunches in front of Laurie and lifted his gimpy leg for her inspection. He made a brave show of it, artfully interjecting a few little moans.

An afternoon of phone calls revealed the hunting fraternity of the Claysville area didn't know Buddy, and, because the license information gave only a post office box number for an address, guesses ranged from far to near as to where his owner might live. The telephone directory, furthermore, wasn't a gold mine of information on the subject. Just my luck to find a dog belonging to a recluse.

Darkness fell, and so did my spirits as I visualized myself going through the rest of my life trying to keep two old dogs from quarreling like a couple of cranky octogenarians having at each other with shuffleboard sticks. There would also be the added challenge of trying to keep Buddy's relationship with Kate platonic.

For all my misgivings, Buddy proved a model boarder through the night, sleeping in an extra dog crate in the basement.

Sunday morning, with Nick again in my office and Kate out harassing chickadees at the bird feeder, Laurie and her mother Becky gave Buddy the run of the basement after he'd been outside to water shrubs. He launched into a long speech as he shuffled around the bottom of the stairs and then began chuffing like a little steam engine about to tackle a steep grade.

"Could be he thinks his people are up here," I called as I stepped into the shower. "Let him come up for a minute to find out they aren't, then maybe he'll settle down."

The needles of hot water on the back of my neck were just starting to work on the headache I'd acquired along with the dog when Becky squawked in outrage from the kitchen. "He's watering the kitchen table leg. Shoo! Shoo! Get out!" The last was accentuated by a slamming door. My headache rallied and clung on despite the hot water spray.

The next report was fast in coming. Buddy had disappeared in the direction of the road. By the time I got dressed enough to face the frosty weather, the only thing I could see of note was Kate out under the bird feeder looking as if she couldn't decide if she would stay and repel an incoming flight of bluejays or follow her new-found love.

I gave her a third option and shoved her into the basement before making for the car. We live ten miles from town, and I could imagine Buddy trying to hobble to Claysville on three good legs, menaced all the while by highballing pickups, farm dogs with a great deal of wolf in their ancestry, and cows that were possibly litter-mates of the dogs.

It all flashed through my mind like the plot of a Disney movie, and I was halfway to Claysville when I realized even my grandfather's foxhound on a hot trail of his favorite quarry—deer—couldn't have covered that distance in so short a time.

When I got home Becky, muffled up in a snowmobile suit, was out in the yard waving toward the bramble field on the hillside across from our house. There was Buddy, sweeping the overgrown field at a sprightly run, snaking smoothly through the occasional clumps of hawthorn.

He disappeared into a little tuck of ground and suddenly the Oriental cussings of an outraged ringneck were leaving scorch marks across the icy morning calm. The rooster clawed for altitude then set sail for parts elsewhere with Buddy after him at a full, joyous gallop.

I caught Buddy while he was casting hopefully through a clump of brambles close to the road. He resisted all of my efforts to lead him, making out that his bum leg was now utterly wrecked.

Carrying an overweight Brittany is no picnic, but he was finally back in the basement, and for the rest of the day he went outside on a checkcord.

On Monday morning, when the world finally opened for business again, I took it as a personal challenge to find Buddy's hearth and home. A check at the county court-house gave me the same number I'd gotten Saturday from the state police; no surprise, because the information at the police barracks is nothing more than a carbon copy of the courthouse data. But a friend at the Claysville Post Office checked the boxholder information and came up with a telephone number with a "1" where my other two sources had given me a "7." I tried the revised number and hit pay dirt. Because my handwriting is often held up to ridicule, I can sympathize with a person whose ones are mistaken for sevens. I can sympathize, but I don't for a while.

When we got Buddy to his home, which was about a quarter of a mile from the post office, there was an old man standing on the porch to greet us. Buddy got out of the car and limped up the walk, muttering something about being kidnapped while he was trying to get home.

"Get in the house, you old faker!" the man bellowed. Buddy scooted by him, legging along in a flawless scuttle. "Had a broken leg when he was a pup," the old man said. "But he gets on awful good when it suits him."

I sighed. Yes, I had seen Buddy getting by awful good—awful good, indeed.

Tom Huggler has had an ongoing love affair with dogs for most of his forty-eight years and cannot imagine hunting without at least one four-footed partner leading the way. He currently owns two English setters, a shorthair, and a golden retriever and wants to get a yellow Lab to fill the void recently created when Holly, the long-time companion described in this story, passed on to hunt in other places. "A heaven for hunting dogs?" Huggler asks. "Why not? An animal that asks so little and brings us so much pleasure surely lives on in another time and place." A full-time freelance writer and author of ten books, Huggler, who lives near Lansing, Michigan, is Hunting Dogs columnist for North American Hunter *magazine.*

OWNED AND DISOWNED BY HUNTING DOGS

by Tom Huggler

According to my mother, who keeps track of such things, by the time I left home at nineteen, a total of thirty-eight dogs had passed through our family of three boys. Some of the dogs actually hunted. I'm forty-eight now and can only guess at how many four-footed partners have shared a finger-fed portion of my lunches served in duck blinds and on truck tailgates. Some of these charges hunted, too, and all are memorable. I have owned and been owned by beagles and Brittanies and goldens and Labs and many doe-eyed English setters—my Achilles heel, to be sure—but I am equally impressed by pointers, retrievers, flushers, and trackers who have a nose for game and are true to the law of their blood.

Let me tell you about some of them.

The hunting instincts are immeasurably strong in certain individuals and within some breeds. For example, although I've never owned one, springer spaniels score high in the sheer guts department. Somewhere in a file I have a black-and-white photo of a bouncy springer named Brandy climbing a barbed-wire fence to get to a South Dakota ring-necked pheasant on the other side. Another spaniel named Molly, an old fat female that looked like a brown-and-white barrel with legs, hadn't hunted in years when she insisted on tagging along one day on our Iowa pheasant hunt. "Let her go with you," the farmer-host hollered across the field when I tried to coax the disobedient dog back to the barnyard. "It'll be good for her."

Snorting and panting all day, Molly tried to keep up with my friends and me and our younger dogs. We got to feeling sorry for her and began waiting for the game old gal to catch up. Groaning, two of us hiked the heavy dog up and over fences. Exhausted from that and miles of tramping, at day's end we stumbled over our long shadows back to the farm with Molly in tow. She barely made it to her doghouse. Next year when we returned I asked the farmer how she was.

"Molly? That hunt was her last hurrah. She died a couple of days later."

A friend of mine once lost a $5,000 champion beagle when the dog literally ran itself to death chasing snowshoe hares in Michigan's Upper Peninsula. In Oklahoma I let a wobble-legged, half-blind English pointer named Sam find a downed bobwhite within my reaching distance. Closing his eyes, Sam gummed the bird awhile, savoring what turned out to be the season's last retrieve. In Colorado, three of us held down a young German shorthaired bitch and removed a faceful of porcupine quills. An hour later she pointed and retrieved her first sage grouse. Such dogs never fail to inspire.

Some of the best ones are tightly meshed to their owners. Sam and his son, Jake, a pair of Chessies owned by Bill Wood of Bismarck, rarely took their eyes off Bill the whole day we hunted the North Dakota prairie.

Later, Jake held a sharp-tailed grouse for the camera until Bill told him he could open his aching jaws.

A drahthaar owned by Iowan Miles Trachel was in the act of killing my young setter who had nosed the bigger dog's fanny until Miles—and only he could have done it—shocked his dog off the doomed pup. One day on Michigan's Saginaw Bay I watched a 110-pound yellow Lab named John break his tether in our blind, leap into the icy water, and challenge dangerous four-foot waves. John wanted to help his owner, who was bouncing around in our small boat, to retrieve a goldeneye a half-mile out into the heaving bay. I wondered if John's heart would burst before he made it back to safety.

For years I have hunted small game and upland birds all over North America in the company of dogs like these and others. I am not a professional trainer or breeder although I have managed to fumble both and still put an occasional star in my kennel over the last thirty years. When good dogs find game, it provides a prologue to the exciting drama of flush or run, swing and shoot, hit or miss, and I live for such hair-trigger tension. But I am familiar with the heartburn that even good dogs produce when they screw up. I know, too, about the heartache all dogs cause when they grow old, are stolen, or die.

Dogless hunters do not make a habit of burying their partners. There is a reason why hunting dogs don't live very long, but I do not know what the reason is. I just know that five years or so, which is the average length of time that canine maturity and experience transect with prime age, is far too short a time.

A Kansas friend of mine, who hunts with Labrador retrievers and who is smarter than I, figured this out many years ago. So whenever his youngest dog turns five, he starts over with a puppy. The last time we walked native prairie together, his Labs were aged twelve, seven, and two. For him, the inevitable changing of the guard is always predictable and much less painful than trying to fill a void with emptiness.

Smelt-Eating Beagle

Memories help me to fill the void. When I was growing up, my dad kenneled his bird dogs, retrievers, and hounds in the backyard where Mother could tolerate them, even feed them when we boys forgot. Most of these dogs were mutts, their ancestry usually questionable, their working ability often as faulty as the guns and hunting gear that Dad had traded for them. A .35 Remington deer rifle with cracked scope was appropriate dicker bait for a retriever with a steel trap for a mouth. And so on. One of these backdoor deals was a beagle pup Dad brought home one day in the pocket of his deer-hunting coat.

Our father steadfastly called the dog "Emil," but to my brothers and me he was always "Boots." No matter; he rarely came by either name. Emil/Boots turned into one of the most unusual dogs I ever knew, even though he spent only a few years with us before becoming a highway traffic statistic.

I was about twelve at the time when I first saw the tri-colored puppy with the impish face peering out from the woolen depths of my father's coat. Placed on the kitchen linoleum, the pup scampered off, his white forelegs prancing like a drum major in white boots.

"Let's call him Boots," Dave, my older brother, said.

"I like Emil," Dad said without explaining why, and then, upon discovering a spreading wet spot in his coat pocket, offered several other names for the newest arrival in our home.

I pause briefly to explain that, although my father loved most pets (especially dogs), they rarely returned the sentiment. Another time he brought home a cardboard box containing a crippled pigeon he had rescued from the roof of a house where he had been installing a television antenna. As Dad sat down to a late supper of spaghetti, he told us boys there was a surprise in the box. We tore it open, and the pigeon flew straight to my father's balding head where it perched just long enough to relieve itself. As I was saying, Dad received little respect from pets, wild or domestic.

The problem was that he had little patience with them. Dad simply expected his hunting dogs to mind and hunt for him, regardless of whether they had been trained to do so. My father met his match with Boots, who was stubborn and completely unafraid of anything. With the right trainer Boots might have turned into a crackerjack hound because he was an excellent cold tracker. But the critters he tracked were not always rabbits and hares. I remember hearing him plodding through the loose snow of a northern Michigan swamp and cutting loose with squeals and an occasional bawl as he puzzled out a snowshoe hare track. Suddenly the swamp would go silent. Then the hound's voice would take on a machine-gun attack—sign of a jumped deer.

If we could get to Boots soon enough, we could pull him off the track. If not, the chase could involve hours and miles. Once Boots was caught, Dad would wail on him a while, put him back down in a new cedar swamp, and twenty minutes later the beagle would sing off louder than before on another deer track. Boots grew to expect the swift and certain punishment, yet he always returned to his deer-running ways.

I never knew a hunting dog to have more moxie. One time we drove to the farmland country to hunt pheasants. Tooling down a rural road in our '57 Chevy, Dad pulled up next to a farmer walking a beautiful Irish setter. I was sitting in the back seat with Boots on my lap while the men talked through the open window.

"Sure, you can hunt," the farmer was saying, and about that time Big Red put his paws on the window for a look inside. In a flash of brown and white, and without even a warning growl, Boots leaped for the interloper's throat. The red dog fell on his back with the crazed beagle all over him, shaking his head like a pup with a huge stuffed toy. Had he fought back, the bigger dog could have bitten Boots in two. Instead, the farmer kicked the beagle off his prize setter while Dad got a finger in Boots's collar.

It took a long time to find another place to hunt that day.

On the subject of former dogs, most hunters think back to golden afternoons replete with head-high setters on point, perfect retrieves, game-heavy hunting coats. When my mind wanders to Boots, I remember cold nights driving two-track roads looking for a worn-out hound, the rush of cold air mixed with the acrid fumes from my father's ever-present Phillip Morris, embarrassment mixed with worry, an empty game pouch—and smelt. Yes, smelt. Boots loved them. I recall one spring evening when I was sixteen or so, I stood at the kitchen sink cleaning smelt for my supper. Only Boots and I were home, and I well remember the hopeful expression on that otherwise mischievous face every time I lifted one of the little fish from an iron skillet on the stove.

I ate one, then tossed him one. It disappeared in a tongue flick, only to be replaced by that expectant look. One for me, one for Boots. Pretty soon the skillet was empty, so I fried another batch. After about twenty fish each, I began to wonder if the beagle could eat more than I. Two hours later we had consumed fifty smelt each, and I looked at my tummy with unease and a little shame. Boots's stomach was slung like a well-fed lion, and a glassy look was fast replacing the eager glint in his eyes.

He must have known he had me because I could barely swallow number fifty-one and stopped halfway through fifty-two. Meanwhile, Boots lay on his side and slowly chewed, his belly curved like a scimitar and taut as a drum. The tail of smelt number fifty-two disappeared. When he nibbled on number fifty-three, I declared him the world champion.

To this day, I do not like smelt, but I suspect that Boots still does. I figure he gets a platter now and then, too, soon after working up a good appetite from chasing deer.

Somewhere on Point

English setters gobble more ground in less time than any other breed of bird hunter. The brain, or maybe it is blood genetics, tell the dog to run hard and run long. Those that are mostly white in color float like elegant spirits over prairie grass and flash through aspen slashings. But their first points are puppy clumsy: the legs misshapen, the body corkscrewed. You can mold such a young dog on point as though she is Play-Do in your hands. "Cock that foreleg now. Keep the head up. Up, up. That's it, girl." You will also not resist closing fingers around and stroking that magnificent tail. Like the feather plume on a musketeer's hat, it must be carried proudly high.

I played with setters long before I understood these things, certainly before I was old enough to hunt, with a gun at least, behind them. The first was a family dog named Queenie, a big out-of-control runner. Queenie was bold, knot-headed, unmanageable in the way that only setters can be, but I suppose that was mostly my fault. On autumn afternoons when the elementary school bus deposited me in front of our rural home, I'd race to change clothes and unleash the excited dog. Then we'd head for the big fields beyond our lawn. We knew our roles well: Queenie's was to chase the pheasants; mine was to chase Queenie.

I remember one time when she slammed, unexpectedly, into a pose as rigid as the cement lion on our front porch. She had been racing, pink tongue to the wheat stubble. Suddenly, it was as though she struck an invisible wall. Her body flag flew up and somehow she managed a pretzel bend to stare back over her front shoulder at me, or so I thought until I approached close enough to see she was mesmerized by a pile of old cornstalks. The pile ignited, and a big cockbird, all on fire, came roaring out.

That day I fell in love with English setters. I was six, maybe seven, years old.

Queenie's last big run occurred a couple of years later when a farmer shot her for trespassing. That is what our family was told, anyway, but never could prove.

When you are grown, you learn to savor life more than during the younger years, or realize you are a fool if you cannot. Perhaps better than most, hunting dog owners know how time always compresses rather than expands. A dog can be born, grow up, and die in the span it takes some people to earn a college degree. The eight years I owned a remarkable setter named Lady Macbeth seemed to pass with the mere snap of fingers.

I am holding a photographic slide of her now, and she is on point. Foreleg cocked, nose haughty and high, it is a classic setter pose, one that Robert Abbett would drool for. The poignancy of Macbeth's points—a certain compactness of energy, a stick-pinned sharpness—always reminds me of a drawn bow. The bracken fern blurs under the ghostly birch, and I swear I can smell the new richness of decaying woods through the celluoid. May it always be that way.

Her death was completely unexpected and remains a mystery today, years later. I found her, dead, in the kennel at feeding time one evening. There were no signs of suffering. I could not bury her on the farm where she was born because I had to leave for a long trip the next morning, and there was an autopsy to do. The autopsy proved nothing.

Those are the facts. They are the easy part to explain.

The evening before, we played on the back lawn and she pretended there were birds hiding under the roses, just blooming. Macbeth's tail chased her nose, wormlike, as though the hunting was for real. When I told her about our plans for the fall, she made that silly grin again. Our travels would take us to many places in search of native grouse. Some of these, such as blue grouse and ptarmigan, Macbeth had never seen. But I was confident that she could handle them, like she had learned to hunt Mearns quail and mountain quail and other game birds on other trips. She was confident, too.

At first, I thought about canceling the grouse journey. What was the purpose, I asked myself, if I could not take along the partner that had shared so much with me in the past?

Now I sort through other stacks of slides, and in my mind's eye I recall other things worth remembering. Scenes when Macbeth would retrieve birds that I was unable to get to—a pheasant that died in the middle of a duck pond, a grouse that fell into shirt-shredding tangle. The day she learned to hunt brushy fencerows for bobwhites by vacuum cleaning them toward me. Her first taste of prairie grouse in Nebraska. How frustrated she grew when scaled quail tried to sprint from New Mexico into Arizona.

I remember other things that were irritating or humorous but are part of any partnership, too. Her general bitchiness with other dogs and sometimes children as she grew older. Her refusal to eat the supper I prepared in a hub cap, pried loose from my Chevy pickup, because I had forgotten her regular dish. The evening in the baggage terminal at Chicago's O'Hare Airport when she barked the instant she recognized me.

Progeny of a field trial mother and a gun dog father, Macbeth's permanence in my kennel was a fluke of sorts. By telephone, I had sold her as a pup to a friend from Kansas, after selecting a male for myself from the litter I was raising. I had her vet's certificate in hand and a reserved spot on an airplane leaving the next day. It is not fair to ship a nameless dog as though the dog was baggage, and so for want of a better name, I called her Ron's Star Point. That night the phone rang. It was Ron.

"I can't take the dog, after all," he said. "My wife left me this morning, and I don't know what I'm going to do. But I know it would be dumb for me to invest in a dog now."

So I kept Point, changing her name when an editor and hunting companion sent a letter telling me of his own new setter, Shakespeare. "You can't get any more English than that," he wrote. "Can you?"

The best dogs are those that form a special bond with their owners. I do not know how to explain that simply except to say that Macbeth and I had such a bond. There were times when I believe she could read my mind, and there is no doubt that I could read hers. She had ways of letting me know if she was happy or not, like the day when I came home from a sharptail hunting trip in North Dakota. I had not taken Macbeth because it was a short trip, and a sudden blast of frigid weather had me concerned about her safety in the cold belly of a DC-10.

I arrived in Michigan on a Sunday afternoon in early November with just enough time for a woodcock hunt in some local coverts. After being able to see forty miles on the treeless Dakota plains, it seemed strange to be tramping through aspen bamboo where I could see only forty feet. Also strange was the behavior of my dog. She ran off to hunt on her own, flushed wild, and refused to retrieve the only bird I shot. I was so mad I could taste copper. I hauled Macbeth into the truck and drove home. "I did this for you, fool!" I scolded. My dog squirmed into her corner of the truck and refused to meet my glare.

Soon, I softened and held out the warm hand of truce. Macbeth craned her pretty white head, sniffed my trousers, twisted her nose, and shrank back to her corner. Only then did I realize I still carried the odors of Dakota prairie and grouse along with the smells of strange dogs whose names I had already forgotten. I washed the clothing before we hunted again.

Macbeth could be headstrong, sure, but only to the degree that you hope for in a bird dog. A dog that does not test the obedience limits once in a while is not worth putting your name on its collar. I shot my last grouse over her on the last day of the calendar year, the final preserve pheasant in early February. I was proud of her both times, and I think she approved of my shooting.

No matter how open or tight the cover, a pointing dog *has to check in.* Unless I had done something to annoy her, Macbeth always checked in. Except when she was on point, and then it was up to me to find her.

Maybe you know. Maybe you, too, remember a time in southwest Kansas when a thirty-knot wind tried to unbutton your hunting coat. The wires between you hunters and your quail dogs were certainly down that day. First Mike lost his golden retriever for a frantic twenty minutes. Then it was Macbeth's turn to disappear. You watched her chase the busted covey she had overrun from the upwind side. Embarrassed, she ran two errant birds downwind for a quarter-mile, finally vanishing as a white speck over a little rise in the cut field of grain. You waited three minutes. Five minutes. No dog.

Remember how the tension mounted, along with your anger? "Excuse me," you tell your hunting partners. "I have a dog to punish."

But you should be the one spanked for not trusting your dog. There she is, locked up, another four hundred yards farther on! The wind stirs her tail feathering. You feel foolish and you apologize to your dog as you creep into shooting position, while she admonishes you with those nervous setter eyes. They dart from you to the bird and you know what she is thinking. "For God's sake, Thomas, where the hell have you been? Here's the quail, right under this milo stalk."

You kill the bird, a young cock, for your dog on a crossing shot. Her perfect retrieve means she has forgiven you. The law allows two more; instead you unload your gun. You have learned that when the cup will hold no more, it is time to stop trying to fill it.

And so that is how you will come to accept the loss of this dog, your favorite hunting partner. You had her at her absolute best, and, in spite of your many mistakes, you were also the instrument for some of her success. You know she was not great, at least not in the way the experts grade hunting dogs, but she was better than good and she made *your* Bird Dog Hall of Fame. Nothing else matters.

It is now several more autumns that you have walked those mountain saddles and aspen whips and windswept plains without her. There have been other dogs and other hunters, and sometimes you have walked alone. But not too often because you find yourself looking for a white setter with black speckling to check back with you. She was right here, wasn't she? And only a moment ago.

When she does not return, you realize she is on point somewhere else. You just have not found her, yet.

The Price

Some dogs do not cut it, in spite of their good looks and great breeding. They have to go, but getting rid of them is never easy. I'm talking about dogs whose synapses are short-circuited because of an aberrant gene or the way they were raised. You know, the old heredity versus environment thing that every parent agonizes over.

A few years ago I sold a setter puppy to an artist friend who fell in love with the litter runt. "Cleo," as we called her because of her gorgeous eyes circled with black, was the most handsome of the ten puppies. She was also an aggressive little bitch who harassed her litter mates and often bit the hands that fed her. I told my friend, who had a family of his own and had never owned setters, that Cleo was the worst possible choice. When he insisted on buying her, I refused to take his money. "Send me a check in a week," I said as he backed out of my driveway, the little furball wriggling like live macaroni in the arms of my friend's five-year-old son.

Two days later my friend was back in the driveway. Leaving the engine running and the door open, he thrust a cage with Cleo in it at me. "Here's your dog back," he blurted. "My kid has been bitten and scratched all to hell."

What do you do with a dog like that? Knock 'em in the head? I, for one, cannot, and so I traded Cleo for two fifty-pound bags of Purina. Then I gave away her mother—a tightly wired ground gobbler who had trouble hearing commands unless you first melted the wax in her ears with electricity—to an enormous Sicilian from Detroit who said he was one of boxer Thomas Hearns' body-guards. I believed him.

You never know for sure what you will get from breeding (or buying). How can you tell, for example, if behind those liquid brown eyes there is functional gray matter? And once you commit yourself to any hunting dog that will not or cannot measure up, at what point do you disconnect and then dispose of the flunky? This much I know: The older I become, the less time I have to waste with dogs that are incorrigible or crazy. I would add "stupid" except I have never owned a dog that was flat-out dumb. Happy in his own ignorance, perhaps, like Odie in the Garfield comic strip, but never dim-witted to the point that the dog had not probed for my weaknesses and then figured out how to capitalize on them.

Such was a powerful, strong-willed male named Chaucer who was a guest in my kennel six years too long, which was also his age when I gave him away. Chaucer had more lives than a cat, and I suspect he is still alive today but do not know for sure.

I got him as a pup in March and all spring and summer we worked with a fly rod and wing, leash, and check cord. By the end of August, he appeared to be ready. Like an optimistic football coach, I broke training camp thinking I had a promising rookie on my team. Things began to fall apart soon after. In early September, when Chaucer was nine months old, he nearly died from a virulent disease. Upon returning home from a fishing trip, I found him in the kennel, lying on his side and covered with flies. He was barely breathing. I rushed Chaucer to the veterinarian, who gave him a shot of cortisone and put him on a drip diet of glucose. The next day the lab report came back: canine parvovirus. It was amazing that Chaucer lived at all, and several weeks passed before his health returned.

So the youngster missed his first hunting season, a critical experience in the life of any gun dog. Late the following summer, I sent him for professional training. "He's a different one," the trainer admitted when I came to pick up the dog. "He's either too willful or not too smart. It's hard to say for sure, but he sure as hell has a mind of his own. He lacks consistency, but I think he'll be okay if you hunt him a lot."

Instead, I spent most of Chaucer's second autumn in Alaska, and he did not get the field work he needed. Even so, I was not overly concerned because many male setters are notoriously slow to develop. So in the fall of 1985, when Chaucer was three, I took him and the other dogs on a three-month, cross-country odyssey to hunt quail. His problems became manifest on that trip.

Because Chaucer was socially ignorant, he behaved shabbily. He picked fights, for instance, with my friends' dogs—until a tough old Labrador changed his mind in Kansas. In Iowa, Chaucer pissed on the pant leg of my host and bared his teeth and growled whenever anyone tried to take a bird away from him. He refused to load in the trailer I pulled behind my motorhome unless I exhausted him first by "roading" him for miles. That wasted a lot of time because Chaucer was the strongest dog I had ever owned and he did not tire easily. About this time I took to calling him "Lunchmeat" and decided to give him away to the next farmer who commented on his handsome black eye patch.

Then Lunchmeat did something remarkable. In Oklahoma, he began to hunt birds instead of chasing deer into Texas. By the time we got to Missouri, he was holding bobwhites with some consistency. He backed Macbeth a time or two and even retrieved an occasional half quail after biting the birds in two to make sure they were dead.

In Arizona, Chaucer turned jerk again when he showed more interest in chasing jackrabbits than in finding Gambel quail. Arizona was also where he experienced how painful cholla can be. The other dogs quickly learned to avoid the prickly cactus, but Chaucer not only tangled with the miserable stuff, he bit at it. I spent half of one afternoon pulling spines from his face, palate, and testicles. One barb was completely through his tongue.

Then in New Mexico, Chaucer fell from an old pickup as we lumbered over corrugated roads at 45 mph. Floyd, my friend who was driving, stopped when he noticed the tailgate had banged open. There were our dogs, sensibly lying away from danger near the cab. All except Chaucer. He was gone.

"Good God!" Floyd said. "He must have fallen out. Where do you suppose he is?"

Five minutes later, we spotted a small dust funnel on the horizon. Borrowing Floyd's binoculars, I could make out my dog, galloping toward us, his pink tongue nearly touching the dry roadbed.

"In forty years of hunting, I've never had a dog fall out of a truck," Floyd said. "No wonder you call him Lunchmeat."

The next year Chaucer had good days and poor days afield. Meanwhile, like a good cabernet Macbeth steadily improved, and so I began to rely even more on her, leaving Chaucer in the dog box of my trailer.

"For pete's sake get rid of him," advised my friends, some of whom are experts on dogs.

I could not bring myself to do it.

Each year before bird season, I run my dogs, one at a time, on a leash alongside the truck. I do this in the cool evenings, along back roads where there is little traffic. The dogs love the exercise. One evening after Chaucer had enjoyed his turn during a two-mile romp, I removed the leash and told him, "Kennel up." He wrinkled a lip in the manner of a snot-nosed sixth grader headed for the principal's office. Could Chaucer have spoken, he might have said, "Kennel up yourself, sucker." Angry, I tried to grab his collar. He scooted backwards, into the other lane and a LeSabre that happened to be roaring by.

If you have ever witnessed an auto accident, you know the sinking feeling when time stops. The low-slung car dragged my dog a long way before it shuddered to a stop and the dust cleared and I could see. There lay Chaucer, misshappen and in certain pain, although he neither yelped nor howled. Two thoughts raced through me: (1) It's over for him, (2) Thank God it wasn't Macbeth. I told the lady driver, who was shaken over hitting her first animal, that it was not her fault and to go home. Then I tried to figure out what to do with my suffering dog.

I could hardly believe he was still alive. I knew he had a broken back and would bite me if I tried to move him. Bending over the stricken dog, I talked gently; amazingly he seemed to know who I was. A plan evolved. My vet lived only a couple of miles away. I would knock on a nearby door, call the doctor, and ask him to come quickly and give Chaucer a mercy needle. But as I walked across the road back to the truck, I was shocked when my dog began dragging himself after me. As gently as possible, I muzzled him with a handkerchief, then found another and daubed at the blood oozing from a nasty gash to his head. He was bleeding through his nose and mouth and his undersides were scraped raw. Carefully I loaded Chaucer into the truck and drove to the vet's office.

I told you this dog had more lives than a cat. The doctor found no broken bones, just severe lacerations and a probable concussion. "We'll keep him here for a couple days," he said. "He may come out of this with just a big headache."

Chaucer healed fast. Two weeks later I took him to Michigan's Upper Peninsula for my annual grouse hunting camp. He thanked me by running off the first time I slipped his leash in a promising cover. Two hours later I found, and punished, my dog. Two weeks after that was the last time I took him hunting.

It was a balmy October afternoon when three friends and I chanced upon a heavy flight of woodcock. The poplar slashings were stiff with birds, and we were getting the kind of gunning that can carry a man through the long winter. Unfortunately, Chaucer had run off on his own adventures earlier in the day and was now missing all the fun—bittersweet action for me because I was furious over my dog's antics. I looked for him until dark, then left a hat in the woods in case he came back. He didn't. I drove home two hundred miles, my neck throbbing from tension. The next day the phone rang. A friend of a friend had found the errant Chaucer—six miles from where I had last seen him—and my name and telephone number on his collar.

"What do you want me to do with him?" Kevin, my friend, asked over the telephone.

I did not hesitate. "Give him away."

"He's a beautiful dog, but I don't think anyone wants him," Kevin said. "Hunting season is about over. But the guy who found him says he'll take him to the pound for you."

I know now how a mother feels when her good-for-nothing son is hauled downtown for questioning. Or a wife tells a skirt-chasing husband goodbye and this time means it.

"Do it," I said and slept well that night.

But two days later, there was a knock at the door. It was Kevin, and in his car was Chaucer, bounding from the back seat to the front seat and back again, happy to be home once more.

"They couldn't turn him in," Kevin explained. "The dog is just too…How do you say it?…a born loser, I guess. You can't put down a dog like that. He has a way of looking at you. It's in his eyes."

"I know."

It was Chaucer's last big roundup. For the next several months he stayed in his chainlink kennel, like a convict, except for brief bouts of exercise in the yard of my farm while I prepared food and changed his water. Sometimes I would take him to the office where he liked to sleep under the desk while I wrote. I stopped calling him Lunchmeat because he never again got the chance to do anything wrong. The following spring I gave him to a young married couple who wanted a pet.

It is the price one sometimes pays for owning bird dogs.

The Problem with Holly

The problem with Holly is that she is growing old much too fast and may not make it to grouse hunting camp next October. At night my wife and I pill the yellow Labrador with Ascriptin, and Holly whimpers when I massage her arthritic hips too hard. Her wheezing reminds me of an old switch engine slowly chugging through the woods. Her eyes have developed the smoky, opaque look of a glass marble that is flawed. This, I feared, was cataracts but is advancing age—according to her vet—and perfectly normal.

I am the one not normal. At nearly thirteen years of age Holly is the oldest hunting dog I have ever owned, and I am writing about her now because I do not have any experience here and am reasonably certain I will fumble the words later. Whoever said we should pay our tribute to the living, not the dead, was right, and the truth is I owe this dog more than I can tell you in a few short paragraphs.

By now, you know that I have an immense soft spot for English setters. The irony is that over many years I have spent thousands buying and training setters only to have them die in their prime, run off, get stolen, sold at loss, or turn into absolute rascals. Holly cost me seventy-five dollars when I bought her in 1980 from a Mayville, Michigan, breeder. I needed a meat-and-potatoes hunter, a clean-up partner to fetch ducks and to rout pheasants from the places the racing setters missed. Training? I spent twenty bucks to enroll Holly in a dog obedience class at the local high school. I admit to being surprised when she took first place, beating out a thousand-dollar golden with the improbable name of Octavius.

Holly has shared kennel space with setters most of her life, and they have all taken advantage of this gentle bear hug of a dog. Puppies whose names I can no longer remember thought she was a hairy medicine ball. One rogue got her pregnant; complications followed the abortion and I had Holly neutered. Another setter nailed Holly on the forehead. Even though she bit back and won the fight, it is she that carries a little hole between her eyes.

About four years ago we brought Holly into our house to live, and she has behaved like the good citizen she always was. I have never owned another dog that did not at least bark at the UPS drivers, but Holly offers a grin and a blockish head to pet. She approves of warm hands. A watchdog she is not.

Holly never messes in the house, does not beg, and knows her boundaries. On the other hand, over the years we have noticed an increasing sense of entitlement in direct proportion to the spread of whiteness across her muzzle. Holly refuses to take her pill unless my wife coats it first with peanut butter. She becomes instantly agitated whenever I pack for a trip, and when we do take her along she insists on riding in the front seat. If dogs could cry! "Insistence" takes the form of squinting eyes, a pink tongue in your face, the disappointed whap of an otterine tail along your leg.

The first time Holly smelled birds was the November day I chose her from the basement litter that was eight weeks old. She looked like one of those furry mitts used for washing cars. After sniffing my Bean boots, freshly worn in pheasant cover, she peed on them with excitement. These are the same boots with the chewed-away finger loops, a reminder that Holly once was a puppy. I still have them, somewhere, and probably always will.

Next year the first pheasant she flushed caused panic, then embarrassment, then a determination to put the boot to every ringneck on the continent. The following October she learned how to knock geese flat with noseguard force. The setters were next. One of Holly's goals in life is to find a setter on point, then slamdunk the dog and take credit for the flush. I lecture her about this often, but she offers those Oriental eyes, grins, and trembles over her skillful revenge. This trait has grown so bad that I have had to attach a twelve-foot checkcord to Holly and tie her to aspens where she howls in misery until released for the retrieve.

Holly has gone everywhere with me, helping to collect game birds from deserts, mountains, plains, and woods. She has tasted all the native grouse and quails, pheasants from a dozen states, and doves, woodcock, partridge, and most species of waterfowl. In Nevada she blundered into a bobcat trap but escaped injury. Another time in Kansas she narrowly missed the strike of a prairie rattler. I have removed Missouri cockleburs, Oklahoma goatshead pickers, and Michigan porcupine quills from her feet, face, belly, and tail.

She has never complained.

Aging is a deceptive process, especially in a yellow Lab whose complexion masks a creeping gray face. I first noticed Holly's advancing age four years ago in the Colorado high country when she flagged behind and I, an out-of-shape flatlander, had to wait. In camp last fall she stole away early from our evening fire and found her bed in my tent. I know her hind legs ached from struggling to pull them over logs all day. I know because she licked my hands while I gently massaged her lower back and hips.

Later in Iowa, for the first time I can remember she did not bark when I unloaded a setter and left her in the truck. The dog ran wild and I kenneled him. I chose Holly and within five minutes she flushed a ringneck and delivered it with her patented soft retrieve. It was the kind of performance I have come to expect for a decade now but only learned to appreciate recently.

On trail you would never know Holly has a bowed back and drooping tail because she changes into a fluid blonde predator. She can make herself as slim as a nervous grouse about to flush. There is a youthful suppleness along with a determined economy to her movement. Holly hunts only where experience tells her birds might be. She knows exactly when I'll rein her in close, so why waste energy going out too far in the first place?

This fall Holly wants to migrate with woodcock throughout eastern North America. We have been sharing thoughts and plans on the subject for several months. As I write this, Holly lies in a yellow pool at my feet, muscles twitching from woodcock fluttering into her dreams.

I thumb through the calendar past too many pages to October.

Editor's Note: A couple of weeks after we received Tom Huggler's manuscript, he called to inform us that Holly had, indeed, passed away and that he had decided to put his travels for woodcock on hold. Huggler mentioned that Holly lies beneath an enormous beech, "wide as an elephant's ass," on his property. The beech commands a view of woodcock tangles and grouse uplands. The other night he flushed a ruffed grouse from its branches.

Diane Vasey says her life went to the dogs by the time she was twelve, when she started taking her family's cocker spaniel to obedience classes. She spent the next two decades learning all she could about every hobby related to canines. Today, she is editor-in-chief of the AKC Gazette magazine for purebred dogs, and lives in Connecticut with her Lab, champion papillons, and cocker spaniels. Former editor of The Pointing Dog Journal, she has participated in field trials with her pointers, enjoys quail and waterfowl hunting—and trout fishing at every opportunity. A conscientious breeder, she says there are few things more fun than raising young puppies—but one pleasure that offers immense satisfaction is being able to see a pup grow to reach his potential and become all he was meant to be.

GILLY

by Diane Vasey

To one who has seen many, there are dogs and then there are *dogs*.

A person who is seasoned in the business of dogs, who has flirted with the fancy long enough to have seen fashionable breeding and training trends become historical lessons of genetic or environmental dysfunction, assumes a sort of circumspect attitude when an enthusiastic neophyte seeks his opinion about a dog or puppy. He responds to such inquiry with casual and vague generalities that are virtually meaningless to the approval-seeking questioner.

To the would-be field trialer with a puppy entry: "Got some fire, doesn't he?"

To the hunt-test enthusiast with a versatile breed: "Thorough little guy, isn't he?"

To the conformation show hopeful: "That pup looks real *nice* right now."

Nice? And the uninitiated walk away without a clue about what they have or what the enlightened really thought of their prospect.

Why does one with expertise respond with such vagueness? Because he knows. The veteran fancier developed this attitude over time, obtaining wisdom from hard-earned firsthand experience. He knows that every prospect may become the "dream" dog for the guy at the other end of the leash, but that most never will achieve their potential—and that, of those who do, most will merely blend with the multitudes, having some good qualities and some weaknesses, the sum of which keeps them from standing out in the crowd.

So it is that most dogs come into our lives and then go, without notorious fanfare. They do what we ask of them while we provide their needs, their contributions ultimately well worth the effort it takes to keep them well and happy. Whether good or bad, they steal our hearts, and we are hooked for life (theirs). When they go, we mourn their departure and they linger in our memories for a time, fading eventually into blurred, shadowy images biased by time and selective retention.

On rare occasion, though, we encounter an exceptional being, one whose uncanny abilities raise the possibility of the purported sixth sense—a mystery that imparts an almost eerie feeling of wonder and awe in those who are fortunate to know the animal beyond casual acquaintance. This is the dog, just one in a multitude, who transcends our common understanding of the species, one whom we ineptly describe as "almost human."

If the dog who possesses this level of intelligence also possesses physical qualities for capable athletic performance, and if the dog ends up with an owner who recognizes potential and has the skills and resources to develop it, we have, in effect, a dog to die for. We have the stuff of which legends are made.

Such was the case with Gilly, a pointer prodigy I had the fortune to raise this past fall—a serendipitous, all-too-brief experience for which I can accept little credit.

I had been editor of *The Pointing Dog Journal* magazine for about a year when I had an opportunity to get a pup that seemed to fulfill all of my rather lengthy prerequisites for adoption. The publisher of the magazine, Dave Meisner, was interested in participating in the development of and in sponsoring a pup for different types of events and competitions. He agreed that my future pup could come to the office each day, and he looked forward to the training ventures that would become a part of the office environment.

Because selection of the line and the breeder of a pup is much more critical than actually choosing the individual, I spent an inordinate amount of time considering characteristics and abilities of generations of producers. I finally settled on the credits and reputation of Bob Wehle, a man who had been breeding pointers for fifty-seven years. His dogs had been bred for function and form, which would contribute to intelligence, biddability, and class. Elhew Kennels had produced gun dogs for bird hunters and field trial dogs that had won every type of competition imaginable, and had done so consistently throughout decades. Arrangements were cinched after Dave and I talked with Bob himself; we were pleased to discover that he truly fit his reputation as a stalwart believer in evaluating the total dog before breeding it, one who will sacrifice an outstanding inheritable trait if the dog should not be bred because of a bad inheritable flaw, a conscientious man of sound principle—and a gentleman's gentleman.

Despite months of homework and careful deliberation, however, I was not prepared for what I saw when I picked up the pup at the Chicago airport. Bob's description of the pup had been accurate: He was orange-and-white, symmetrically marked with a black nose and black eyeliner. But more important, Bob also had said that the pup was special, his pick puppy in an outstanding litter that he planned to keep himself.

From the moment he stepped out of his crate, the little pup carried himself with an air of nobility. A dignified puppy is oxymoronic—yet if the concept were possible, this puppy would have been dignified. His aura was subtle and is hard to describe, and perhaps only a connoisseur of canines would even have noticed—but I sensed it within ten minutes after letting him out of the crate to potty.

This ten-week-old pointer stepped into grass near the office, blinked, yawned, blinked again, took a quick survey of the scene while he relieved himself, saw me and made a beeline. When he reached me, he tugged my ruffled ponytail hairpiece from its place, flipped it into the air and then stalked it, freezing into a picture-perfect, classic, poker-straight high-tailed point. Dave and I looked at each other and I saw wonder in his eyes.

"Sheeesh," he said. "Wow; Diane—that dog is incredible."

We tossed the hairpiece and played the game repeatedly with similar results. Smiling, I scooped up the puppy, and Dave and I looked at each other and shook our heads.

"This is gonna be fun."

◆

The next six months were filled with a mixture of joy and heartache.

He was named Elhew's Upland Gilly, after the hunting and fishing guides of the Scottish Highlands.

Gil went along everywhere I could take a dog, and some places where they normally were not allowed. At about twelve weeks old, he went along with magazine staff on a press check to St. Croix Press near Minneapolis. Employees were intrigued when they heard there was a pointer puppy in the CEO's office. They wanted to see him point. We didn't have a rod-and-wing handy, so we improvised with what was available in the office. Those who came in to see him spread the word after they left, and by late afternoon there had been a steady stream of visitors who had come to see him do his stuff. He was a predictably consistent and reliable performer. When people came, we would pull out a white tissue and snap it to the end of a leash. We tossed it to the floor and he would transform into a statue—no, a sculpture—of a bird dog on a classic point, tail straight to the ceiling. And he would remain on point until the tissue was flipped out of sight and hidden. At one time, there were about a dozen people standing in the room talking and watching him. They would come in, marvel, and leave, but through all the commotion, he never acknowledged anything except the tissue for as long as it remained on the floor.

Truth is, when the Good Lord passed out personality, Gilly must have been first in line. He was full of it, and full of himself, and he burst with it in all he did.

Gilly's puppyhood was riddled with mischief and adventure. When some kids took their sleds to a snowy hillside, he perceived it as an opportunity to create games the kids had never played. He would start down the hill chasing the kids and wind up sliding, like an otter, his mouth wide open and tongue lolling out the side. Once at the bottom, he figured it must be a race to the top, and he'd win the race if he could pull the kids down on his way. When the kids threw snow to retaliate, he would leap to catch all he could.

He loved "happy time" on the soft couch, where he would tunnel between the cushions and flip upside down, burying his head and snorting. It was on the couch that he learned to love being rubbed all over, and to this day he greets people he likes with a catlike rub against their legs.

When faced with a canine dilemma, he would cock his head in thought, assessing the situation and devising a plan for solution or disaster—whichever came first.

When he wanted something out of his reach on the kitchen counter, he would figure out an alternative route to get it—even if it meant starting at the other end of the kitchen and using the trash can to climb up, walk across the range top, around the microwave, over the sink, and past the toaster to get to his destination.

I don't think Gilly was born with all of that problem-solving braininess, though—I think he got some of his smarts and much of his rebelliousness from watching too much television. He liked to lay on the couch or sit in front of the TV and watch the Discovery channel. I know he preferred that channel to MTV because he would stand up with his ears perked forward every time birds flew across the screen, as if waiting for them to fly out of tube into the family room.

One thing he did not like was bears, and if a grizzly showed up on the screen, he would get up and walk stiff-legged, with hair on end, to peer behind the TV. I think he wanted to make sure that no bears would sneak out the TV's back door to join us.

His all-time favorite late-night viewing was when I would pop popcorn ("one for you, three for me"), start a bird-dog training video produced by his breeder, and invite him to curl up on the couch. There was no doubt in anyone's mind that he recognized Bob Wehle and the familiar bobwhite whistle that Bob uses in early training. Gil would stand up and freeze, like he was honoring the dog in the video. After the birds flew, he would get excited and paw me, as if asking me to rewind it!

◆

Life seemed grand at the time to both of us, he without a care in the world and me with grandiose plans for shared trips afield and in hunt tests and field trials. We lived in blissful ignorance of the events that would change our lives and signify the end of our time together.

When the publisher of *The Pointing Dog Journal* first told me he was considering selling a part of the ownership of the magazine to other investors, I was not concerned for the welfare of the magazine or my position as editor. We had thousands of devoted subscribers; we had won the highest quality award and recognition possible to us in 1993 from the Dog Writers Association of America; and our first set of renewals had just started to come in. The wind shifted for me personally, however, when greed bungled the first investor's offer and the deal fell apart. A second investor, a publishing company complete with its own several magazines and existing editorial and production staff, became interested in the *Journal*. A merger took place shortly thereafter. Soon I was trying to decide the direction to take for the rest of my career: editing for a different employer, becoming self-employed as a publisher or freelance writer, or going back to school.

Eventually I opted for returning to school to pursue becoming a veterinarian. My biggest challenge, I thought, would be figuring out how to do that without giving up my pointer, Labrador retriever, cocker spaniel, and papillon. I had grown accustomed to owning a home, and renting is problematic when you have dogs. Tuition money was a problem, too, I found, because federal loans were not available to "special students," or people who already had a master's degree. To save every penny I could, I hoped to find a place that would not charge rent, or charge as little as possible, in exchange for some kind of service I could offer—perhaps assistance for an elderly person.

It was tough. I had offers that would take me without the dogs, or with just one small dog. But no one really wanted to deal with a growing pointer puppy. It was beginning to look like I would need a miracle. That's how we came to live with the Doneffs.

Nick and Kris Doneff are a good Christian couple who took pity on me and offered to put a roof over my head until I found something else. They thought that having Gilly temporarily might be fun for their kids, who were ten and twelve. They also had two toy poodles and two cockatiels, but we had it all figured out: The Lab would stay temporarily with a friend in Missouri who hunts waterfowl, and he would get a litter out of her in return; the cocker would stay with another friend in Wisconsin, and they would get a puppy in return; and the papillon and Gilly could stay at the Doneffs.

Problem was, no one knew what to expect from the Gil Monster. All I could do was cross my fingers and hope for the best. Things seemed to start out okay, but...

Gilly kept on growing. As his muscles developed, he became more coordinated and athletic. He began to show us what a true, powerful, gutsy bird dog should be made of—and it wasn't sugar and spice. I have to admit that I was awed by his prowess—I had seen a lot of bird dogs grow up, but this one never stopped surprising me. Unfortunately, I seemed to be alone in true appreciation of his physical capabilities. One day his impressive agility led to his exile.

I had just brought him in from a romp outside, which was intended to burn off pent-up energy that had earlier caused him to accumulate a series of not-so-delicate etiquette-related offenses. We were headed through the house toward my bedroom when he decided to take a shortcut. Suddenly, he leapt over the couch without touching it, landed on the other side, and launched himself onto the table beyond, scattering papers and such in all directions. Quite pleased with his new Olympian feat, he looked down from the table at the Doneff's two toy poodles, who were now barking at him from below, glanced over at me, and grinned.

It was an ill-fated circumstance that, at that precise moment, Kris happened to walk into the room. Her eyes widened as she stopped and stared at our Pegasus, and I quickly tried to reassure her.

"This, too, will pass." I smiled weakly.

"Yes," she said, ever so politely, stifling a laugh (lest, perhaps, Gil be encouraged?). "Of course. When do you think it'll pass?"

I looked at Gil, still obviously pleased with himself, and I knew that my answer would have significant ramifications for his being welcome in the house. Mustering all the credibility of an expert in canine development, I said, "Well, you know, these hunting dogs are bred to be athletes. We expect them to have the physical ability to leap over rivers and cross mountains in pursuit of birds."

"I see."

"Yeah, and then we expect them to come into the house and lie quietly at our feet, causing no disruption, and basically just snooze away time."

"Uh huh."

"Well, you know, it takes time to teach them that..." I seemed to be losing ground.

"Hmm."

I looked back at Gilly, who wriggled with pleasure, wagged a high tail, and appeared to be challenging me to a game of King-of-the-Mountain from the tabletop.

"Okay, okay," I said, resigning myself to straight-from-the-shoulder candidness: "In about two or three years, he'll be so calm in the house, you wouldn't know he was the same dog."

"Really."

So it was that the Gil Monster received "time-out" in the kennel without parole, to think about his manners. To his misfortune, it happened to be the coldest

Wisconsin winter in twenty-five years, and no one in the family wanted to live outside in the doghouse with him. I felt bad about his new quarters, but reminded him that he had brought it upon himself, and that he was lucky they were letting me run electricity out to the doghouse for heat.

He accepted his lot without complaint, and I tried to make up for it by increasing our time afield. Our daily romps out back through the woods and fields grew longer as he grew stronger. Often the snow was deep and he would bound through it like a jackrabbit, his ears flying as he appeared and disappeared with each leap.

Like no other dog I've seen, Gil had a spirit of profuse and unfettered joy. Unrestrained as it was, his exuberance was contagious, and it was on these walks that I felt my spirit mesh with his, lifting ever higher, and I thrilled to it vicariously. When the snow melted, he would sail past with gazelle-like grace, seeming to float effortlessly back and forth ahead of me, savoring through his nostrils all that the earth had to offer.

Watching him get into birds would raise goose bumps on the arms of an honest dog man. Catching scent, Gilly would pivot midair to land on point, with style that would make your blood race nearly as fast as his. He would quiver with controlled eagerness, as if every muscle was in tetany, overdosed for the flush. He was rigid on the tips of his toes, mesmerized by the irresistible fragrance that teased his nose and stirred his hair to its end. He was at once both inebriated and impassioned; and when the birds flew, he was so deeply entranced that at first he could not move—then he seemed to regain consciousness, collect himself and charge for all he was worth after the birds, sure that he would sprout wings and soar until he caught them.

With Gilly, nothing was ordinary or mundane. To him, everything was recklessly fun and fascinating, and he experienced life in a venturous frame of mind that was fueled by a supercharged engine. You could not walk with this dog and watch him run without smiling and feeling yourself come alive, too.

But as the days and weeks went by, school became more demanding, my time became more limited, and our walks became shorter and less frequent. The commute to school was an hour and a half each way; classes sometimes went from morning till night, and some nights I could not make it home at all.

On those nights, the Doneffs took care of Gilly's needs. I encouraged the kids to let him out of the kennel for play, but I knew he needed more structured exercise and training. He was far too intelligent to spend hour upon hour in a kennel, and I became concerned that boredom would make dull his mind and limit his development—or worse, lead to behavior problems.

Had he been less intelligent, less physically capable, or less—humanlike, I might have been able to invent creative ways to ensure his well-being without feeling that my absence was depriving him of reaching his potential. But his was such a rare combination of ability and intelligence that I knew he would be better off with someone who had the time and resources to help him develop into all that he could be.

I believed that keeping Gil from attaining his potential could be likened to keeping Beethoven from developing and composing a symphony. Gil had the potential to become a bird dog exemplar, but if I did not have the time or resources to direct his growth, he would not ever become the artisan that Beethoven was—he would never make fine music.

I knew, too, that my motives for keeping him were selfish. But selfish motives are strong ones. At a time in my life that was riddled with hardship and stress, he was my joy—my freedom. He was my relief from all that was painful, and I loved him.

Because I loved him, I could not bring myself to let him go to someone else; I knew that I would never have another like him. But because I could not give him the time he needed and deserved, I was hurting him. Both options had bleak consequences; I was torn between selfish desire and selfless devotion.

Then one day I returned to him after a two-day bout at school and I thought he had lost weight. I checked his self-feeder. It was full of food, but the magnetic swinging door on the side of the feeder, which was designed to keep the food dry but allow the dog to eat when he pushes against it, was in its closed position. I had been propping it open because Gil, never a hearty eater, would rather not eat than push against the door to feed. I suspected that when my prop fell aside and the door swung closed, he probably quit eating.

I was frustrated and discouraged, and worried about his health. Keeping weight on him was almost impossible; he was growing like a weed and his ribs stuck out like ripples in a pond. I had tried every trick known to entice his appetite, yet I could not put a layer of fat on him to protect him from the low outdoor temperatures.

To heighten my torment, each time I talked to Dave, he asked about Gilly. He saw the dog's potential and always offered to take Gil and give him the best that life could offer a bird dog. Gil would live in a house on a shooting preserve, be exercised daily in bird country, spend his days lounging in the editorial office, travel throughout the country on hunts, participate in trials and tests, and be by Dave's side everywhere he went. I imagined Gilly at the preserve, trembling on point with a noseful of hypnotic quail scent, wide-eyed and in a trance. Then I thought of him in his snow-topped dog-house, waiting for me to return from classes.

Late one Friday, with a heart like a shipwreck at sea, I called Dave and offered him the dog. I told him that whatever we did, we'd better do it quickly—before I got too weak to follow through.

The next day, I loaded Gilly and his favorite belongings into the wagon and headed for the office. When we arrived, Dave had everything ready for Gil: a new crate and bed cushion, new feeding bowls, and assorted bones and toys. Gil was happy to return to the office—one of his favorite places to visit—and ran about gaily, bent for joyful destruction and wreaking havoc wherever he could.

"Guess we should make this short and sweet," I said feebly, feeling a bit nauseated.

We stood for a moment and watched Gilly celebrate. Neither spoke for a while while he romped, terrorizing anything he thought he could get away with destroying. I broke the silence.

"We got a Thing, you know—he and I."

"I know."

Gilly grabbed a rawhide bone and carried it aloft, strutting down the hallway and growling at phantom littermates. Soon he returned without the bone, and I guessed that he had done what he'd done a hundred times before: He probably deposited it in a safe place while we talked—maybe changed his mind a time or two, sneaking from room to room to hide the bone where he thought no one would find it. He'd come out of the room into the hallway and look to see if anyone had noticed him carry it into the room. If he thought we had, he'd go back and get the bone and start all over.

"You'll keep in touch and tell me everything he does?"

Dave nodded silently at the request he'd heard the night before.

"I'd like to hunt with him sometime."

"We can do that."

"If anything ever happens and you can't keep him, he has to come back to me," I reiterated. "You can't sell him to anyone else without offering him to me first."

"You know I wouldn't."

"I know you wouldn't," I said, nodding apologetically.

We paused again as Gilly shredded pieces of cardboard, all that remained of an empty box he had selected to pulverize.

"I'd like a puppy out of him someday..."

"I told you you could have pick."

"I'm sorry. I guess I'm clinging, huh?" I said softly.

"Take your time," he said gently, and walked out of the room.

Alone with Gil, I squatted and looked at him. He immediately came over and leaned into me, putting all his weight against me, and slid down my legs, eventually turning upside down and flailing his legs about in comic relief. Since I didn't respond by rough-housing, he sat up and looked at me, and I rubbed both sides of his neck behind his ears.

Sensing the gravity of the moment, Gil offered a paw and leaned in to lick a salty rivulet from my cheek. Then, capricious as only a puppy can be, he pushed off me, grabbed a nearby tennis ball, and bounded away in an invitation to play.

Dave returned quietly to the room, and I stood to put on my coat. Gil stopped his rowdy sport, dropped his ball and looked me squarely in the eyes. Studying me, he cocked his head, and his tail sank slowly to the ground.

"Take care of him," I said lamely, my eyes riveted to the dog's.

"He'll have the best," Dave replied unnecessarily, his head turned away from mine.

There was nothing left to do but go. Gilly followed me to the door, but my silent wave told him I would be leaving alone. I let the door close slowly behind me and bent my head into the wind. I looked back only once, long enough to see Gilly's face in the window, his paws on the sill, with his new owner's hand resting on the back of his neck.

"Go make music, my Beethoven," I whispered.

Glen Sheppard, a newspaperman for forty years, was raised hunting birds and chasing trout and bluegill in northern Michigan. Since 1969 he has published The North Woods Call *from the drumlins along Lake Michigan near Charlevoix. Sometimes described as the bible of Michigan conservation, the bi-weekly newspaper highlights exclusive conservation and outdoor recreation reports. Mary Lou and Shep share life with a bird dog named Nails and a retriever named Rusty. "Toots, 1975–85" is etched into a bluebird house made of mahogany on a post near the barn.*

TOOTS

by Glen Sheppard

It was a Christmas Eve in the 1950s when I
realized that bird dogs would dominate life.

I'd gone down the line talking to each guy. Their
attitudes ranged from bitter to depressed. They'd
counted on being freshly showered, in clean uni-
forms, warm and well fed—maybe even enjoying
the afterglow of a few beers—and taking in the Bob
Hope Christmas show.

It hadn't turned out that way.

They talked about family and sweethearts. About
the big Christmas meal. The decorations and the
tree. How they'd kick back in a big, warm, soft chair
after Christmas dinner and sleep the rest of the day
away. How, if they wanted to, they'd take a shower
in the morning, another in the evening, and change
their socks and underwear twice a day. Exactly the
kind of visions young American men should be having on a Christmas eve in a cold, dreary foxhole.

Back at my position, I hunkered down to catch
some sleep. It was going to be a long and, with any

luck, boring night. When the radio guy shook me awake to tell me the squad was ready for patrol, I was sitting on a stump along a tote road in northern Michigan's Dead Stream Swamp. The leaves were down. Everything was brown, yellow, or conifer-green. I was rubbing my dog's ear. As I came out of the grog, I realized my right hand was stroking a gas mask bag in which I kept tobacco, candy bars, and a book, thinking it was a dog.

That nagged at me as the squad fell in and we headed into the night. Everyone else was trying to escape their reality by filling their minds with loving faces, a warm, cheerful home, mounds of hot food, and clean bodies and clothes.

Not me. I'm sitting on a stump talking to a dog.

Clearing my head for the business at hand, I vowed to never again be without a dog and to do as much October stump sitting as possible.

And I have.

Early on I became bullheaded about that sorta stuff. Bird dogs are English setters. It may be the best hunter in the township, but if it ain't an English setter it is just another dog, no matter how good it hunts or behaves. Nothing against it, but it isn't a bird dog. You hunt birds with guns that have two barrels. No matter how deadly you are with it, if it has only one tube it isn't fit for hunting birds. (You fish trout only with long rods made of cane.) Birds are ruffed grouse and woodcock. Pheasants, quail, and other game that fly are whatever they are named, but they aren't "birds."

Dad used to brag that "I'm too smart to be dumb enough to think I'll ever understand women." Time taught me he might better have been talking about bird dogs. (But, maybe, he wasn't that smart.) It took many frustrating, teeth-gnashing, larynx-strained years to figure out that if you take a dog too seriously, demand that she do it your way ("right"), she's gonna make a fool of you. And, more important, you aren't going to like her or yourself.

Look for a pup that comes from pure hunting stock. From parents that live for the hunt. Don't give a hoot about their pedigree or how stylish or colorful they are. Just that their brains are in their nose and their hearts are stuffed with grouse and woodcock feathers. Their instincts will handle the rest.

Get 'em young. As young as possible, but never over eight weeks old. Teach them the rudiments. But make it fun. Always remember that bird hunting is supposed to be a happy game. That's what the pup must learn from day one. There are no scores in this business. No losers. If you spend time together where birds live you're winners. (Remember: God was at his best when he made the places where brook trout and ruffed grouse live.)

The hard part comes next and you need a special housemate to make it work. The first day the pup is with you, make it a partner. I mean, be serious about it: take the little critter to bed with you for the first couple of weeks. (Synchronize your turnovers so you don't squash the pup.) Not only does this bond you, it potty trains the pup in a hurry. The pup won't do it in bed, so it will let you know when the time has come, allowing the two of you to scoot outside.

We, finally, got this down pat in July of 1975. That's when Toots came to us. I'd lost Thorne the previous winter and had been looking for a replacement. I found her in a big litter in the Upper Peninsula of Michigan. I forget how many pups there were, but at four weeks they were already on the bottle. The mother couldn't keep up.

Previously, I'd agonized over several litter picks. Not Toots. As many choices as there were, somehow the eyes, the spinning wormy little tail, the confidence displayed in her eager curiosity, and the flat head with a long, squarish nose and jaw sent an instant signal.

At that age she was pure white. I prefer white dogs, easier to see when working. Her parents were mostly white, with flecks of blue, gray, and amber. (She would end up with a few splotches of tan.)

Jack Jorgenson, a state waterways supervisor, wanted her gone, now. He was over his head hand feeding them. It was risky, but she was no longer dependent on her mother for nourishment. Jorgenson directed us to a local market for a particular type of baby formula and instructions on how to feed her. She fit easily in the pocket of my sweatshirt (reminding me of a pup from my bachelor days who lived part time in the half-open bottom drawer of a newsroom desk in Detroit).

We were camping, so Toots went into the world immediately experiencing the outdoors. That first day, she alternated between snuggling, sleeping in my pocket, whining, seemingly trying to find her mother and litter-mates, and vomiting the formula we had to half force down her. By evening, I was on the verge of taking her back, afraid she wasn't going to make it. Mary Lou's mothering instinct and experience told her she would be just fine, once her (and my) nerves settled down and she felt secure.

That night she joined us in the big sleeping bag and soon cuddled and slept. Sometime in the night I was awakened by a sandpapery tongue on my neck. Taking her out she did her job and returned to my hands as naturally as if she'd always belonged there. Mary Lou halted my move to warm some milk for the pup.

It wasn't full daybreak when she was tugging on my ear, then nursing on a finger, not sure if she wanted to play, potty, or eat. We did all three and she never again thought she'd known another home.

By seven weeks she had mastered her manners and responded to her name, came when called, sometimes, and had destroyed a handmade pair of Indian caribou boots I'd picked up years before in Alaska. She completely ignored the cap gun I fired when she ate and played. She was alternately attacking and pointing the woodcock wing that fluttered off the end of the long fishing rod. We were still working on stop and stay. By ten weeks she lived for the woodcock wing and had made wobbly points on several birds and dozens of songbirds and butterflies. She also had stop and stay down, but it had taken some stern drilling.

◆

During the bird season opener September 15, 1975, when Toots was three months old (that's right, three months), she became a legend, the standard by which I will always measure bird dogs.

About a quarter mile from our old farmhouse in the headwaters of the Elk River watershed was a feral orchard. It was flanked by a rather steep slope covered with pole-size pines. Near the center of the orchard was a tilting tool shed. The first tree south of the shed was the most productive early season apple tree in the orchard. A fine, thick old apple tree. We'd wild flushed a grouse from under the tree several times.

It was about 4:30 P.M. and I wasn't about to alert that bird again, if he was there. My plan was to sneak from the north end of the orchard, with Toots on a short leash, releasing her while we were still behind that tool shed.

I was hoping for her first kill.

Letting her loose, she dashed around the shed before I could move. Stepping briskly, I expected to hear a bird flush. Coming around the shed, there was Toots, still a scrawny pup, dead on point. The bird was not more than eight feet in front of her, on the ground, tail fanned.

The bird, a big mature male, died not fifteen feet from her nose and fell in clear view. Cracking the gun to slide another round in the empty barrel, I told her to fetch.

Damn pup! She just held that silly puppy point, ignoring several demands that she fetch. As the shell dropped into the barrel I raised a boot to give her a push, not a kick.

Two birds flushed from within the tree! She hadn't broken point because she knew they were there. I got off a fast, awkward shot and dumped one of the birds at the edge of the pines. It was thrashing on the ground, out of sight.

Again, I told Toots to fetch. She was off like a streak, down the hill, then up, heading toward me, with a glob of flailing wings in a tiny mouth, her head obscured by the bird. She dropped it several times, but pounced and managed to get her mouth around it again.

I'd died and gone to bird hunter's heaven. Of course, it wasn't always, or usually, that good. How could it be?

She quickly developed several quirks. Toots was a quick character study. If she didn't like someone, she would not hunt with them. Several times, she simply trotted behind me, refusing to hunt.

She didn't like being left alone, except at home or in the car, and she'd get even if you left her in a strange place, like the motel room where she destroyed a one hundred dollar set of drapes and a bedspread, or the cabin where she mangled a screen door.

So we didn't leave her alone, which produced one of my proudest moments. Mary Lou and I were staying at the Holiday Inn in Grayling. I bumped into some friends who wanted me to join them for a presupper drink. I wasn't interested, so used the excuse that Toots was back in the room. They made some derogatory remarks about not being able to trust that lousy mutt. I told them I'd meet them in the bar. Going back to the room, I put Toots on heel. She casually followed me through the halls, ignoring every distraction. At the table in the bar I put her on sit. She sat there nearly an hour, moving only her head, eyes, and tail, with several dozen people moving and talking.

I kept hearing about that performance from other people for years.

But she wasn't perfect. She liked to point rabbits. You knew when she was on a rabbit; she would hop, stiff-legged, up and down, maybe four to six inches in the air. When the rabbit broke cover she'd ignore it.

And she never liked retrieving dead birds. If they were alive she'd grab them and bring them to you. But not dead, which led to an embarrassing moment along the Jordan River.

I still hadn't accepted this flaw. It was early season and we'd broken a young covey, downing three in, maybe, a minute or so, in a snarl of berry bushes. The second bird was thrashing. She grabbed it and I picked up the first one. Then I told her to fetch the third one, which I "knew" had fallen about twenty-five yards to the south. No way. She went and squatted beside a big boulder to the west, ignoring my repeated demands that she find the bird.

Just as I was about to lose my temper, I noticed another hunter walking toward me. Fine shooting and dog work, the elderly hunter applauded. Why are you mad at the dog? he wondered. I told him she wouldn't fetch the third bird, as we walked toward her. The bird was no more than a foot from her. The guy, probably in his early seventies, smiled and rubbed Toots's head. He knew who had the smarts in this pair.

After that when she wouldn't fetch, I just followed her to the bird and picked it up myself. It was a small compromise to make in return for her bird-finding and bird-holding qualities.

A week hunting in the Copper Country comes to mind. We were staying in a resort about a block from downtown Copper Harbor. We would walk to the restaurant, Toots following and then sitting on the porch until we finished. Folks, including hunters, asked what kind of dog she was; they weren't familiar with bird dogs. (Retired Michigan wildlife chief Nels Johnson has a great line about the tendency of Upper Peninsula hunters to drive two-tracks and ground swat birds they see ahead of the car. "Know how they shoot trap in the U.P.?" Nels asks. The answer: "They put twenty-five blue rock in a grocery bag, back off twenty-five yards, and open fire.")

I'd arranged to be dropped off and my car left about a mile down Brockway Mountain Road. This is rugged hunting. You must scramble over steep rock ridges. The dog can be twenty yards away, but you have to move a hundred yards to get to her.

Within the first fifteen minutes, we had killed our limit of grouse—five. Before we reached the car, we had seventeen more points. Fantastic hunting; twenty-two points in less than two hours. She held every one of those birds steady while I climbed up, down, and around those rock cliffs to get to her. (That was also the last time I allowed myself to take a limit, except on migratory woodcock.)

She was in her second year when Mary Lou wanted to see her hunt. It was the first week of October. I had parked the car at the high banks on the South Branch of the Au Sable, intending to fish for a while and then hunt. Woodcock flights were in.

Toots slid down the slope and onto the boggy bank along the river, coming to point while we were still edging down the hill. She was in the open. Easy shot. Mary Lou was right behind me, as I told her Toots had a woodcock pinned and that I would walk up until I was no more than a few feet behind her. The bird would then flush and, if it didn't fly over the river, I'd shoot it, I explained, like it was gospel.

Sure as hell. The bird flushed, leveled off at no more than fifteen feet and flew in the open along the riverbank. I emptied both barrels. The bird kept flying and then landed in brush maybe twenty yards down the river. The three of us moved up. Toots went back on point. The bird flushed. I emptied both barrels, again. The bird flew on and landed once more.

We moved up. Toots pointed. The bird flushed. I fired. Nothing. Then again, my sixth shot, at the bird flying in the open. This time it dropped, loudly flogging the ground with a busted wing. Toots fetched.

"Geez! Is it always like this? Good thing you have Toots," she quipped, between smirks.

◆

Several years later, Toots put on another all-star performance for Dad and my two youngest brothers. I'd agreed to meet them at the forks in the Dead Stream Swamp at noon. A business emergency came up and I got there about 4 P.M. I was surprised to see them standing around a fire, their guns stashed. It was cold and wet. They were tired and fixing to singe some steaks, which they'd brought in case there were no birds. They hadn't had a shot all day. I was surprised because flight birds were in where I live, about seventy-five miles north.

When I said I was going to hunt for a few minutes, Dad made some biting comments about wasting my time "with that dog!" Some bad experiences with wild, wide-ranging English setters had soured him.

A half hour later, I was back with four birds. We wrapped them in tinfoil with butter and onions and put them in the coals. Dad didn't comment, except that they sure made super hors d'oeuvres.

Michigan's November 15–30 deer season was hard on Toots. She couldn't understand my leaving the house with a gun and not taking her. Mary Lou said she would lay by the gun cabinet and moan until I came back. So, while I object to Michigan's December bird season, as soon as deer hunting ended I'd take her hunting daily, whenever possible, for a week or so. The shotgun was empty. But I figured I owed her that much.

One year, I had pegged the habits of a really fine buck during bird season. Thought I had him down pat. Opening day of rifle season he took on a new character. Never saw his tracks that season, but heard that someone had missed a huge thirteen pointer in the swamp south of my eighty acres.

December 1, with deer hunters out of the woods and the weather balmy for that time of year, Toots and I headed out for our charade hunt. We were in the pines below the same orchard where as a three-month-old pup she had made her fabulous emergence as a bird dog. Suddenly she started a contorted dance around a large fallen pine. She would charge toward the tree, stop, yap shrilly several times, spin around, fall back, and then charge again. After a half-dozen or so charges a trophy buck calmly stood up and slowly, almost disdainfully, limped off. He'd been knocked in the right rear leg but was putting some weight on it. I could have killed him with birdshot he was so close. He had probably been hiding there for days.

She loved to go fishing with me, which came close to being our undoing. She would sit at the edge of the stream watching me cast. Fishing the Jordan in June, I spotted a steelhead in shallow water near the east shore. Clipping off the dry fly, I knotted a streamer on the 5X tippet and cast. The fish took after several casts. As it barreled out of the water, Toots nearly fell over on herself. Then, perhaps her dignity at stake, she raced into the water, yapping and following the fish as it dove and then headed upstream. I couldn't hold the fish—a six- to eight-pounder—on the light leader and four-weight rod. It broke off around a bend, with Toots in hot pursuit.

A few seconds later she came around the bend on the opposite side of the river, swimming frantically, only part of her head out of the water. The current surges through this spot in a torrent, smashing under a twenty-five- to thirty-foot-long string of cedar sweepers. It is so powerful and deep that I've never been able to rescue flies that have hung up in the sweepers. At the end of the sweepers the river rages over and down a narrow chute filled with boulders and debris that could crush man or dog.

Toots wasn't going to make it. The current was sucking her into the sweepers. Flinging the Bob Summers fly rod some men might die for onto the bank, I plunged across the stream. She disappeared under the first sweeper. An instant later I saw she had tumbled over, her legs toward the surface, her paws smashing through the cedar boughs.

If I didn't hit my head on something, I could hold my breath until I got through the sweepers. I dove, desperately lunging for her. By some miracle I, finally, got her collar. Kicking wildly, my right foot found something solid (a rock or sunken log) and I managed to propel us into the open and to the surface.

After some thrashing, my feet found the bottom and I dragged her toward shore. Finally getting my arms around her, she was limp, perhaps briefly in shock. As the water level receded to about my waist, she came alive, scrambling up my stomach until her chest was in my face, her legs around my neck.

On shore, I set her down. She stood there, legs splayed, neck and head drooping. My waders and vest pockets bulged with water. Shedding them, I sat on the bank, rubbing water out of her feathers and darn near crying as she stood there dazed. In a few seconds, she crawled into my lap and started shaking. Leaving the waders, vest, and rod, I carried her to the car. Putting her on the sweatshirt and under the old down coat I keep in the Suburban year around, I started the rear heater, even though it was June, and went back for the fishing tackle. Standing there, looking at the current slamming along the opposite bank, I realized, for the first time, neither one of us should have made it with me encumbered with the waders and packed vest.

She didn't eat for a day and a half, and rarely moved. By the third day she seemed to have recovered. Which was better than I'd done. Though I hadn't felt them during the dive into the river, I was a mass of bruises, apparently from smashing into the sweepers.

During her last season we could hunt only about an hour at a time. She was feeble, but begged to be in the field. On her last hunt we were working along a creek about a half mile south of the house, in a three-mile stretch of wild country. She'd pointed seven birds—three grouse and four woodcock. I had a grouse and two woodcock in the bag. I was ready to cross the creek and take her home before she was so weak that I had to carry her. She went on point not ten feet from the edge of the creek. She had worked the area for a couple of minutes, so I doubted a bird had suddenly materialized, but as I came up behind her a grouse flushed. I shot it. Picking it up, I waded across the creek, expecting her to follow. When she didn't I turned to call her. She was on point again. Walking back through the creek, a woodcock flushed not two feet from her nose. I shot it. I have never been able to explain to myself how those two birds suddenly materialized where she had found none seconds before and after I had milled around the area looking for a creek crossing.

From then on she was too weak. I kept the shotgun and vest in the heated portion of the garage for the rest of the season, so she wouldn't see me take them from the gun cabinet.

Irv Drost, an old hunting buddy, used to declare: "God only gives you one good woman and one good dog." Irv has a lot more experience with women than I do, so I can't comment on that (besides, what would you do with more than one?). But I've never had a bad dog and I've had many good ones.

Toots wasn't one of them.

She was majestic.

If there is a billet in heaven for old newspapermen, I expect to find her waiting for me by that stump along the long ago overgrown tote road in the Dead Stream Swamp.

Stuart Williams has had a birdshooting career as extensive as it has been intensive, with over a hundred trips to twenty-four countries. He got his start with hunting dogs at a very early age, shooting quail over a brace of his uncle's grand setters. Later he trained Brittainy spanies. He has shot quail over pointers on classic Georgia plantations and in the brush of south Texas; partridges over pointers in the Andes of Peru and Ecuador; pheasants over Drathaars in Bulgaria; and pheasants, chukars, and Hungarian partridges over springer spaniels in Turkey. His favorite birdshooting destination is Argentina, which he has visited twenty-four times.

Williams is regular contributor to Gun Dog, Wing and Shot, Shooting Sportsman, Sporting Clays, *and other publications. He is international editor of* Hunting Report, Birdshooters' Edition. *His major work is* Birds on the Horizon: Wingshooting Adventures Around the World, *published by Countrysport Press.*

INTERNATIONAL BIRD DOGS

by Stuart Williams

Considered on a worldwide basis, shooting birds over dogs has fallen on evil days. Aside from the United States and Canada, "dogging" is commonly practiced in just four countries: Mexico, Argentina, Uruguay, and Scotland.

The *chaparral*, or brush, of Tamaulipas state in northeastern Mexico offers the finest quail shooting in the world. Almost every plant there grows in enmity to the flesh of man: *cholla*, *nopal*, *yucca*, Spanish dagger and, most malevolent of all, *tasajilla*, a pencil-shaped cactus that, the more you try to free yourself from it, the more deeply it impales you. There is not a more protective quail cover anywhere.

Where the brush has been cleared away the land has been planted in corn and sorghum and sunflowers. Under the *ejido*, or cooperative, system of farming, which is based on a socialist model and is thus highly inefficient, lots of grain and seeds are never harvested and much is wasted on the ground. It is a kind of benign neglect, and the quail love it. A team of wildlife biologists with unlimited funds could not create better conditions for bobwhite quail.

Over the years I have hunted quail in Tamaulipas a dozen times, but of those dozen times the season of 1992–93 certainly shines as the finest. In the spring and summer of 1992 Tamaulipas received the heaviest rainfalls in many years, and quail populations exploded in response. When I shot whitewing doves there in September 1992, I routinely saw twenty to twenty-five coveys every day just traveling to and from the dove fields.

In December of that year I shot quail out of El Tejón, a lodge long known for the consistently high quality of shooting it produces. The first afternoon David Gregory—booking agent and hunting impresario par excellence—and I enjoyed a slam dunk of a quail shoot with David McBee, a well-known dog handler from Texas.

The previous day he had scouted a field where he had seen twelve coveys in the last fifteen minutes of daylight. That is the field we would hunt.

On the first day conditions were perfect: temperature in the sixties, a breeze of eight to ten miles per hour, and vegetation that had been moistened to the proper degree by an early morning drizzle.

Upon arrival in The Happy Hunting Grounds, McBee put down Jodie and Queenie, pointers; Ruby, a German shorthair; and Annie, a setter. We worked a fallow field about one-half mile square, grown up in mixed weeds, wild daisies, and wild *tomatillos*, or miniature green tomatoes, the seeds of which quail love.

Annie made game within fifty yards of the truck, and Jodie backed. The birds were evidently running because time and again Annie would move forward and readjust her point. Then Jodie got in the game, moving ahead of Annie as the birds ran ahead. Some of the way the dogs moved forward side by side precisely in step. I have seen some extraordinary dog work but never anything like that. The dogs kept up this relay for nearly a hundred yards until the birds could stand the pressure no longer. They flushed just ahead of Jodie's nose; I took two birds from the air and David Gregory one.

On the next point Ruby, the shorthair, made game solidly. I moved in quickly but before I could get close she laid down on her belly, continuing to point rigidly. I stepped in front of her, a single rocketed away, and I put it down.

On the next point two birds got up and flew to the left and right, respectively. I put down the left bird and Gregory the right bird at precisely the same instant as McBee shouted his applause.

For the most part the birds were difficult to see and shoot that afternoon because they simply wouldn't fly high enough to make themselves visible against the sky. We did, however, make a number of long shots on low, crossing birds that dropped in long slants, and finished the day with fifty birds.

The next afternoon Eduardo "Lalo" Maraboto, manager of El Sargento Lodge, joined me. McBee manipulated the mutts and Gregory immortalized the grand deeds with his cameras.

We went out to a ranch of rolling hills covered with a dense yellow carpet of wild daisies, and with recently harvested sorghum and tall grass. For the first two hours we concentrated primarily on photography.

The final hour was perhaps the finest hour of quail shooting I have ever enjoyed. McBee put down Jodie, Annie, and Diamond, a littermate of Jodie's, in a weed field of about sixty acres surrounded by dense thornbrush and cactus. In the final hour the dogs moved just five very large coveys, but between the covey rises they pointed singles almost continuously. I counted thirty-five points, and undoubtedly missed some. Many times all three dogs were on point. Annie would have a bird, Jodie another

100 yards away, and Diamond still another 135 yards away in a different direction. At other times all three dogs would be pointing the same bird, surrounding it in triangular fashion. Many of the birds were runners, and the dogs—sometimes two, sometimes all three—would continuously move forward with them, side by side. In the cool fragrant gloom of evening birds roared up and away, and shooting and shouting filled the air with a joyous cacophony. It ended all too soon, as all good things do, when we could no longer see to shoot. The dogs were still pointing in the thickening darkness and they hated to give it up. With difficulty did McBee get them back into the truck.

During the course of that evening I saw some of the most elegant, disciplined, exhilarating dog work I hope to see in this world or the next; tails rigidly erect, mouths tightly shut, bodies quivering with excitement like a high tension wire, leaning toward the bird with head well extended, honoring and backing with perfect teamwork, all beyond reproach.

In January 1993 I returned to Tamaulipas, this time to shoot at No Le Hace Lodge, an opulent shooting resort built by Lloyd Bentsen, Sr., in the middle 1960s. It was originally intended to be a corporate entertainment retreat for the oil industry. Now it is open to the public.

During the 1992–93 season No Le Hace Lodge retained Gerry Glasco as head dog-handler. Gerry annually trucks about forty dogs and two assistant dog-handlers to Mexico for the quail season. He is the only handler in Mexico who has enough dogs to keep four fully finished, fresh dogs on the ground at all times for each party of two shooters. (He calls them his four dog dragnet.) I have shot with him at times when he had no less than seven dogs on the ground—all pointing at the same time.

The first three days at No Le Hace I shot with Mike Fitzgerald II, director of Mexican programs for Fish and

Game Frontiers of Wexford, Pennsylvania. Then Mike left, and on the fourth day I went out with Glasco and his assistant dog-handler, Joe Dan Carter, who were taking a busman's holiday. We drove far to the west, arriving at the field of choice just at sunrise. Conditions were perfect: a heavy dew, temperature in the sixties, a gentle breeze, excellent cover, and plenty of food. Gerry put down his dragnet, and they sifted through every centimeter of cover. Suddenly one dog pointed and the others were immediately paralyzed in response. I moved ahead, a small covey leaped into air, and I shot two birds going straight away.

As soon as the sun climbed a ways in the sky, the heat forced the birds to take refuge in the cool shade of the dense fencerows, or *cortinas*.

At the first *cortina* Gerry put down Buck, a setter, and Radar, a Drahthaar, his two most finished dogs. I went down the left side and Joe Dan down the right, and Gerry followed in his truck. A covey exploded out to my side, and I took down two birds with the first shot and one with the second for a two-shot triple. A bit farther Buck pointed, and I dropped a bird that got up high and tried to fly back over my head. Every minute or so the dogs would make game, and in ten minutes we shot more birds than in the previous two hours. On one flurry Joe Dan and I put down six birds in as many seconds, and Radar retrieved two at a time—something I had never seen before.

Much of the time I rode on the specially built bucket seats which were mounted on the front of the truck. They greatly facilitated getting into action. When we called it a morning at 1:30 P.M. we had seventy-six birds picked up.

We headed to San Fernando, the closest town of any size, for lunch. We ate at an excellent small restaurant called Los Caporales, where Gerry regularly took his clients. We started out with their famous appetizer, *queso flameado*, which is a dense melted cheese flavored with sausage drippings. Smeared on tortillas, it is absolutely irresistible. We moved on to the house specialty, the *Parilla los Caporales*, a mixed grill of sweetbreads, short ribs, pieces of chicken, and chunks of sausage. The finale of the feast was cheesecake, and lemon meringue pie with graham cracker crust—the best I ever tasted. We washed it all down with Bohemia, that wonderful Mexican beer. Gerry said that the feast had been "mighty high-powered hoggings," and he should certainly know, because he is a pig farmer in the off season.

However, it was not lunch, but the last hour of shooting that was *la mejor hora del dia*—the best hour of the day. Gerry put down his dragnet of dogs in a mile-long field of harvested sorghum overgrown with crabgrass and weeds, parallel to a dense thicket of cactus and thornbrush. I rode in the right bucket seat and Gerry in the left while Joe Dan drove along the edge of the thicket. On the first covey rise the birds flew right in front of us toward the thicket. I took down two with my first shot and one with my second. Gerry emptied his eight-shot Benelli, and empty shells kept hitting me in the face, but nary a bird did I see fall.

Then Gerry and Joe Dan got down and walked, Gerry about fifty yards out and Joe Dan about a hundred yards out from the brush, all of us following a parallel course, while I continued to ride up on the front of the truck. A Mexican boy drove. As the dogs pointed and the birds flushed, they would invariably fly toward the brush, thus passing over or to the side of me. I was the beneficiary of what you might call a driven quail shoot. On one covey rise a dozen birds flew over high, and I knocked down one stone dead from forty yards up. It fell in the midst of the thornbrush, and *mirabile dictu*, a birdboy, crawled on his belly far into that brush and fetched it.

Then came the high point of the day for me. Two dogs pointed, Gerry put up the birds, and they came right toward the truck. While the truck was still moving I took down a bird to my left, which fell far behind the truck, and then one to the right, which fell far in front. Gerry missed a low bird, which crossed in front of me at forty yards, and I snatched it down in the waning light. In one day I had become a master drive-by quail shooter.

I shall never forget that last delightful hour: riding up on the front of the truck, with waves of cool, delicious air washing over me; the dogs quartering back and forth, searching out bird scent; birds bursting into air on all sides; and shotguns roaring out their peremptory orders to cease and desist from flight—all of it laid out before me like a grand show enacted for an emperor riding in his chariot.

The dogs wanted to hunt into the darkness, and we had to collect them using the headlights. In fact, we shot the last covey rise in the light of the high beams. We finished the day with 143 birds picked up—my best day of quail shooting ever.

That may seem like a lot of birds, and it is, but the average life expectancy of a quail in the Tamaulipas brush is only about 1½ years, so even very intensive shooting by the very few shooters who go down that way doesn't even replace the natural rate of mortality.

The rolling grasslands of Argentina and Uruguay are home of the tailless tinamou partridge, one of the world's great game birds. The tinamou is a drab brown bird about twice the size of the bobwhite quail that thrives in fields of short grass and sparse cover and is therefore dependent on man and cattle for its well-being. To the upland hunter whose experience is with pheasants, ruffed grouse, and bobwhite quail, it would scarcely seem credible that a game bird would inhabit fields with grass so short and cover so thin that they would hardly hide a sparrow. Yet the tinamou is a different kind of bird altogether. It is primarily a running bird, not a flying one, and thick cover would impede its movement as well as block its view of avian enemies. Finally, it is so perfectly camouflaged that it hardly needs any cover at all. I have on many occasions seen a dog go on point out on bare ground where I could have sworn there wasn't a bird within half a mile. Yet in every instance there was indeed a bird there.

The tinamou is an even more incorrigible runner than the pheasant. It simply will not fly unless hunter and dog put firm and consistent pressure on it—usually after it has run at least fifty yards, sometimes over a hundred yards, from the place where it was pointed. Furthermore, when it does get up, it blasts off with such explosiveness that it leaves the inexperienced gunner haplessly blowing holes in the air.

The tinamou feeds and moves about singly. I have never seen a simultaneous double, or even a consecutive double. I have, however, on several occasions got into a hot corner where I had six to eight flushes in rapid succession. There is simply nothing in the world of upland shooting to compare with this experience.

Shoot operators use pointers almost exclusively. These dogs are anything but field-trial dogs. They work in close, and when they make game and the tinamou runs out ahead of them, they creep forward, quickly readjusting their point as they go. A staunch dog is totally worthless on tinamou.

Because tinamou usually get up at considerable distance and get away quite rapidly, shooting them is strictly a 12-gauge game. The little 20- and 28-bore guns affected by "gentlemen" gunners in this country will quickly put you out of the tinamou game. I like an over-under with barrels at least twenty-eight inches long bored modified and full, or a semi-auto with twenty-eight inch barrel with modified choke tube.

The best load is one throwing a full 1¼ ounces of nickel-plated 7s or buffered, copper-plated 7s. Fired out of a modified or full choke gun, any of these loads will cleanly kill tinamou at forty yards.

I have shot tinamou at the world-renowned Estancia Santa Emilia in Uruguay, out of the opulent Goya Lodge in the rice-growing country of Corrientes Province in northeastern Argentina, and in the fertile fields of the Río Negro Valley in south-central Argentina. I had one of my most memorable shoots with outfitter Carlos Sanchez in the lush uplands of Entre Ríos Province, which lies between the mighty Uruguay and Paraná rivers.

We were working through a field of emerald-green grass not six inches high. Quartering back and forth into the breeze were Carlos's pointers, Ossie and Camila, most efficient meat dogs. Suddenly Ossie stopped in midstride, and his body quivered as if ten thousand volts of electricity were flowing through it. Camila backed and honored.

Carlos ordered: "Move out smartly in front of Ossie and take the bird!"

The bird, however, did not cooperate. I stepped out smartly, but Ossie broke point and crept forward five yards and pointed again. I moved up ahead of him, and he again moved forward and pointed. Clearly we were dealing with a runner.

Carlos exhorted: "Move out faster or the bird will just run away from you!"

I walked as fast as I could for twenty-five yards, and a brown bombshell exploded underfoot and rocketed off low and straight. I dropped the bird softly onto the grass at thirty-five yards. Ossie and Camila raced to fetch.

Within minutes Camila had another bird, and Ossie backed precisely, tail extended straight back in the European manner. Clearly this bird was also a runner, because Camila broke point and raced forward and pointed again. Then Ossie dashed in front of her and pointed for a few seconds, and Camila once again raced out ahead and pointed. Some of the way they crept forward side by side. They kept up this *pas de deux* for nearly a hundred yards, while Carlos continually urged me: "Get out ahead of the dogs! Put pressure on the bird! Bear down on the bird! Make it fly!"

I did precisely that, and after 125 yards of this footrace the bird could stand the pressure no longer. It burst into air, headed out over a fence toward a road, and I dropped it squarely in the middle of the road. Ossie snaked under the fence, grabbed the bird, and sailed back over the fence.

On the next point I almost had to run ahead of the dogs to make the bird fly, and when it did get up it was a full forty yards in front. It likewise veered off toward the road, and I sent three shots after it. Not a hint did it show of a hit, but nonetheless I felt sure that all three shots had been well delivered. Surely enough, just as the bird reached the adjacent field it began to falter. It flew another hundred yards and dropped stone dead. Carlos and his dog-handler and I gave out a shout. The dog-handler marked it down precisely, crossed two fences, walked two hundred yards, bent down, and picked it up without searching in the least.

Then two birds got up wild in rapid succession at thirty to forty-five yards, and I laid them both on the grass. The shooting kept up like this for about three hours. The final action capped off the morning in a most spectacular and satisfying manner. The dogs made game, the bird raced out ahead, and the dogs ran along with it until they forced it to fly at thirty yards, squarely between them. The bird flew straight up, and at the apex of its flight I plucked it back down to earth. Ossie snatched it out of midair.

It had been a near-perfect morning. The heavy dew held bird scent wondrously well, hanging in pearls from every blade of grass. Along the edges of the field, enormous windbreak Lombardy popular and eucalyptus and drunken, or *palo borracho*, trees swayed in the cloudless sky, and the limbs of the *ombu* trees reached out chaotically in all directions. The mid-winter temperature was a perfect sixty-seven degrees, and the air was filled with a most exhilarating fragrance, even though I could not discern a single flower. It was a rare and wonderful day to be alive and afield.

We moved back to the grand manor house at Estancia El Garbón for lunch. Helen Calderón, lady of the manor, served a magnificent luncheon. She started out with a fine quiche of eggs, bacon, and nettle leaves; followed with roast pork, pureed spinach, and roast potatoes; and topped off the feast with peach upside-down cake à la mode. Carlos and I grunted most contentedly as we staggered back to our rooms for a siesta.

Such are the delights of shooting tinamou in the fertile farmlands of Uruguay and Argentina.

◆

Shooting Scottish grouse on the heather-covered moors of Scotland over dogs, or "dogging," as it is commonly known, has long been the poor cousin of shooting driven grouse. It simply does not have the mystique, prestige, or cachet of driven grouse shooting, and it permits the shooter to kill only a fraction of the birds he might get on a day of driving. Nevertheless, dogging has its devotees, who stoutly maintain that it is a superior sport to driving.

Dogging is generally practiced only in the northern parts of Scotland, in Sutherland and Caithness. There the number of birds are insufficient to justify the high costs of driving. It is also practiced on other moors where the lay of the land does not permit driving. It is used as a technique to herd the birds away from the periphery of the moor to the inner areas where they are more easily controlled. Finally, it is practiced in the first week of the season to agitate the birds—especially the young birds— and make them wilder so that they will fly better when the driving begins.

English setters and pointers are far and away the most commonly used breeds. Other breeds occasionally seen are Gordon and Irish setters, springer spaniels, and the so-called versatile dogs: German shorthairs, vizslas, and Weimaraners. These dogs find the birds. After the birds have been shot, other breeds—yellow and black Labs— move in and retrieve. There is generally a strict division of labor, especially if pointers and setters are used. If in the exceptional case that one or more of the versatile breeds are used, they might also do the retrieving.

Dogging fell into neglect for many years but is now enjoying something of a comeback. To a great extent that is because shooting driven grouse has become hideously expensive. One can enjoy a day of sport over the dogs for a fraction of what a day of driven shooting costs.

I had the good fortune to enjoy a week of dogging at the famous Seafield Sporting Club—alas a destination of the past—in Banffshire, Scotland, several years back. I shot with two fellow Americans, Jim Walter and Burke Kibler, and George Drummond, a dog-handler known far and wide for his beautifully trained springer spaniels. The estate manager, Colin Whittle, completed the foursome.

On the first day—a beautiful day—George put down a brace of his irrepressible dogs, Jack and Lady, and a lady dog-handler put down a brace of Irish setters (which are almost never seen afield in Scotland nowadays). Colin and I shot with George Drummond, and Burke and Jim with the lady dog-handler. Keepers followed Jim and Burke with black Labs to pick up fallen birds.

The date was the Twelfth of August, the opening of the grouse season and the most sacrosanct date on the British sporting calendar. The heather was at the peak of its violet bloom. As we waded through it, it enveloped us with a mellow fragrance.

Colin and I had not gone two hundred yards when the urgent wagging of the spaniels' tails commanded our close attention. George blew a shrill blast on his whistle:

"Mark, mark, sirs, there'll be birds just ahead of ye here! A covey, I should think!"

Just then the covey lifted up out of the heather, and Colin and I put down birds simultaneously. I dispatched a second futile shot just as the birds were getting out of range. The covey sailed away down the slope, skimming along just over the heather.

"Not a bad beginning at all!" George commented. Jack and Lady each dumped a bird at his feet and climbed up on him seeking approbation. After a couple of pats he sent them back to work.

"Doun, laddie, doun, doun! Doun, garrl, doun!"

Within 150 yards those tails went into paroxysms again. This time the birds, evidently young and uninitiated, held closely. Then they arose and scooted out across the heather. I killed one bird and wounded a second with my first shot and put it down cleanly with the second shot.

"What a lovely right and left, sir!"

On the next flush a huge pack of birds got up in staggered fashion. Colin and I each doubled, reloaded, and took down a third bird. The birds unwisely swung downhill, arrogantly uttering their "go-back! go-back! go-back!" as they went. George blew a warning blast, and the birds flew right over Jim and Burke. They were ready, and pulled down three birds with four shots. Nine birds in as many seconds! There were wild congratulations all around.

"Lovely gunwork, sirs, lovely gunwork!"

"Oh aye, oh aye! That it was indeed! Very rare gunwork!"

The whole force of Labs and springers nosed out the heather for fallen birds.

By lunchtime we had 17½ brace of birds—a very respectable start for the Glorious Twelfth.

We sprawled out languorously in the heather and feasted on smoked salmon on pumpernickel sandwiches; caviar on black bread; cold sliced Prague ham; Stilton and Port Salut cheeses; champagne grapes; a crisp salad; and a good Pouilly Fuissé and Beaujolais to wash it all down. Afterwards, sated and dulled by the rich foods, relaxed by the wines, and warmed by the sun, we dozed on the fragrant hillside.

A half-hour later I was awakened by an enormous Lab giving me a sloppy kiss on the ear. I sat up reflecting on that line of Shakespeare: "Thou hast neither youth nor age, but as it were an after-dinner sleep, dreaming on both."

Geoffrey Norman is the author of eight books and numerous magazine articles, many of them on the outdoors. He grew up in panhandle Florida and southeast Alabama where he hunted quail and learned to appreciate the big running pointers and setters. He lives in Vermont where he hunts grouse and woodcock over dogs that stay much closer. For ten years, Norman hunted the grown-over orchards and the alder swamps with a fine-boned Brittany named "Molly." When he reached the age of fifty, however, Norman's old longings asserted themselves. He is now trailing a hard charging liver-and-white pointer by the name of J.E.B. Stuart. "If we don't find any grouse," Norman says, "then we'll go find us some Yankee railroad bridges to burn."

A DOG NAMED BERNIE

by Geoffrey Norman

Bunch of us were sitting around talking about dogs. Hunters like to do this when they aren't hunting…talk about dogs, that is. They tell dog epics in a way that I imagine isn't too very far from the way the ancient Greeks used to sit around and tell stories about their warrior heroes. In fact, if you had a strong, big running pointer and named him Hector, you could tell of his deeds in iambic pentameter.

> Long ago, in the Wiregrass of Georgia
> There lived a creature of stout heart
> Firm on the point; steady to wing and shot…

Well, you get my drift and anyway, I digress. The conversation I have in mind was not about heroic deeds so much as the comic kind. The mood was Aristophanes more than Sophocles, don't you see. The subject was dogs that, while they wouldn't win any trophies at the field trials, sure knew how to leave 'em laughing. People who have never spent any time around field dogs probably don't believe that a dog can have a sense of humor. Anyone who has hunted much with dogs knows otherwise. Emphatically. Some dogs are just born clowns. They can hunt—some of them are real good, as a matter of fact—but they live for laughs.

"You know," one of the men at the table said, "I had an old black Lab, several years back. Male. Name of Mose. That old dog was like one of those comedians who makes a living bumping into things or falling down. Mose couldn't get out of his own way. Walked right through the screen door to our kitchen one time, just like it wasn't there. That dog drove my wife right straight up the wall."

"Some women are like that," one of the philosophers said. A medievalist, probably.

"Yeah," the tale teller continued, "but there were plenty of times when I felt the same way. The dog loved to hunt and he was good in a duck marsh. But he was the *clumsiest* dog.

"If we were in a blind together, and I opened a Thermos and poured a cup of coffee, then it was for certain that Mose would decide that was the time to get up and turn around and spill my coffee. I don't know how many times he knocked the Thermos out of my hand, right when I was pouring the first cup of the day. One time, he hit it hard enough to knock it clean out of the blind. And the thing was, no matter how mad you were, no matter how much you wanted that hot coffee, there was always something funny about it."

Everyone agreed that there is something comically redeeming about a clumsy dog.

"Probably," the teller went on, "old Mose put on his greatest performance with somebody else in the blind. Friend of mine came down to hunt and he just fell in love with that dog. I tried to tell him the dog was a little bit…oh, *unpredictable*. But he wasn't having any. Said he and Mose would make an unbeatable team. So I dropped them off at one blind, in the dark, and went on around the marsh and set up in another blind. I was maybe two hundred yards away. I could hear my friend talking to Mose, telling him to 'sit' and 'stay.' Then it was quiet until the sun came up and the ducks came in.

"Now, Mose didn't cause any problems when the ducks were overhead. He was first class, that way. And after a couple of passes, six or seven mallards came into the decoys in front of my friend's blind. I heard him shoot. Heard the splash when the duck hit the water. Then I heard him say, kind of soft and confident, 'Okay, Mose. Fetch.'

"And then, the next thing I heard was him yelling like he'd been stabbed with a hot fork.

"'No, Mose. No. *Whoa*, Mose.'

"But it was too late. I heard the dog hit the water. A little later, I heard my friend say, sort of soft and mournful, 'Oh, no.'

"I shouted across the marsh, kind of nervous, 'What happened?'"

"'My *camera*,' my friend said.

"I figured Mose had knocked it off the ledge and into the mud, or something. So I hollered, 'How bad is it?'

"'I don't know,' my friend said. 'I'll let you know when Mose gets back.'

"Now, at first I had a hard time figuring what he was talking about but when he explained it later on, it all came clear. It seems like he'd carried this brand new, very expensive Nikon camera with a zoom lens to the blind in his bag. If I'd have seen it, I would have told him to leave it at home or get another dog.

"Anyway, when he got settled, he took the camera out of the bag and hung it from a peg, by the strap, so he could reach up and get it. Probably figured he was going to get a nice shot of Mose coming in with a retrieve.

"Well...what happened was, he downed that first duck and told Mose to fetch. Mose took off and put his head through the loop of that camera strap and kept right on going. Hit the water with that Nikon around his neck. Like I say, he was a good worker, so he just swam on out to where that mallard was floating and picked him up, then turned around and swam back in. Of course, my friend didn't have a camera when he *really* needed one. I'd have given anything for a picture of old Mose, coming out of the water with a drake mallard in his mouth and a Nikon camera hanging around his neck. My friend was laughing so hard he couldn't hunt. And it was his camera."

Everyone agreed that this was pretty good stuff. More to the point, nobody doubted the story. Of course the Lab had taken off out of the blind with a camera around its neck. That was *fated*, as the Greeks would have said, from the moment that fellow stepped into the duck blind carrying his camera.

"You know," one of the other men at the table said, "that's pretty tough about ruining that camera. But I had an old Chesapeake that did that to a car one time."

"Went into the water with a car around its neck?" Chesapeakes have a reputation for feats of strength but this was pushing it.

"Nah," the man said. "What I meant was he *ruined* a car, same as that Lab ruined a camera. But actually—now that I think on it—it was a *van*, not a car."

"Oh. Well in *that* case..."

"Yeah," the teller went on, undeterred. "It was a silver van. Belonged to Avis. Kind of a hard bunch, in my view.

"Anyway, three of us were using this van. Three men and one Chesapeake, name of Tiny. Dog was built like a linebacker. With a similar disposition. But he was a hunter. He'd been swimming in freezing cold water all morning, retrieving bluebills, and when we decided it was time to quit, he looked at us like he thought we were a bunch of wimps.

"It was lunchtime and we drove a couple of miles to a restaurant. We left the shotguns and everything else, including Tiny, in the van so we figured we didn't need to lock it. What we didn't count on was *Tiny* locking it. But he did. Every single door. When we came out of the restaurant there was Tiny, sitting in the front seat of the van, with all the doors locked, and the keys in the ignition.

"We were all still wearing our hunting clothes and when Tiny saw us, he must have decided it was time to go again. He got excited. So he started eating the van.

"He started with the dash, then he moved on to the steering wheel. When he finished there, he went after the upholstery. We kept trying to talk to him and calm him down but, like I say, Tiny was a linebacker and hard to reason with. Somebody finally said, 'Let's break a window while there's still something left of the car.'

"So, we took a big old rock and smashed the window on the driver's side and got inside. There wasn't much left. We turned the van in to the Avis people the next day and had a real hard time convincing them that one dog had done all that. I told the manager that if she would supply the car, Tiny would be glad to give her a demonstration. She didn't think that was funny. I figure she was probably a cat lover."

Everybody agreed that this was a pretty good story: dog tearing a van apart from the inside while a bunch of helpless men stood around pleading with the dog to spare the vehicle. Then one of the men who had been silent up to this point said, "I knew of a dog, one time, did something that will top that."

Oh?

"Yeah, this dog was a Lab. A chocolate. Fellow who owned him called the dog Yoo Hoo, after the drink, you know.

"Anyway, Yoo Hoo was like most Labs. He was a good-timer and he just couldn't stand to be left alone. The fellow who owned him—name was Paul—was kind of a soft touch and instead of leaving Yoo Hoo at home, by himself and sad, he'd let him ride around with him in his truck while he did his errands. The dog spent so much time in the truck that I believe Paul had him to where he could wear a seat belt and work the radio.

"Well, one day Paul has to go into town from the house, which is out on a country road, and he whistles up Yoo Hoo and puts him in the shotgun seat. Paul gets in on the driver's side and starts down the driveway. It's about a quarter of a mile to the road and halfway there, Paul remembers something.

"It's a narrow drive so he can't just turn around. And, since he doesn't want to back all the way to the house, he throws it in park and leaves Yoo Hoo in the truck, with the motor running, while he goes back to the house. Won't be but a minute, you see."

"Uh oh," one of the listeners said.

"Yeah buddy," the narrator answered. "That was just too much opportunity for a Lab. And Paul made it worse by answering the phone and doing a couple of other things so he wound up spending fifteen or twenty minutes in the house. Then he walked out the front door, strolled down the driveway, and discovered that this truck was gone.

"Now, his first thought was that somebody had stolen his truck. Which was bad enough. But what made it worse was that the thief had also gotten Yoo Hoo. What's running through Paul's mind is that you can always get another truck but he'll never be able to replace that Lab.

"He's standing there in the driveway, feeling terrible and just about to turn around and go back to the house and call the cops when he hears something. The sound of an engine, down in the woods off the high bank where he built his driveway. He walks over and looks down into the woods. There is a clear set of tracks running, oh, about two hundred yards out into the woods and at the end of the tracks, there is the pickup with Yoo Hoo at the wheel. Paul figured that the dog had spent so much time in the truck, watching him, that he knew about the gearshift and how it worked. He said that if the dog had just had an opposable thumb, he might have been able to get the truck down the driveway and gone on into town. Question was, what did he have in mind once he got there?"

◆

I listened to all these stories, and more, and I enjoyed them. But I didn't have much to contribute. My dogs have come from the pointing breeds and they are the stoics. Some pointing dogs will work until they literally drop. They generally don't have the time for stunts. The comics come from among the retrievers. Especially the Lab. Since the day I sat and listened to those stories, I have met a Lab whose legend would hold up whenever the tales of great comic deeds are told. His name is Bernie.

He comes from Cleveland and the breeder named him after the Brown's great quarterback, Bernie Kosar. The name fits the dog as perfectly as a stretch sock. You could never think of him as "Bernard." He is a "Bernie" if ever there was one.

Bernie is a big yellow Lab with the kind of easy amiability that you see in a lot of big men. When you are big you can come on gentle and nobody is likely to think it is because you are weak. I suppose Bernie can fight. I've seen him nicked up. But he is a party animal, not a fighter.

Bernie has a good nose and lots of drive. He is an excellent retriever both as a pickup dog off a mule wagon or out of a duck blind. But he seems to have sensed early in the game that he is not any better at this sort of basic, meat-and-potatoes dog work than a lot of other yellow Labs. And Bernie wanted to be thought of as special. He was not content with a future that consisted of hundreds of competent, straightforward retrieves. Bringing duck after duck and quail after quail to the hand of a moderately grateful master in return for a few 'attaboys' was not the sort of vision to stir Bernie's soul. He was after bigger things and like the starlet whose acting skills are no better than average but is determined to be a star, Bernie decided to make himself outrageous—to become a legend.

Nobody remembers Oscar Wilde for his poetry. Bernie is probably as good at sniffing out a freshly shot quail in the broomweed as Wilde was with verse. Maybe better. But an ordinary pickup doesn't really get Bernie's juices flowing and sometimes he will get down off the wagon and run right past the spot where the bird has fallen. He will then proceed to run the country while the handler yells at him and the shooters mumble under their breaths about ill-trained dogs, and the pointers, which are still on point, must be wondering why this bozo is allowed to get away with murder while they get whipped if they bust one lousy covey.

Bernie seems to know just exactly how long this sort of behavior will be tolerated before serious repercussions result. He does not want to be left in the kennel next time or whipped too hard, for that matter, this time. He'll take a whipping but he is no masochist.

So, just when patience has been stretched to the breaking point, Bernie will suddenly remember what he has been sent out to do. He will make a straight line back to where the bobwhite fell, sniff around in the grass, make a show of picking up the scent and trailing—even if the bird fell stone dead and never moved an inch—and then dash in the last ten feet and with the bird safely in his mouth, lift his head very high so everyone on the wagon or riding horseback can admire his form. Then, if this doesn't get results, Bernie will take a victory lap or two around the wagon before he brings the bird in to his handler.

A routine pickup is never really routine when Bernie is involved. He has a way of making the easy ones look hard.

Then, there are the hard ones. When Bernie has to trail a runner, he milks it for every ounce of drama. You'd think the bird was armed and dangerous. And, of course, once the chase has ended, Bernie takes a victory lap.

On an unorthodox retrieve, he is even better. I watched him go after a runner that had gone down a gopher hole to hide and I consider it one of Bernie's finest moments. Bernie put his head into the gopher hole, then his feet, then his entire body until only his hindquarters were above ground. He moved approximately a truckload of red clay to get at that bird.

"Seems like old Bernie would rather be a coal miner than a bird hunter," one of the shooters, watching the show from the mule wagon, said.

"I just hope he doesn't find a rattlesnake down there," another shooter said.

At about that time, Bernie emerged from his excavations with the bird in his mouth. He got a round of applause from everyone on the wagon and that just made his day.

While Bernie's technique on land is colorful, it is when he gets around water that his instinct for theater truly comes through.

Like most retrievers, Bernie quivers with anticipation when the ducks are coming in. In Bernie's case, I think it is something like stage fright. He knows he'll be on soon (provided the human does his rather humdrum part and shoots a duck or two) and for an artist, no matter how many times you have done it before, it is always opening night.

First thing that happens when a duck hits the water and a shooter says "fetch," is that Bernie *launches* himself like one of those NBA basketball players going for a dunk on the cover of *Sports Illustrated*. Bernie milks his entry into the water for everything it is worth. Usually this means the shooter is soaked.

This dramatic entry is especially interesting when it is done from a canoe. Bernie goes about ninety pounds and if your canoe does not have a lot of wetted surface, you can go right over. Shotguns and all. But this is a minor thing up against the making of a legend.

Occasionally, this big splash is enough to satisfy the ham in Bernie and the remainder of the retrieve will follow the normal pattern. Bernie will swim out to the duck, pick it up in his mouth, swim back, and give the duck to the shooter. But this is no sure thing. It is not possible to know when the ham in Bernie will take over and he will decide that theatrics are somehow called for.

This can take the form of something that might be called "hide the duck," which is pretty much what it sounds like. There is, however, no way to convey, on paper and in mere words, the kind of passions this seemingly harmless game can inspire. You wouldn't think grown men could be forced to such rhetorical heights by the actions of a mere dog. Bernie seems to think that the objective of this game is to get someone to go in over his waders and about half the time he is successful.

Bernie also likes another game which might be called "Where is the duck?" This game is best played when Bernie is taken to a blind and asked to retrieve a duck that he did not actually see fall. In those cases where the duck is floating out in the middle of open water, plainly visible to all, Bernie might just swim past it, so close that the duck is swamped by his wake. Hunters on shore will scream things like, "Right there, Bernie. Right there."

Bernie will then begin to circle. First the circles will grow wider. Then, as the screaming of the hunters grows louder and more shrill, the circles will grow tighter and tighter, with the duck in the precise center like the ten ring on a target. Finally, Bernie will locate the duck and return to shore in triumph.

A variation on this one occurs when the duck has fallen someplace where he can't been seen from shore. Say, in a patch of cattails. In a case like this, when Bernie is told to "fetch," he responds with a look and something like a shrug as though to say, "Fetch *what*?"

You can point as urgently as Napoleon directing his men through the Alps and Bernie will continue to give you the look. Finally, you decide to throw something out in the area where the duck has fallen. Then, of course, Bernie leaps into action. Big leap, lots of water splashed back on everyone on shore.

The basic comic script, here, calls for the dog to swim out and pick up the stick that the hunter has thrown to mark the duck. Bernie does this with the best of them. But he also seems to realize that this is pretty humdrum, pie-in-the-face sort of stuff. That what it needs is a *twist*.

Bernie has come up with a couple of variations on this theme and is, no doubt, working on others. The first variation calls for Bernie to swim right past the duck and even bump into it on his way to fetch the stick. He can do this with an absolutely straight face so that the hunter can believe that Bernie was actually unaware the duck was even there. Bernie's expression does not change even when three or four hunters scream, in unison, *Right there*. The deadpan is worthy of Johnny Carson.

A second, more elaborate variation calls for Bernie to swim out where the stick has fallen close to the duck. He ignores the stick, picks up the duck, and turns back for the shore where the chorus is chanting *Good boy, thataway Bernie, bring him here*. About half way back to shore, Bernie drops the duck, turns around, and picks up the stick which he then brings to shore. It is as though Bernie wants everyone to understand that while he certainly knows the difference between a duck and a stick, he is not going to be locked into some rigid, orthodox thinking according to which a duck is *always* preferable to a stick. Some days, you see, he just feels more like retrieving sticks, even if there is a duck around.

It was on the day when I first saw this performance that I decided Bernie was interested, above all, in creating a legend. Now, while Bernie is certainly a ham, he is not necessarily a *prima Donahue*. He will jump—literally—at the opportunity to share the stage with other actors, though it is better if they are not dogs. He seems, in fact, to prefer beaver.

Take Bernie up to a quiet, concealed pond in the hour before dawn and everything will be fine unless he hears the slap of a beaver tail. Then he is off. Swimming, diving, running, and barking. Just putting on a hell of a show which, in turn, inspires the beaver.

Usually beaver are pretty dour and phlegmatic. No time for fun and games as long as there is an undammed stream or an ungirdled aspen tree anywhere on the planet. But when Bernie comes around, beaver seem to turn into good-time-Charlies and hell-raisers with nothing to do but swim around the pond slapping the water with their tails. Near as I can tell, the game has a lot in common with tag and Bernie is always "it." One thing is certain, no duck has ever been inclined to join in the fun, so on those mornings when Bernie and the beaver are at play, you have to be content to watch them and forget the hunt.

Bernie will also chase a deer or a turkey. Get close to a porcupine or a skunk. He is just naturally gregarious that way. He will run with just about anything that is alive and roll in just about anything that is dead. While he doesn't exactly play with insects, he will eat them. I've seen him wake up from a dead sleep to nail a grasshopper on the wing, which was not half as funny as the time he chomped down on a hornet that happened to fly by.

Bernie eats lots of interesting things, including some that were meant to be dinner. He has been thrown out of a lot of kitchens. Once, when he was inadvertently left in one where there was a ham on the counter, he managed to knock over a planter, open a faucet, and turn on a blender in his attempt (successful) to get at that meat. He spent several days in a maximum security kennel after that. Most dogs would have gotten life but Bernie always seems able to wrangle a pardon.

Part of the reason is that he is always glad to see you. Genuinely glad. Bernie does not have to be called. If you are a kid, he is always ready to play. It would take three ten-year-olds, working in shifts, to wear him out. Kids have pulled his tail, stuck fingers in his eyes, and generally abused him, but he has never raised his voice or shown anyone his teeth. Bernie will go anywhere and do anything for kicks so it doesn't seem so terrible if he can't be relied upon to stay with the script. He is an improviser and a comic. Aristotle, who could appreciate the Greek epics as well as anyone, wrote that man is the only animal that laughs. Which may be. I'm not going to argue with Aristotle.

But he never knew Bernie. And while I've never actually seen Bernie laugh, I know that he is a comic and that if nothing else, he lives for the laughter of others. There is just no other way to account for him.

Jerome Robinson is a lifelong grouse hunter who lives in Lyme, New Hampshire, among the foothills of the white Mountains. He raises English Setters and trains them in the grouse woods that straddle the New Hampshire-Vermont border. Robinson has been writing about birds and bird hunting for the nation's leading outdoor magazines since 1967. He was gun dog editor at Sports Afield *for more than twenty years and is currently contributing editor and feature writer at* Field & Stream. *Robinson is the author of two gun-dog training classics:* Hunt Close, *a guide to training pointing dogs for tight cover situations, and* Training the Hunting Retriever, *a step-by-step guide to training retrievers for real hunting situations.*

GUN-DOG TRAINING

by Jerome Robinson

A glance through the sporting dog supply catalogs can give the mistaken impression that successful dog training relies upon varying degrees of punishment applied with whips, choke collars, pellet guns, and electronic shocking devices. So, before you become convinced that tools of punishment are necessary to dog training's everyday problems, let's make a few subtle observations.

The little old lady whose dog sits quietly beside her wherever she goes did not steady the dog with a sling shot, she probably just gave it a food tidbit whenever the dog sat quietly and withheld the treat when it did not.

Likewise, the old man whose dog delivers the newspaper to him each afternoon did not force-break the dog to retrieve by punishing it, he probably just rewarded the dog with a treat and a kind pat when it naturally copied him by picking up the newspaper and carrying it.

Given the opportunity, most dogs try to please the person who feeds them. They do this by copying that person; going where he goes, sitting when he sits, hunting if he hunts and bringing him whatever things he seems to like. Dogs do that without any so-called "training" at all if given the opportunity to learn what their masters like them to do.

Unfortunately, the idea that force and punishment are required to train sporting dogs has become widely accepted in spite of the fact that all other animals are primarily trained by rewarding them with food treats and affection when they behave as their trainers wish. So much emphasis has been placed on using sophisticated methods of force and punishment to train sporting dogs that training with food treats has been made to seem amateurish, yet logic tells us that the use of food treats should be the most effective means of getting a dog to do what you want.

Learning how to get food is any animal's strongest instinct. From the instant it draws its first breath an animal devotes its intellect to figuring out where food comes from and how to get it. Dogs are among the quickest animals to learn how to get food and are, therefore, among the easiest to train.

When a pup learns that it can win food treats by behaving in certain ways, it begins trying very hard to figure out which behaviors earn rewards and which do not. In no time you have a pupil that is not only willing, but eager, to comprehend what you want it to do.

There are no tricks to training with food rewards. Your job is simply to show the pup how to behave in certain ways and then to give each behavior a name that the dog can distinguish.

For instance, you can teach a pup to "sit" by holding a food treat (thin slices of hot dog make good treats—pups love them and always want more) over the pup's head.

Move your hand back over the pup's head towards its tail. The pup will follow your hand with its nose and will fall backwards into a sitting position. The instant its fanny hits the floor, open your hand and let the pup have the treat.

Repeat the same maneuver three or four times, each time giving the pup the treat the instant it sits. Soon the pup will begin anticipating that it can win the treat by sitting and will sit automatically when your treat-bearing hand appears. That's the behavior you want. Now give it a name. Say "sit" as you hold out the next treat and give the reward the instant the pup obeys.

In very short order the pup will learn what the word "sit" means and will be quick to respond to the command if you are always quick to reward it with a treat. Now begin encouraging it to sit for longer periods of time by withholding the treat. When the pup begins to stand up, repeat "sit" and reward the pup instantly when it obeys.

You can teach the pup to "lie down" by holding the hot dog treat in your closed fist and letting the pup smell it. Then drop your treat-bearing hand to the floor and move it slowly along the floor. The pup will follow your hand with its nose and will get down on its belly as you extend your hand away. The instant its belly hits the floor, open your hand and let the pup have the treat.

With a few repetitions the pup will automatically anticipate that lying down is another behavior that wins food rewards and will begin lying down as soon as your hand goes to the floor. That's the behavior you want, so give it a name. Say "lie down" next time you extend your hand and reward the pup the instant it complies.

Even a very young pup will learn to obey these simple commands quickly in order to win food rewards. You are appealing to its strongest instinct. The pup is learning how to make food happen.

Expand on the pup's eagerness to win a reward by gradually increasing the distance from which you give the command and by extending the time you make the pup continue the required behavior before you give the treat. Once it learns that compliance always wins a reward regardless of where you are when the command is given it will obey reliably. When it understands that it always gets the reward at the end, it will wait as you increase the length of time you require the command to stay in effect before the treat is given.

As you give the pup its treat at the end of each successful lesson, say "okay." This is a signal that the command it obeyed is no longer in effect and helps the pup to comprehend that it has completed the requirement of your command.

Already, you have a pup that has learned it can win food treats and your affection by obeying word commands. And you haven't punished it or forced it to do anything. Your pup likes you, trusts you and has no reason to fear you. Pups trained this way want to do things that please you.

You can easily teach a pup to "heel" by walking with it on a leash and holding the food treat at your knee. When the pup falls in beside you, say "heel" and give the reward at your knee as you proceed.

If you are consistent at restraining the pup with the leash when it pulls forward, using the leash to prevent it from dragging behind and giving it a food treat at your knee if it walks beside you when you say "heel", you will quickly have a pup that understands what "heel" means and knows what to do to get a food treat when it hears that command.

Teaching a pup to "come" on command is a cinch when food treats are used. When the pup has romped away from you for a short distance, get down on one knee, clap your hands to attract its attention and have a food treat ready to give when the pup bounds up to you.

Next time, don't bother clapping; just say "come" and the pup's name. Be sure to have the food treat ready. Practice at increasing distances and you will soon have a pup that is absolutely reliable at coming when called.

From the pup's point of view an interesting phenomenon is taking place. At an early age, without ever being punished or forced to do anything, the pup has formed a deeply rooted habit of obeying your commands. It knows how the system works. It has learned a few ways to win food rewards and please you at the same time and that knowledge gives the pup confidence and makes it want to learn more.

As the pup develops you can continue to build on that knowledge.

If you are wondering how you're going to keep a supply of hot dog slices on hand for all this treating, the answer is simple. Carry a sliced hot dog in a plastic sandwich bag in your pocket whenever you are with the pup and put the bag in the refrigerator when you're apart. The hot dogs will cost less than any tool of punishment and will enable you to train your pup to obey out of habit, not out of fear.

A pup that reliably comes, sits, lies down, and heels on command, has learned the basics on which all degrees of higher training are founded. Once your pup responds reliably to those four basic commands, you can gradually replace hot dog treats with words of praise. Say "Good dog" and give the pup an affectionate pat each time it responds properly. Let your praise become the reward the dog earns by proper response and save the hot dog treats for teaching the proper responses to new lessons.

Well-bred sporting dogs come with certain special characteristics that have been established by many generations of selective breeding. You should not have to train a pointing dog to point, for instance, or a retriever to retrieve. Given the opportunity to rely on their own instincts, well-bred pointing dog pups will naturally hesitate before jumping in on a bird they smell but cannot see and well-bred retriever pups will pick things up and carry them without being trained to do so.

You will, however, need to train the pointing dog pup to hold its point for unnatural periods of time and the retriever will have to be trained to carry things straight back to you without fooling around and to deliver gently to your hand.

The easiest way to teach a dog to retrieve directly and gently to hand is, once again, to offer food treat rewards.

Most pups, regardless of breed, have some degree of natural retrieving instinct. If you toss a rolled up sock a few feet from a ten week old pup, it will probably run over and pick it up. Remain silent. Not knowing what to do next, the pup is very likely to run to you carrying the sock.

Have a hot dog slice ready and when the pup brings you the sock make a trade. Take hold of the sock and offer the hot dog slice simultaneously. The pup will automatically drop the sock in order to accept the treat and, presto, you have accomplished a completed retrieve and a gentle delivery to hand.

With repetition, the pup will get into the habit at a very early age of completing the retrieve quickly in order to win the reward and will relinquish the retrieved object instantly in trade for the hot dog slice. Two of retriever training's most troublesome tasks, the direct retrieve and a soft-mouthed delivery, will become a natural habit if you start a pup's retrieving training in this manner.

People usually don't send their dogs to professional trainers until the dogs are well grown, so the pros have had to develop training methods that apply to headstrong older dogs that probably have been allowed to develop habits that must be broken. That is why their training methods often depend on force and punishment.

As a puppy owner, however, you have a chance to start your pup off with good habits that make advanced training much easier for the dog to understand and force and punishment become unnecessary.

For example, there is no reason to wait for a pointing dog to grow up before putting it on birds. A well-bred pointing dog pup will point at eight to ten weeks of age if given the right introduction.

Here's how:

Dizzy a pigeon and place it in short grass with its head tucked under its wing, then lead your puppy up to the bird on leash. The pup will investigate the bird and probably will prod it with its nose or mouth it. When prodded the bird will flush and its flapping wings may startle the pup momentarily but within a moment the pup will settle down and want to sniff where the bird was.

Let it sniff. You are introducing it to the thrilling scent of birds.

Dizzy another pigeon and tuck it into short grass in the same place. This time bring the pup up on leash from the downwind side. When it smells the bird the pup may show excitement or it may show timidness. Say nothing and let Nature take its course.

Eventually, the pup will creep in close to the bird, using its nose. It may pounce on the bird or it may show a fear of touching it. Don't interfere, just watch. If the pup doesn't pounce on the bird and flush it, the bird will shortly wake up and flush on its own. Once the bird is gone, let the pup investigate where it was.

Now repeat the whole procedure one more time, planting a third dizzied pigeon in the same place, but this time hide the bird in the grass so that it cannot be seen from a distance. Again bring the pup up slowly from the downwind side.

Let the pup advance on slack leash at its own speed. This time, when the pup smells the bird but does not see it, it will freeze in hesitation knowing that the bird is close and not wanting to stumble into it. That hesitation is the foundation of the pointing instinct.

Let the pup stand there as long as it will. Imagine what the pup is experiencing. Bird scent is flooding its senses and the pup is awakening to the demands of its genetic instincts. At this tender age, you have introduced the pup to the thrill of bird scent and allowed its instincts to demand that it freeze and remain motionless.

As it stands on point, gently push the pup forward towards the bird. It will automatically resist being pushed into the bird and will stiffen back against your pressure and intensify its point. Stroke its tail up into a rigid position. Trail your fingers along its back from tail to head in a soothing gesture that assures the pup that its rigid attitude pleases you.

A pointing dog pup that is introduced to birds in this manner at eight to ten weeks of age forms a pointing habit before it is ever tempted to chase. With repetition of this lesson several times a week, you can develop a solid pointing dog that would rather point birds than flush and chase them.

If you follow this method and develop the pointing habit in a puppy before it is big enough to want to chase its birds, the rest of training becomes remarkably easy.

As the pup grows bigger, have it trail a short rope so that you can tie it to a bush or tree whenever it points. With the pup restrained, you can move past it to flush its bird and be assured that the pup cannot chase it. In this way you prevent the pup from ever having the chance to chase a bird that it pointed. A pup that points from instinct and lets you flush its birds without trying to chase forms a natural behavior pattern that avoids the need for force or punishment in training.

Controlling a gun dog's hunting range is one of training's biggest headaches, particularly for those who buy pups from field trial stock which has been selectively bred for generations to run big. Nothing is harder than trying to keep a dog hunting close when its genes are goosing it to become a horizon-buster.

If you want a gun dog that hunts at a pace suited to a man walking, buy a pup whose ancestors have been used successfully by hunters who hunt on their feet—it's as simple as that. With a dog that is bred to hunt at close to moderate range, you will be training in harmony with nature rather than against it.

When you have a pup that naturally wants to hunt near you, range control can be accomplished as a natural extension of the "come" command that you taught using food treats.

Once the pup is reliable at coming to you when you command "come," begin replacing the "come" command with a whistle signal. Call "come" followed by three beeps on your whistle. When the pup responds, slip it a food treat.

With a few repetitions, you can drop the verbal command and use the whistle signal alone, always rewarding the pup with a treat and an affectionate pat when it comes to you.

Use the whistle signal and a food treat to call the pup to you whenever it begins to range too far when hunting. Through repetition, show it that when it reaches a certain distance from you it is always called back. Eventually, the pup will recognize this distance and will begin to turn automatically when it gets out about that far.

From time to time, pause in your hunting and call the pup all the way to your side and give it a food treat when it comes up to you. Pat the pup. Take a break and have a moment of affection. Then send the pup ahead again and resume hunting. The pup will learn to look forward to these breaks and will be alert to where you are at all times. Its range will settle naturally into a comfortable pattern if you make it pleasant for the pup to be near you and reward it for responding correctly to your whistle signals.

All dogs respond eagerly to commands if they fully understand what they are being asked to do and have learned from experience that there is a desirable reward for responding correctly. Using food treats as bribes for correct responses is by far the most effective means of getting dogs to do things your way.

As you can see, food treats make it easy to teach the dog to come when it is called, sit and lie down on command, walk at heel, retrieve directly, deliver gently to hand, and obey whistle signals with which you can control its hunting range. These methods are effective because they enable you to work with, rather than against, the dog's nature.

Encouraging bird dog pups to point before they are big enough to chase is effective for the same reason; you are working with the pup's raw basic instincts and teaching it behavior that pleases you before it discovers behavior that does not.

When dogs form desirable habits early, those habits are deeply ingrained and continue to influence how the dog will behave as it matures. If you continue to use logical training methods which are based upon reward for proper responses rather than punishment for incorrect responses, training will be fun for you and your dog and your days in the field together will be wonderfully satisfying.

Remember, a dog that fears your punishment learns to fear you. On the other hand, a dog that expects rewards tries hard to learn how to earn them and becomes intensely devoted to the person who shows it how to succeed.